SCIENCE
AND THE
NEAR-DEATH
EXPERIENCE

"The belief that consciousness itself is somehow produced within the brain will topple under the momentum of observations this theory simply cannot explain. Chris Carter's second book, as well organized and accessible as his first, details the history, physics, and observed phenomena that will forever change how we look at the brain. A readable, informative, and devastating critique of materialism."

ROBERT BOBROW, M.D., CLINICAL ASSOCIATE PROFESSOR OF
FAMILY MEDICINE AT STONY BROOK UNIVERSITY
AND AUTHOR OF *THE WITCH IN THE WAITING ROOM*

"Chris Carter's tightly reasoned approach and his encyclopedic grasp of the research make *Science and the Near-Death Experience* the best book on NDEs in years. The clarity of Carter's work and the breadth of his scholarship make this an ideal book for experts and those new to the field. This brings insight and common sense to our understanding.

BRUCE GREYSON, M.D., CARLSON PROFESSOR OF PSYCHIATRY
AND NEUROBEHAVIORAL SCIENCES, UNIVERSITY OF VIRGINIA

"As a physicist and neurosurgeon, I find Chris Carter's *Science and the Near-Death Experience* to be a comprehensive analysis of NDEs, and a book that allows one to understand that consciousness persists beyond the death of the physical body. It is beautifully written!"

JOHN L. TURNER, M.D., AUTHOR OF
MEDICINE, MIRACLES, AND MANIFESTATIONS

"In this important book, author Chris Carter does a masterful job at demonstrating how the evidence does not support the mainstream scientific view that consciousness and mind are produced by the brain. In addition, Carter objectively reviews the empirical data on near-death experiences and rightly concludes that these data fully support the notion that mind and consciousness can continue to operate after the cessation of brain activity."

MARIO BEAUREGARD, PH.D., PROFESSOR OF NEUROSCIENCE,
UNIVERSITY OF MONTREAL, AND COAUTHOR OF
THE SPIRITUAL BRAIN

"There has been a spate of books on the afterlife and the immortality of consciousness lately, indicating a resurgence of interest in what is surely one of the most important—and I would argue THE most important—question a conscious human being can pose in his or her life. Carter's book is not only an important contribution to this literature; it is its current crowning achievement. For he masters both the theoretical and the evidential approach, showing that belief to the contrary of the survival of consciousness is mere, and now entirely obsolete, dogma, and that the evidence for survival is clear and rationally convincing. A book to read and to remember for the rest of one's life—and perhaps beyond. . . ."

ERVIN LASZLO, AUTHOR OF *SCIENCE AND THE AKASHIC FIELD*
AND FOUNDER OF THE CLUB OF BUDAPEST

SCIENCE
AND THE
NEAR-DEATH
EXPERIENCE

How Consciousness
Survives Death

CHRIS CARTER

Inner Traditions
Rochester, Vermont • Toronto, Canada

Inner Traditions
One Park Street
Rochester, Vermont 05767
www.InnerTraditions.com

Library of Congress Cataloging-in-Publication Data

Carter, Chris.
  Science and the near-death experience : how consciousness survives death / Chris
Carter.
      p. cm.
  Includes bibliographical references and index.
  Summary: "The scientific evidence for life after death"—Provided by publisher.
  ISBN 978-1-59477-356-3
  1. Near-death experiences. 2. Consciousness—Miscellanea. 3. Future life.
I. Title.
  BF1045.N4C38 2010
  133.901'3—dc22

                                                                    2010019267

Printed and bound in the United States by Lake Book Manufacturing

10   9   8   7   6   5   4   3   2   1

Text design by Jon Desautels
Text layout by Virginia Scott Bowman
This book was typeset in Garamond Premier Pro with Perpetua Titling and Swiss
721 as display typefaces

To send correspondence to the author of this book, mail a first-class letter to the
author c/o Inner Traditions • Bear & Company, One Park Street, Rochester, VT
05767, and we will forward the communication.

Dedicated to the memories of Henri Bergson,
William James, and Ferdinand Schiller,
three remarkable individuals
who never let fashion dictate their opinions.

We can easily forgive a child who is afraid of the dark; the real tragedy of life is when men are afraid of the light.

PLATO

CONTENTS

PART III

Deathbed Visions

FOREWORD

If, like most contemporary Western philosophers and scientists,
I were completely ignorant of, or blandly indifferent to, these
phenomena, I should, like them, leave the matter there.
But I do not share their ignorance, and I am not content to
emulate the ostrich.

C. D. Broad

The history of science is replete with examples of ideas, concepts, and theories that at one time were accepted as true, but which are now known to be false. Once upon a time, it was quite reasonable to believe that Earth is the center of the universe, that it is flat, that it is less than eight thousand years old, that an unregulated free market is the best way to run an economy, that women are by nature inferior to men, that the material world consists of independently existing particles, that the world we observe exists independent of our observing it, and so on. All of these beliefs have been proved false by science.

However, as history shows, there is usually a generation time gap between when the old theory has in fact been empirically proved false and when so-called "mainstream" science finally is able to accept the new idea. Hence the quip that science advances "one funeral at a time."[1]*

---

*The quip is a distillation of a famous quote from Max Planck. Frustrated by the inability of his contemporaries to grasp the new ideas in physics, Planck wrote, "A new scientific truth does not triumph by convincing its opponents and making them see the light, but rather because its opponents eventually die, and a new generation grows up that is familiar with it."

Materialism—the belief that consciousness is produced by or is the same thing as the physical brain—is one of those beliefs that have already been proved false by science. However, although science has in fact already established that consciousness can exist independent of the brain and that materialism is therefore empirically false, it will take another generation before these facts are recognized by mainstream academia. Old paradigms never go gently into the night: they go screaming and kicking. And the defenders of materialism today are indeed screaming and kicking ever more loudly, perhaps because of a total lack of evidential support for their respective ideology.

The scientific evidence against materialism, and hence in support of the hypothesis that consciousness is independent of matter, has been steadily accumulating for over one hundred years. Even back in the time of the great philosopher and psychologist William James, the evidence was sufficiently strong to convince the majority of scientists and philosophers who took the time to examine it carefully and conscientiously that there was something to it. Today the collective evidence is conclusive: I know of no responsible investigator who has concluded otherwise. For example, after a careful, scientifically rigorous analysis of the near-death experience (NDE), Edward Kelly, Bruce Greyson, and Emily Kelly conclude:

> The central challenge of NDEs lies in asking how these complex states of consciousness, including vivid mentation, sensory perception, and memory, can occur under conditions in which current neurophysiologic models of the production of mind by brain deem such states impossible. This conflict between current neuroscientific orthodoxy and the occurrence of NDEs under conditions of general anesthesia and/or cardiac arrest is head-on, profound, and inescapable. In our opinion, no future scientific or philosophic discussion of the mind-brain problem can be fully responsible, intellectually, without taking these challenging data into account.[2]

Thus, it is only because the materialist is deeply ignorant of the empirical data that have decisively refuted his or her cherished beliefs that he or she is able to sustain belief in what is false. The situation for the materialist is logically the same as that of the creationist. Both materialist and creationist must ignore, debunk, and ridicule the scientific findings that have refuted their beliefs.

The analogy here is useful. The belief that Earth is less than ten thousand years old has been decisively refuted by science. The fact that over 40 percent of Americans still believe otherwise has no bearing on the truth of what they believe. Similarly, the belief that consciousness is produced by the brain has also been decisively refuted by science. The fact that the majority of scientists and academics do not yet believe this has no bearing on the truth or falsity of the belief itself. What does have bearing on the materialist's hypothesis is empirical data, collected for over one hundred years, that have led every responsible investigator to the same conclusion as that of the scientists in the above quote. And just as the creationist is more concerned with preserving his religious ideology than he is with discovering empirical truth, so also the materialist is more concerned with preserving ideology than discovering empirical truth, and is quite happy to ignore an incredibly large body of empirical data that proves his ideology false. This is why I said that the evidence is already in, regardless of whether academics choose to examine it or continue to ignore it. The data were already quite considerable at the time of physicist and philosopher C. D. Broad (1887–1971); the data are overwhelming now.

I have recently retired after teaching philosophy for forty years at one of the major state universities in the United States. For the last thirty years, I have been carefully following scientific research on the NDE, as well as other areas of investigation that prove fatal for the materialist's ideology (including mediumship studies, reincarnation studies, and after-death communications). During those thirty years, not once did a colleague come into my office to inquire why I was interested in things that my profession considered "bizarre," "crazy," and "off the deep end." On the contrary, my interest in parapsychology and survival research was taken as "evidence" that I had "lost it," and my opinions were marginalized.

At the time, I accepted being professionally ostracized as the price one has to pay for thinking outside the materialist box. Greater thinkers than

I, as the history of science shows, have met similar, if not worse, fates. Yet now, looking back on it, it seems that my colleagues' total lack of interest in my work demonstrates at best a failure of curiosity of monumental proportion; at worst, it is intellectually irresponsible. There is perhaps no philosophical question more important than the question of whether consciousness is independent of the body and, hence, whether the consciousness that constitutes our very selves survives the death of our body. Given that there is a large body of empirical data that (1) is highly relevant to this question and (2) has convinced virtually everyone that has taken the time to examine it that materialism cannot explain it, I find myself agreeing with Kelly, Greyson, and Grosso that it is intellectually irresponsible for a philosopher or psychologist to be ignorant of this data.

At the same time, I was beginning to incorporate these data in my teaching, and during the last fifteen years was teaching courses that centered primarily on these data. The overwhelmingly positive reactions of my students to these data removed any lingering doubts I may have had about teaching this material and allowed me to stay in academia with integrity, my colleagues negative opinions of me notwithstanding. It is not merely that my students found this material intrinsically fascinating and philosophically relevant. More importantly, this material has the power to change lives, and to change them for the better. Students—or at least those who find their way into philosophy courses—are searching for something that gives meaning and purpose to their lives. Reading about the NDE in some detail gives students—and myself—a sense of meaning and purpose; it gives them a framework that greatly helps them with the conduct of their lives, giving their lives direction and meaning that they did not have before.

So my experiences teaching this material have brought me much hope and a little sadness. The sadness revolves around the fact that my colleagues will never be able to wrap their minds around these data and, as such, will never be able to receive the personal benefits that come from embracing a nonmaterialistic worldview. They illustrate the "one funeral at a time" quip. My hope revolves around the fact that the future belongs to the students. Many of my students are tomorrow's doctors, psychologists, and neuroscientists. Because they have been exposed to these data before they become effectively brainwashed by materialist graduate programs to believe that such things are impossible and ridiculous, they go forth into their professions with an open mind and, more importantly, with an open heart.

I wish this book had been available when I was teaching, because I would certainly have used it. The author examines in detail virtually all the various hypotheses that materialists have historically advanced to explain, or explain away, the NDE. I use the word "historically" here (even thought the history is just thirty years or so) to indicate my opinion that there is no materialist hypothesis left that any scientist who is highly knowledgeable about the NDE takes seriously. For example, at one point back in the 1980s, some materialists proposed that the NDE was caused by a buildup of carbon dioxide in the brain. Granted, this is not an intrinsically unreasonable hypothesis. But subsequent research has shown (1) that many NDEs occur without a buildup of carbon dioxide in the brain, and (2) that there are plenty of cases of carbon dioxide in the brain without an accompanying NDE. So the presence of carbon dioxide in the brain is neither necessary nor sufficient for an NDE and, hence, has nothing to do with causing the experience. As Chris Carter so convincingly demonstrates in this book, every proposed attempt to explain the NDE in physiological terms has met a similar fate.* All such proposals have been directly falsified by empirical evidence, and hence it is no longer rational to believe in such things. One of my brighter students—a neuroscience major—after examining the data extensively, concluded that the abysmal poverty and sheer irrationality of the materialist arguments against dualism must themselves constitute some evidence for the opposite position.

Science is a rational enterprise. Indeed, science is the epitome of what it is to be a rational enterprise. Although it may not be possible to give a precise definition of the term "rational," everyone will surely agree that it is rational to base our beliefs about the world on empirical data. It is rational to modify, revise, or abandon our hypotheses in the face of evidence

---

*This, I take it, is the upshot of van Lommel's study in *The Lancet*.

that proves them false. It is irrational to cling to beliefs that have been shown to be false. And it is irrational to refuse to examine data because the data might be threatening to one's preconceived opinions.

Although science is a rational enterprise, we human beings are not rational creatures, neither in our personal lives nor when we are trying to do science. When one is confronted with empirical data that challenge deeply held a priori beliefs, such as geologic facts for creationists or the NDE for materialists, there are various logic tricks that are customarily used to defend beliefs that one is unwilling to relinquish. If the facts are not on your side, you can always "spin" things with words and twisted logic so as not to appear as silly as you really are. These tricks and fancy word games have been exposed by various writers over the years, from the time of William James[3] to the present, including both myself[4] and Chris Carter.[5]* But the issues here go much deeper than mere logic. Logic pertains to the process of reasoning from premises to conclusion, from data to hypothesis. But if one remains studiously ignorant of the empirical facts, then there can be no honest discussion of the logic. Just as creationists will tend to avoid information from geology, paleontology, and biology that undercuts their cherished beliefs, so today's materialists steadfastly ignore and ridicule the data from parapsychology and survival research that proves their cherished beliefs false.

Thus it is imperative for the materialists, if they are to maintain their beliefs, to avoid being exposed to data that run against the contours of their ideology, as my colleagues successfully did for thirty years. To be sure, there are always logic tricks and semantic sleights-of-hand that the materialists can fall back on, should any uncomfortable information come their way. But avoidance of such information is by far the best way to cling to the materialist paradigm. This is surely irrational and very unscientific behavior. Scientific rationality, as philosopher of science Karl Popper maintained, requires that one be constantly on the alert for data that contradict one's cherished beliefs, rather than constantly avoid-

---

*An excellent in-depth philosophical discussion of these logical errors and fallacies can be found in R. Almeder, *Death and Personal Survival* (Lanham, Md.: Rowman and Littlefield, 1992).

ing such data. If materialists were rational, they would regard it as their business to seek out and examine data, such as the NDE, mediumship research, and so forth, that challenge their hypothesis. The nature of the human mind is the most important question for philosophers, psychologists, and psychiatrists. One might think that standards of rationality and intellectual responsibility would require that they be fully up-to-date on the findings of parapsychology and survival research, but academics are human first and rational thinkers second. Thirty years ago I would not have believed that an educated person could be as dogmatically and irrationally attached to materialism as creationists are dogmatically attached to their silly beliefs. But I believe it now.

Thus far, I have been regarding the materialism paradigm as on a par with other such paradigms that have been overturned in the course of the history of science, but I believe that there is something rather special and different about the present situation. There is a message hidden in all this research, and it is a message that successful academics do not wish to hear. The message is universal love. Every near-death experiencer is convinced that the purpose of life is to grow in our ability to give and receive love. And NDE researchers—as well as mediumship researchers—have themselves come to this same conclusion, but academic life is the opposite of loving.

Both science and academia are organized around the same principles that structure the corporate world: success in one's career depends a little on talent, but mostly on competition, self-promotion, and so forth, that is, on personality traits that have little to do with curiosity, intelligence, or intellectual honesty, to say nothing of love. Those who have been most successful at this—the ones who control the journals, decide who gets funding, decide who gets tenure—hold power in science and academia because of personality qualities that are opposed to the message of universal love. They believe, and need to believe, that the purpose of life is to "win," to be successful and influential in their field of study.

Many academics would be horrified to learn what all near-death experiencers have learned. A successful life is not measured by fame, prestige, wealth, or number of publications; it is measured by how we treat one another, by our ability to live according to the golden rule, and by growth in our ability to feel compassion for others. But try mentioning this at any professional meeting and you will be laughed out of the conference room, and those with the most power and prestige will be laughing the hardest. One of the reasons this research is resisted with exceptional fierceness is because the message of this research—the message of universal love—is threatening to the power structures that govern science and academia. *Science and the Near-Death Experience* is a splendid presentation of thirty years of NDE research. The author does an excellent job of presenting the empirical data and discussing in detail the materialist's efforts to explain it away. For any open-minded skeptic, or anyone just curious to learn about the NDE, this is a great book to start with, but it is also good for a different category of person: the believer! Often I have had students who already accept the reality of the NDE—perhaps because of their religious faith or because they have had such an experience themselves—and they are resistant to learning the details of argumentation and all the philosophy of science that I make them study. They will say, but I already believe, why do I need to go into the details? My response is, this is not merely a matter of forming certain beliefs: it is also a matter of understanding the scientific, rational basis for our beliefs. *Science and the Near-Death Experience* is as much about rationality itself as it is about the NDE. The author will guide you, step by step, into this fascinating, and very important, area of scientific research.

NEAL GROSSMAN

Neal Grossman received his Ph.D. in the History and Philosophy of Science from Indiana University in 1970. He has taught philosophy at the University of Illinois at Chicago for over forty years and, for the past fifteen years, has incorporated the Near-Death Experience in almost every course he teaches. His book *Healing the Mind: The Philosophy of Spinoza Adapted for a New Age* presents Spinoza's elegant system of spiritual psychotherapy in terms accessible to a lay reader.

INTRODUCTION

I do not believe we can go back to an age of simple belief. Many of the explanations once given by religion, especially those about the material world, have been shown to be scientifically invalid. The general denial of any possible spiritual reality, however, and the active ignoring of evidence pointing toward the reality of some sort of spiritual aspect of humanity, is scientism, not science.

CHARLES TART, PH.D., INSTITUTE
OF TRANSPERSONAL PSYCHOLOGY

The belief in an afterlife dates back at least to the Neanderthals, who buried their dead with flowers, jewelry, and utensils, presumably for use in the next world. Although many people today associate belief in an afterlife with religious faith, it is important to remember that this belief predates any organized religion. It is found in the old shamanic spiritual beliefs of hunter-gatherers from around the world, and usually without any elaborate theological baggage.

For instance, the explorer and writer H. R. Schoolcraft, in his travels through the United States in the early 1800s, was greatly impressed with how the Native Americans handled their dead without apparent emotion.

The Indians do not regard the approach of death with horror. Deists in religion, they look upon it as a change of state, which is mainly for the better. It is regarded as the close of a series of wanderings and hardships, which must sooner or later cease, which it is desirable should not take place until old age, but which, happen when it may, if it puts a period to their worldly enjoyments, also puts a period to their miseries. Most of them look to an existence in a future state, and expect to lead a happier life in another sphere. And they are not without the idea of rewards and punishments. But what this happiness is to be, where it is to be enjoyed, and what is to be the nature of the rewards and punishments, does not appear to be definitely fixed in the minds of any. If a man dies, it is said, he has gone to the happy land before us—he has outrun us in the race, but we shall soon follow.[1]

In 1913, nearly a century later, the anthropologist J. G. Frazer wrote,

It is impossible not to be struck by the strength, and perhaps we may say the universality, of the natural belief in immortality among the savage races of mankind. With them a life after death is not a matter of speculation and conjecture, of hope and fear; it is a practical certainty which the individual has little dreams of doubting as he doubts the reality of his own existence.[2]

Of course, civilizations all over the world have built breathtaking monuments to the belief in an afterlife. The Great Pyramids of Egypt, the lost temples of Angkor, the Notre Dame Cathedral in Paris and many other magnificent structures around the world testify to the power of the belief in an afterlife to motivate people to the most extraordinary effort.

What is the source of this belief? At this point the skeptic offers various explanations: tribal people dreamed of their dead and mistook these dreams for visits; people tend to fear death and yearn to be reunited with their loved ones, and so are willing to follow anyone who promises eternal life in return for certain forms of behavior; and so on.

However, there is another possibility. Throughout recorded history people have reported many phenomena that would seem to indicate evidence of survival past the point of bodily death. Could the nearly universal nature of cultural belief in some sort of survival be based on experiences humans have reported in all known cultures for thousands of years?

Even today, reported contact with the dead is surprisingly common. In 1973, University of Chicago sociologist Andrew Greely asked a representative sample of 1,467 Americans, "Have you ever felt that you were really in touch with someone who had died?" Twenty-seven percent said they had.[3] In 1975, professor of psychology Erlendur Haraldsson asked in a representative national survey in Iceland, "Have you ever perceived or felt the nearness of a deceased person?" Thirty-one percent answered yes. Ten years later Haraldsson asked the question again in the European Human Values Survey: this time every fourth person in Western Europe reported contact with the dead.[4]

In fact, evidence for the survival hypothesis—the idea that our consciousness survives the death of our bodies—is vast and varied, and comes from several different lines of evidence: NDEs, deathbed visions, reported memories of a previous life, apparitions, and even messages from the dead. All of these lines of evidence have been examined by many first-rate researchers, scientists, and philosophers. However, opinions differ on how all of this data should be interpreted and what it all means.

Webster's dictionary defines prima facie evidence as "evidence having such a degree of probability that it must prevail unless the contrary be proved." In terms of sheer quantity and variety, the evidence in favor of the survival hypothesis certainly does seem to provide a strong prima facie case in its favor. However, many alternative explanations have been proposed, some crude, some clever. All attempt to account for this evidence in terms that do not require the survival of the mind after death of the body. So if we are to make up our minds regarding the reality of survival on rational grounds rather than on religious or materialistic faith, then we must demonstrate that these alternative explanations are either more or less compelling than the hypothesis of survival.

The purpose of this book is to examine and evaluate evidence for the survival hypothesis from near-death experiences and deathbed visions, those strange and often wonderful experiences people frequently report when they have suddenly or finally arrived at the brink of death. But first, we must closely examine the relationship between the mind and the brain, in order to deal with the most common skeptical objection to survival of consciousness beyond the point of biological death.

PART I

Does Consciousness Depend on the Brain?

In this materialistic age, dualists are often accused of smuggling outmoded religious beliefs back into science, of introducing superfluous spiritual forces into biology, and of venerating an invisible "ghost in the machine." However, our utter ignorance concerning the real origins of human consciousness marks such criticism more a matter of taste than of logical thinking. At this stage of mind science, dualism is not irrational, merely somewhat unfashionable.

PHYSICIST NICK HERBERT,
ELEMENTAL MIND

ONE

ANCIENT
AND MODERN THEORIES

The strongest arguments against the existence of an afterlife are those that deny the possibility of consciousness existing apart from the biological brain. These arguments derive their strongest force from common and undeniable facts of experience and from their supposed association with the findings of modern science. In fact, these arguments have an ancient history.

The Greek atomists were the first to define the soul in terms of material atoms. Epicurus (342–270 BCE) defined the soul as "a body of fine particles . . . most resembling breath with an admixture of heat." He stressed the complete dependence of soul on body, so that when the body loses breath and heat, the soul is dispersed and extinguished. The Roman poet Lucretius (99–55 BCE) took up the arguments of Epicurus and continued the atomist tradition of describing the mind as composed of extremely fine particles. Lucretius wrote one of the earliest and most cogent treatises advancing the argument that the relationship between mind and body is so close that the mind depends on the body and therefore cannot exist without it. First, he argued that the mind matures and ages with the growth and decay of the body; second, that wine and disease of the body can affect the mind; third, that the mind is disturbed when the body is stunned by a blow; and finally, if the soul is immortal, why does it have no memories of its previous existence?

Similar arguments, to the effect that the mind is a function of the brain, were taken up with greater force nineteen centuries later in the work of men such as Thomas Huxley, who wrote that the consciousness of men and animals "would appear to be related to the mechanism of their body simply as a collateral product of its working, and to be completely without any power of modifying that working as the steam whistle which accompanies the working of a locomotive engine is without influence upon its machinery."[1] In other words, consciousness is a mere *epiphenomenon* of brain activity, that is, an effect and not a cause of brain activity, and is produced by the working of the brain the way a whistle is produced by the working of a steam engine.* It follows from this, of course, that the mind cannot exist in the absence of a brain.

Bertrand Russell started his analysis of matter and mind with his premises that "a piece of matter is a group of events connected by causal laws, namely, the causal laws of physics. A mind is a group of events connected by causal laws, namely the causal laws of psychology." He admitted that at the time of writing (1956), "We have not yet learned to talk about the human brain in the accurate language of quantum mechanics," but that the "chief relevance, to our problem, of the mysteries of quantum physics consists in their showing us how very little we know about matter." He then submitted a hypothesis "which is simple and unifying although not demonstrable" to explain the connection between mind and matter, namely that "the events which make a living brain are actually identical with those that make the corresponding mind." He writes:

> An event is not rendered either mental or material by any intrinsic quality, but only by its causal relations. It is perfectly possible for an event to have both the causal relations characteristic of physics and those characteristic of psychology. In that case, the event is

---

*Huxley based his arguments in part on Darwin's lack of a clear distinction between animals and men, but Darwin vehemently disagreed with Huxley concerning the uselessness of the consciousness of both animals and men. He correctly realized that Huxley's thesis contradicted his life's work. For if consciousness were useless, he asked, then why did it evolve?

both mental and physical at once. Since we know nothing about the intrinsic quality of physical events except when these are mental events that we directly experience, we cannot say either that the physical world outside our heads is different from the mental world or that it is not.[2]

In other words, Russell argues that both matter and minds can be defined as groups of events and that we know almost nothing about the intrinsic nature of matter. *If* we assume that an event can only be rendered mental or physical "by its causal relations," and since it is logically possible for "an event to have both the causal relations characteristic of physics and those characteristic of psychology," *then* it is logically possible that an event "is both mental and physical at once." Russell's argument is abstract but logically cogent as far as it goes.

However, Russell seems to be mistaken in his view that quantum mechanics has completely abandoned "the assumption of particles that persist through time" and that "now we have to confess to a complete and absolute and eternally ineradicable ignorance as to what the atom does in quiet times." He means that atoms can no longer be regarded as ordinary objects because "sameness at different times has completely disappeared."[3] However, recently physicist Nick Herbert wrote, "An electron does possess certain innate attributes—mass, charge, and spin, for instance—which serve to distinguish it from other kinds of quantum entities. The value of these attributes is the same for every electron under all measurement conditions. With respect to these particular attributes, even the electron behaves like an ordinary object."[4] It seems we can still know something about the persistent nature of matter after all. Does it make sense to attribute mass, charge, and spin to thoughts?

Russell's argument is purely of a logical variety, starting with the premise that both matter and mind are groups of events and that since we know almost nothing about matter, for all we know mental and physical events can be one and the same. However, Russell realizes that his argument leaves open a logical possibility:

I do not think that it can be laid down absolutely, if the above is right, that there can be no such thing as disembodied mind. There would be disembodied mind if there were groups of events connected according to the laws of psychology, but not according to the laws of physics. We readily believe that dead matter consists of groups of events arranged according to the laws of physics, but not according to the laws of psychology. And there seems no *a priori* reason why the opposite should not occur. We can say we have no empirical evidence of it, but more than this we cannot say.[5]

Russell has not taken into account considerations from neuroscientists such as Nobel laureate Sir John Eccles, who has noted with regard to the identity theory that "this extraordinary belief cannot be accommodated to the fact that only a minute amount of cortical activity finds expression in conscious experience."[6] The most Russell can really say is that a minute fraction of events in the brain are identical with mental events, but he is not concerned here with empirical considerations, from either parapsychology or neuroscience.

Russell also wrote two articles on the question of survival of bodily death, in which he argued that memory is bound up with the structure of the brain, and so when the brain is destroyed the memories must also cease to exist. He ignores the possibility that memory may not be exclusively physical, and bases his arguments entirely on physics and biology. He also makes no mention of phenomena his theory cannot explain.[7]

In his enormously influential work *The Concept of Mind,* philosopher Gilbert Ryle set out to demonstrate the absurdity of what he termed the "official doctrine," which he attempted to ridicule by calling it the dogma of the "ghost in the machine." Ryle states the doctrine as follows: "Every human being has both a body and a mind. Some would prefer to say that every human being is both a body and a mind. His body and his mind are ordinarily harnessed together, but after the death of the body his mind may continue to exist and function."[8]

Ryle thinks that talking of the body and the mind as two separate entities governed by two separate sets of laws (physical and psychological) is to commit what he calls a category mistake, by which he means the mistake of speaking as though something belongs to one category when it really belongs to another. For example, someone would commit a category mistake if he were shown the buildings, faculty, and students of a college, and then asked where the university is. He would commit the same mistake if he were shown battalions, batteries, squadrons, and so forth, and then asked where the division is.

Similarly, Ryle argues that we commit a category mistake when we talk about a mind existing over and above a set of dispositions to behave in certain ways under certain circumstances. And he thinks it is a mistake to refer to thinking over and above the behavior that is supposed to be caused by the thinking. For Ryle, nothing else is going on over and above the behavior: thinking *is* the behavior, and nothing more.

Ryle's theory is therefore an attempt to explain away the mind with a sort of behaviorism. He argues that the mind is not another entity in addition to the body, it is just the way the body is disposed to behave, and thinking is how it actually behaves. So for Ryle, the mind is not the kind of thing that could cause anything. Ryle maintains that we refer to people correctly as wholes, not as minds and bodies together, and that adequate descriptions of human behavior need not refer to anything other than human behavior.

Ryle does not refer his arguments to empirical issues, either from neurophysiology or parapsychology. Instead, his arguments refer to purely verbal issues; instead of reducing mind to body and mental events to physical events, they reduce all *talk* of minds and mental events to talk of dispositions and behavior.

An example should illustrate the limitations of Ryle's analysis. Consider a Spartan soldier who feels pain but usually does not show it. It will sometimes be true that the statement "he is in pain" will be true, but that the statement "he is displaying aversion behavior" is false. Therefore, the statements cannot have the same meaning, unless either (1) we arbitrarily define pain as aversion behavior, or (2) we simply assume that the subjective experience of pain does not exist. The first is a purely verbal tactic, and the second tries to assume the issue away. It should be obvious that we cannot settle empirical issues, such as whether conscious experience exists, has causal influence, or can exist independent of a body, by verbal analysis alone.

Corliss Lamont, former president of the American Humanist Association, has written one of the most extensive statements of the materialist positions in his book *The Illusion of Immortality,* the title of which speaks for itself. He tells us in the preface that he started out as a believer in a future life, but does not give us the reasons why he held the belief against which he reacted so strongly.

Lamont rightly contends that the fundamental issue is the relationship of personality to body and divides the various positions into two broad categories: monism, which asserts that body and personality are bound together and cannot exist apart, and dualism, which asserts that body and personality are separable entities that may exist apart. Lamont is convinced that the facts of modern science weigh heavily in favor of monism and offers the following as scientific evidence that the mind depends on the body:

- In the evolutionary process, the versatility of living forms increases with the development and complexity of their nervous systems.
- The mind matures and ages with the growth and decay of the body.
- Alcohol, caffeine, and other drugs can affect the mind.
- Destruction of brain tissue by disease or by a severe blow to the head can impair normal mental activity; the functions of seeing, hearing, and speech are correlated with specific areas of the brain.
- Thinking and memory depend on the cortex of the brain, and so "it is difficult beyond measure to understand how they could survive after the dissolution, decay or destruction of the living brain in which they had their original locus."[9]

These considerations led Lamont to the conclusion that the connection between mind and body "is so exceedingly intimate that it becomes inconceivable how one could function without the other . . . man is a unified whole of mind-body or personality-body so closely and completely integrated that dividing him up into two separate and more or less independent parts becomes impermissible and unintelligible."[10]

Lamont briefly considered the findings of psychical research, but contends that they do not alter the picture because of the possibility of other interpretations, such as fraud and telepathy.*

In summary, the various arguments against the possibility of survival are: (1) the effects of age, disease, and drugs on the mind; (2) the effect of brain damage on mental activity and, specifically, the fact that lesions of certain regions of the brain eliminate or impair particular capacities; and (3) the idea that memories are stored in the brain and therefore cannot survive the destruction of the brain. The inference drawn from these observations is that the correlation of mental and physical processes is so close that it is inconceivable how the mind could exist apart from the brain. Except for the appeals of the modern writers to the terminology of neuroscience, the arguments advanced in favor of the dependence of the mental on the physical are essentially the same as those advanced by Lucretius.

THE ISSUES AT STAKE

There are really two separate issues here: one is the logical possibility of survival, and the other is the empirical possibility. The arguments of the epiphenomenalists, the identity theorists, and the behaviorists are logically inconsistent with the idea of survival: if consciousness is merely a useless by-product of brain activity, is identical with brain activity, or does not really exist except as observed behavior, then obviously what we call consciousness cannot survive the destruction of the brain. However, as we will see later, there seem to be highly compelling reasons for rejecting the first of these theories, and it is questionable if the latter two theories are at all consistent with observation and introspection or, for that matter, are anything more than just silly.

---

*Lamont's portrayal of psychic research is extremely superficial and contains several false and misleading statements. For an excellent critique of Lamont's book, exposing a mass of inconsistencies and *non-sequitur*, see chapter 18 of *A Critical Examination of the Belief in a Life after Death* by C. J. Ducasse.

If, however, we are willing to admit the existence of consciousness, and not only as a useless by-product, then the postmortem existence of consciousness is at least a logical possibility, that is, there is no self-contradiction in the assertion that consciousness may exist in the absence of a brain. Then the question becomes whether survival is an empirical possibility, that is, whether the idea of survival is compatible with the facts and laws of nature as currently understood.

IMPLICIT ASSUMPTION BEHIND THE EMPIRICAL ARGUMENTS AGAINST THE POSSIBILITY OF SURVIVAL

All the arguments mentioned above that are opposed to the empirical possibility of survival are based on a certain assumption of the relationship between mind and body that usually goes unstated. For instance, one of the arguments mentioned earlier starts with the observation that a severe blow to the head can cause the cessation of consciousness; from this it is concluded that consciousness is produced by a properly functioning brain, and so cannot exist in its absence.

However, this conclusion is not based on the evidence alone. There is an implicit, unstated assumption behind this argument, and it is often unconsciously employed. The hidden premise behind this argument can be illustrated with the analogy of listening to music on a radio, smashing the radio's receiver, and thereby concluding that the radio was producing the music. The implicit assumption made in all the arguments discussed above was that the relationship between brain activity and consciousness was always one of *cause to effect,* and never that of *effect to cause.* But this assumption is not known to be true, and it is not the only conceivable one consistent with the observed facts mentioned earlier. Just as consistent with the observed facts is the idea that the brain's function is that of an intermediary between mind and body, or in other words, that the brain's function is that of a two-way receiver-transmitter—sometimes from body to mind, and sometimes from mind to body.

The idea that the brain functions as an intermediary between mind and body is an ancient one. Hippocrates described the brain as "the messenger to consciousness" and as "the interpreter for consciousness." But, like the materialist theory, this ancient argument also has its modern proponents, most notably Ferdinand Schiller, Henri Bergson, and William James.

Ferdinand Schiller was an Oxford philosopher in 1891 when a book titled *Riddles of the Sphinx* appeared that, according to the cover, was written by a "Troglodyte" (cave dweller). This troglodyte turned out to be Schiller, who in his book attacked the prevailing materialism of the late nineteenth century without revealing his name in order to avoid "the barren honours of a useless martyrdom." Schiller likened himself to the man in Plato's *Republic* who has glimpsed the truth but finds that his fellow cave dwellers simply do not believe his accounts, and so consider him ridiculous.

In his book, Schiller proposes that "matter is admirably calculated machinery for regulating, limiting and restraining the consciousness which it encases." He argues that the simpler physical structure of "lower beings" depresses their consciousness to a lower point and that the higher organizational complexity of man allows a higher level of consciousness. In other words, "Matter is not what *produces* consciousness but what *limits* it and confines its intensity within certain limits. . . . This explanation admits the connection of Matter and Consciousness, but contends that the course of interpretation must proceed in the contrary direction. Thus it will fit the facts which Materialism rejected as 'supernatural' and thereby attains to an explanation which is ultimately tenable instead of one which is ultimately absurd. And it is an explanation the possibility of which no evidence in favour of Materialism can possibly affect."[11]

As for the effects of brain injury, Schiller argues that an equally good explanation is to say that the manifestation of consciousness has been prevented by the injury, rather than extinguished by it. With regard to memory, he thinks that it is forgetfulness rather than memory that is in need of a physical explanation: pointing out the total recall experienced under hypnosis and "the extraordinary memories of the drowning and dying generally," he argues that we never really forget anything, but rather are prevented from recalling it by the limitations of the brain.

French philosopher Henri Bergson held similar ideas to those of Schiller, although it is unclear if he ever read *Riddles of the Sphinx*. Bergson attempted to reconcile physical determinism with the apparent freedom of human behavior by proposing a theory of evolution whereby matter is crossed by creative consciousness: matter and consciousness interact, with both being elemental components of the universe, neither reducible to the other.

According to Bergson, the brain canalizes and limits the mind, restricting its focus of attention and excluding factors irrelevant for the organism's survival and propagation. He assumed that memories have an extracerebral location, but that most are normally screened out for practical purposes, and in support of this, referred to NDEs in which the subjects' entire life histories flashed before their eyes. The brain is therefore both "the organ of attention to life" and an obstacle to wider awareness. He speculated that if the brain is a limiting obstacle, filtering out forms of consciousness not necessary for the organism's biological needs, then freedom from the body may well result in a more extended form of consciousness, which continues along its path of creative evolution.

In 1898, American psychologist and philosopher William James delivered the Ingersoll Lecture. At the start of the lecture, he first remarked, "Every one knows that arrests of brain development occasion imbecility, that blows on the head abolish memory or consciousness, and that brain-stimulants and poisons change the quality of our ideas." He then made the point that modern physiologists "have only shown this generally admitted fact of a dependence to be detailed and minute" in that "the various special forms of thinking are functions of special portions of the brain."

James then explored the various possibilities for the exact *type* of functional dependence between the brain and consciousness. It is normally thought of as productive, in the sense that steam is produced as a function of the kettle. But this is not the only form of function that we find in nature. We also have at least two other forms of functional dependence: the permissive function, as found in the trigger of a crossbow, and the transmissive function, as of a lens or a prism. The lens or prism does not produce the light but merely transmits it in a different form. James added that

> similarly, the keys of an organ have only a transmissive function. They open successively the various pipes and let the wind in the air-chest escape in various ways. The voices of the various pipes are constituted by the columns of air trembling as they emerge. But the air is not engendered in the organ. The organ proper, as distinguished from its air-chest, is only an apparatus for letting portions of it loose upon the world in these peculiarly limited shapes.
>
> My thesis now is this, that, when we think of the law that thought is a function of the brain, we are not required to think of productive function only; we are entitled also to consider permissive or transmissive function. And this, the ordinary psychophysiologist leaves out of his account.[12]

James then raises an objection to the transmissive theory of the body-mind relationship: yes, the transmission hypothesis may be a logical possibility, but isn't it just unbridled speculation? Isn't the production hypothesis simpler? Is it not more rigorously scientific to take the relationship between brain and mind to be one of production, not transmission?

As James points out, from the standpoint of strictly empirical science, these objections carry no weight whatsoever. Strictly speaking, the most we can ever observe is concomitant variation between states of the brain and states of mind, that is, when brain activity changes in a certain way, then consciousness changes also. The hypothesis of production, or of transmission, is something that we add to the observations of concomitant variation in order to account for it. A scientist never observes states of the brain producing states of consciousness. Indeed, it is not even clear what we could possibly mean by observing such production.

As for the objection that the transmission hypothesis is somehow fantastic, exactly the same objection can be raised against the production theory. In the case of the production of steam by a kettle, we have an easily understood model of alterations of molecular motion because the components that change are physically homogenous with each other. But part of the reason the mind-body relationship has seemed so puzzling for so long is because mental and physical events seem so completely unlike each other. This radical difference in their natures makes it exceedingly difficult to conceptualize the relationship between the two in terms of anything of which we are familiar. It is partly for this reason that even though it has been more than a century since James delivered his lecture, in all that time neither psychology nor physiology has been able to produce any intelligible model of how biochemical processes could possibly be transformed into conscious experience.

It has been pointed out many times that there is no logical requirement that only "like can cause like," or in other words, that only things of a similar nature can affect each other; but this consideration has not removed the mystery from the mind-body relationship. As James wrote, the production of consciousness by the brain, if it does in fact occur, is "as far as our understanding goes, as great a miracle as if we said, thought is 'spontaneously generated,' or 'created out of nothing.'" He goes on to write:

> The theory of production is therefore not a jot more simple or credible in itself than any other conceivable theory. It is only a little more popular. All that one need do, therefore, if the ordinary materialist should challenge one to explain how the brain *can* be an organ for limiting and determining to a certain form a consciousness elsewhere produced, is to ask him in turn to explain how it can be an organ for producing consciousness out of whole cloth. For polemic purposes, the two theories are thus exactly on a par.[13]

In short, James elaborated lines of reasoning laid out earlier by Schiller and argued that the dependence of consciousness on the brain for the manner of its manifestation in the material world does not imply that consciousness depends on the brain for its existence. At the end of his book *The Varieties of Religious Experience,* he admits to being impressed by the research of Frederic Myers and other members of the Society for

Psychical Research and concludes that the issue of survival is a case for the testimony of the facts to settle.

James wrote these works around the turn of the twentieth century, but since then these arguments have been endorsed and developed by several more recent philosophers, neurologists, and psychologists, such as philosophers Curt Ducasse and David Lund, neurologist Gary Schwartz, and psychologist Cyril Burt. The latter elegantly summarized the position set forth earlier by Schiller, Bergson, and James, writing,

> The brain is not an organ that generates consciousness, but rather an instrument evolved to transmit and limit the processes of consciousness and of conscious attention so as to restrict them to those aspects of the material environment which at any moment are crucial for the terrestrial success of the individual. In that case such phenomena as telepathy and clairvoyance would be merely instances in which some of the limitations were removed.[14]

The argument in its essence is that the transmission and production hypotheses are equally compatible with the facts materialism tries to explain—such as the effects of senility, drugs, and brain damage on consciousness—but that the hypothesis of transmission has the advantage of providing a framework for understanding other phenomena that must remain utterly inexplicable by the hypothesis of materialism.

TWO

OBJECTIONS OF SKEPTICS

It is time for more scientists and interpreters of science to come forward to explain what science tells us about the universe: for example . . . that the evidence points to a biological basis for the mind, and that there is no evidence for reincarnation or immortality.

PAUL KURTZ, CHAIRMAN OF THE COMMITTEE FOR
THE SCIENTIFIC INVESTIGATION OF CLAIMS
OF THE PARANORMAL, 1994

Some modern philosophers continue to argue that the physical evidence is evidence *against* the transmission hypothesis and *for* the hypothesis of production. This confusion is most recently found in the writings of Paul Edwards, a well-known philosopher of materialism, who begins his argument quite reasonably with the statement, "The weightiest argument against reincarnation which, if valid, would also undermine most other forms of belief in survival, is based on the dependence of consciousness on the body and more particularly on the brain. . . . The issue is one of weighing the evidence from brain physiology against that from parapsychology. For my part I do not see how any rational person can hesitate in regarding the former evidence as *vastly* more impressive."[1]

Let us examine Edwards' arguments. First of all, apart from a brief description of the brains of people with Alzheimer's disease "culled from articles about Alzheimer's that have appeared in magazines and popular science monthlies in recent years," Edwards does not offer any detailed arguments from physiology. Instead, he simply passes the buck to his fellow philosopher of materialism Colin McGinn, whom Edwards quotes as saying that the facts of neurology "compellingly demonstrate . . . that everything about the mind, from the sensory-motor periphery to the inner sense of self, is minutely controlled by the brain: if your brain lacks certain chemicals or gets locally damaged, your mind is apt to fall apart at the seams. . . . If parts of the mind depend for their existence upon parts of the brain, then the whole of the mind must so depend, too. Hence the soul dies with the brain, which is to say, it is mortal."[2]

McGinn is not a brain physiologist, but a philosopher, and should know better than to argue like this.* The crucial sentence above is "If parts of the mind depend for their existence upon parts of the brain, then the whole of the mind must so depend, too." This statement is logically correct, but McGinn has certainly not shown that "parts of the mind depend for their existence upon parts of the brain." The facts of neurology, as James remarked, "have only shown this generally admitted fact of a dependence to be detailed and minute" in that "the various special forms of thinking are functions of special portions of the brain." As James took pains to point out one hundred years earlier, the issue at stake is the *nature* of this functional dependence, that is, whether it is one of production or of selective transmission. McGinn has simply assumed that the functional relationship is one of production, and so has gone far beyond what the facts themselves indicate.†

Furthermore, what does McGinn mean by "parts of the mind"? Is he referring to abilities, memories, or emotions? Intoxication or damage

---

*To be fair, I am basing this conclusion only on the above quote as found in Edwards' book. Unfortunately, I could not check the original source, as Edwards does not provide it.
†The word *function* (from the Latin *fungere,* to perform) has a variety of meanings. Most broadly, when two things A and B vary concomitantly, then the two sets of variations are said to be functionally related. Either can be said to be a function of the other, and in the absence of other considerations or assumptions regarding cause and effect, either one can be considered the dependent or independent variable.

to the brain may indeed affect our mental life, but that does not mean that "parts of the mind" no longer exist; equally consistent with this fact is that the abilities or memories are impaired, inactivated, or inaccessible.

Edwards considers the case of a patient with Alzheimer's disease, which he thinks illustrates that "the instrument theory is absurd." It concerns the mother of a friend of his, a "Mrs. D.," who in her pre-Alzheimer's days was "courteous and well-behaved," but who ended up in a nursing home and in the later stages of the disease not only no longer recognized her daughter, but also became violent.

> Let us now see what the survival theorists would say about Mrs. D.'s behavior. It should be remembered that on this view Mrs. D., after her death, will exist with her mind intact and will only lack the means of communicating with people on earth. This view implies that throughout her affliction with Alzheimer's Mrs. D.'s mind *was* intact. She recognized her daughter but had lost her ability to express this recognition. She had no wish to beat up an inoffensive paralyzed old woman. On the contrary, "inside" she was the same considerate person as before the onset of the illness. It is simply that her brain disease prevented her from acting in accordance with her true emotions. I must insist these *are* the implications of the theory that the mind survives the death of the brain and that the brain is only an instrument for communication. Surely these consequences are absurd.[3]

However, these are *not* necessarily the implications of the theory that the brain is an instrument of the mind, but only of Edwards' crude caricature of this theory. The disputed issue is not the fact of functional dependence of mind on brain, but only the nature of this functional dependence, that is, whether it is productive, transmissive, or permissive. It is perfectly conceivable that Mrs. D.'s damaged brain prevented her from accessing memories of her daughter, so that she genuinely did not recognize her. If, following Ducasse, we define the mind as "a set of capacities,"[4] then by this definition[5] Mrs. D.'s mind was not "intact" (from the Latin word *intactus,* meaning "untouched"), since it would seem that several capacities were indeed affected. However, the fact that certain capacities do not appear to currently function because of impairment due to disease, injury, or intoxication does not imply that they have been permanently destroyed.

If the mind must inhabit a biological machine in order to operate in and manifest itself in the material world, then as long as it is bound to this machine we should expect its operation and manifestation to be affected by the condition and limitations of the machine. If the machine is impaired, then under both the production hypothesis *and* the transmission hypothesis, so too will be the operation and manifestation of mind. Both of these theoretical possibilities are consistent with the observed facts of this case.

However, the effects of brain damage and old age on the mind are *not* consistent with Edwards' crude caricature of the transmission theory, in which causal effect only seems to run from mind to body, and never from body to mind. This seems to be the basis for Edwards' repeated characterization of the instrument theory, and its implications, as "absurd."

Yet it is conceivable that only as long as an individual has a body is consciousness dependent on it for its operation and its manifestation and that when the body dies the individual is freed from this dependency. Consciousness may be joined with a brain during life; the interaction may run both ways, as it apparently does with every causal relationship in the physical world;* and at death the connection may be severed. The fact that up until the brain's death the mind can be affected by the condition and limitations of the brain does *not* entail that the mind cannot continue to exist without the brain and carry on at least some of its processes.

After presenting his case with Mrs. D., Edwards then switches to an ancient argument of the materialists:

------

*In the essay "Remarks on the Mind-Body Question," which argues the scientific case for interactive dualism, Nobel prize–winning physicist Eugene Wigner wrote that "we do not know of any phenomenon in nature in which one subject is influenced by another without exerting an influence thereupon" (Wigner, 1983).

It might be added that quite aside from such disastrous brain disturbances as Alzheimer's, it is well known that many, perhaps most, people deteriorate with age, both intellectually and emotionally. Their memory declines, they are less capable of absorbing new ideas, they get less interested in the world around them, they constantly look for compliments and they also become crankier, more impatient, and more dogmatic in their views. This is far from universal and it is an interesting question why so many people deteriorate while a few do not. However, regardless of how this last question is answered, it is very generally agreed that the intellectual and emotional deterioration, where it does occur, is due to changes in the brain, although undoubtedly other factors are also at work. *It is perfectly natural to say in such situations—and all of us speak and think like this, even believers in survival—that the person's mind has deteriorated with age. The annihilation theory is completely consistent with such a statement but the instrument theory is not.* An advocate of the latter would have to say that the mind itself has not deteriorated and that the changes we note are due to the fact that the mind does not have an undamaged instrument at its disposal.[6] (emphasis added)

Edwards wrote above, "It is perfectly natural to say in such situations— and all of us speak and think like this, even believers in survival—that the person's mind has deteriorated with age." It is debatable whether "*all* of us speak and think like this." Regardless, it is also "perfectly natural" to say that the sun rises and sets, but that does not mean that the sun in fact revolves around the planet Earth. The fact that an idea clashes with our current habits of speech and thought does not automatically imply that it is absurd. It is testimony to the desperation of the materialists and the weakness of their case that one of the strongest arguments Edwards can invoke for his cause is that "the annihilation theory is completely consistent" with what he feels it is "perfectly natural to say."

At any rate, neither Edwards nor McGinn are scientists, so it seems appropriate to now examine some of the arguments from three neuroscientists who have examined the physiological evidence in great detail.

THREE

OPINIONS FROM
NEUROSCIENCE

Wilder Penfield started his career as a neurosurgeon trying to explain the mind in terms of physical processes in the brain. In the course of surgical treatment of patients who have temporal lobe seizures, Penfield stumbled upon the fact that electrical stimulation of certain areas of the cortex could activate a stream of memories that had been laid down years or even decades earlier. In fact, the patient would "relive" the earlier episode, recalling incidents in far greater detail than would be possible by voluntary recall, but during the flashback, the patient would remain completely aware of what was happening in the operating room. Penfield summed up the conclusions he formed on the basis of these experiments by stating:

> The patient's mind, which is considering the situation in such an aloof and critical manner, can only be something quite apart from neuronal reflex action. It is noteworthy that two streams of consciousness are flowing, the one driven by input from the environment, the other by an electrode delivering sixty pulses per second to the cortex. The fact that there should be no confusion in the conscious state suggests that, although the content of consciousness depends in large measure on neuronal activity, awareness itself does not.[1]

On the basis of his experiments and examinations of patients with various forms of epilepsy, Penfield concluded that the mind interacts with the brain in the upper brain stem, an ancient structure that humans share with reptiles. Penfield, who won the Nobel Prize for his work, considers the rest of the brain to be a magnificent biological computer, programmed by the mind. He found that electrical stimulation of most parts of the brain resulted either in memories relived in vivid detail, involuntary movement of a part of the body, or paralysis of some function, such as speech. By contrast, injury to or epileptic discharge in the higher brain stem always simply resulted in loss of consciousness, leading Penfield to conclude, "Here is the meeting of mind and brain. The psychico-physical frontier is here."

Penfield thought that the brain as a computer could accomplish a great deal by automatic mechanisms, but that "what the mind does is different. It is not to be accounted for by any neuronal mechanism that I can discover." He also stated:

> There is *no* area of gray matter, as far as my experience goes, in which local epileptic discharge brings to pass what could be called "mind-action" . . . there is no valid evidence that either epileptic discharge or electrical stimulation can activate the mind.
>
> If one stops to consider it, this is an arresting fact. The record of consciousness can be set in motion, complicated though it is, by the electrode or by epileptic discharge. An illusion of interpretation can be produced in the same way. But none of the actions that we attribute to the mind has been initiated by electrode stimulation or epileptic discharge. If there were a mechanism in the brain that could do what the mind does, one might expect that the mechanism would betray its presence in a convincing manner by some better evidence of epileptic or electrode activation.[2]

In other words, Penfield argues that if the brain produced or generated consciousness, then we would expect that consciousness itself could be influenced by epilepsy or electrical stimulation in some way other than simply being switched off; that is, we would expect beliefs or decisions to be produced. The complete absence of any such effect in Penfield's experience led him to reject the production hypothesis in favor of dualistic interaction.

Edwards argues that the most Penfield has shown is that brain activity is not a *sufficient* condition of consciousness; Edwards argues that it may still be a *necessary* condition. Edwards refers to this alleged confusion of sufficient and necessary conditions as "the confusions of Penfield."[3] Edwards wrote, "The fact that Penfield could not produce beliefs or decisions by electrical stimulation of the brain in no way shows that they do not need what we may call a brain-base any less than memories and sensations." But Penfield fully agrees that the brain *might* still be a necessary condition for consciousness. He wrote, "When death at last blows out the candle that was life . . . what can one really conclude? What is the reasonable hypothesis in regard to this matter, considering the physiological evidence? Only this: the brain has not explained the mind fully."[4]* Penfield's point is simply that there is nothing in brain physiology that precludes the possibility of consciousness in the absence of a brain, contrary to what Edwards would have us believe. Once again it is Edwards who is confused—in this case, about what Penfield actually thought.

In direct contrast to Edwards' statement that "the instrument theory is absurd," Penfield writes: "To expect the highest brain-mechanism or any set of reflexes, however complicated, to carry out what the mind does,

---

*This is Penfield's analysis of what happens when consciousness is interrupted by injury, epileptic seizure, drugs, or deep sleep:

"*What happens when the mind vanishes?* There are two obvious answers to that question; they arise from Sherington's two alternatives—whether man's being is to be explained on the basis of one or two elements. If the first alternative is chosen, the mind no longer exists when it vanishes, since it is only a function of brain action. Mind is recreated each time the highest brain-mechanism goes into normal action.

"Or, if one chooses the second, the dualistic alternative, the mind must be viewed as a basic element in itself. . . . That is to say, it has a continuing existence. On this basis, one must assume that although the mind is silent when it no longer has its special connection to the brain, it exists in the silent intervals and takes over control when the highest brain-mechanism does go into action.

"Thus, it would seem that this specialized brain-mechanism switches off the power that energizes the mind each time it falls asleep. This is the daily automatic routine to which all mammals are committed and by which the brain recovers from fatigue" (Penfield 1975, 81).

and thus perform all the functions of the mind, is quite absurd."[5]

Penfield sums up what he thinks the physiological evidence suggests for the relationship between mind and body.

> On the basis of mind and brain as two semi-independent elements, one would still be forced to assume that the mind makes its impact upon the brain through the highest brain-mechanism. The mind must act upon it. The mind must also be acted upon by the highest brain-mechanism. The mind must remember by making use of the brain's recording mechanisms. . . . And yet the mind seems to act independently of the brain in the same sense that a programmer acts independently of his computer, however much he may depend upon the action of that computer for certain purposes.[6]

On the final pages of his book he states:

> I worked as a scientist trying to prove that the brain accounted for the mind and demonstrating as many brain-mechanisms as possible hoping to show *how* the brain did so. In presenting this monograph I do not begin with a conclusion and I do not end by making a final and unalterable one. Instead, I reconsider the present-day neuro-physiological evidence on the basis of two hypotheses: (a) that man's being consists of one fundamental element, and (b) that it consists of two. In the end I conclude that there is no good evidence, in spite of new methods, such as the employment of stimulating electrodes, the study of conscious patients and the analysis of epileptic attacks, that the brain alone can carry out the work that the mind does. I conclude that it is easier to rationalize man's being on the basis of two elements than on the basis of one.[7]

The relevance of Penfield's arguments can be summarized as this: if the neurophysiological evidence suggests that man's being consists of two elements rather than one, then the separate existence of these two elements cannot be ruled out by consideration of this evidence.

A second prominent neuroscientist to endorse a dualistic model of mind-brain interaction was John Eccles, who found the conscious integration of visual experience impossible to account for in terms of known neurological processes because nerve impulses related to visual experience appear to be fragmented and sent to divergent areas of the brain. This difficulty led Eccles to postulate the existence of a conscious mind existing separate from and in addition to the physical brain, with the raison d'etre of the former being the integration of neural activity.

In addition to noting that there is a unitary character about the experiences of the self-conscious mind despite the fragmentary nature of brain activity, Eccles also held that there can be a temporal discrepancy between neural events and conscious experiences* and that there is a continual experience that the mind can act on brain events, which is most apparent in voluntary action or the attempt to recall a word or a memory. These considerations, combined with his lifelong study of the brain and its neurons, form the basis of his opinions on the mind-body relationship.

Eccles hypothesizes that the mind may influence the brain by exerting spatio-temporal patterns of influence on the brain, which operates as a detector of these fields of influence. In his book *Facing Reality: Philosophical Adventures of a Brain Scientist,* Eccles first discusses the structure and activity of the brain in great detail and then writes:

> In this discussion of the functioning of the brain, it has initially been regarded as a "machine" operating according to the laws of physics and chemistry. In conscious states it has been shown that it could be in a state of extreme sensitivity as a detector of minute spatio-temporal fields of influence. The hypothesis is here developed that these spatio-temporal fields of influence are exerted by the mind on the brain in willed action. If one uses the expressive terminol-

---

*These experiments are described in detail in my previous book *Parapsychology and the Skeptics.*

ogy of Ryle, the "ghost" operates a "machine," not of ropes and pulleys, valves and pipes, but of microscopic spatio-temporal patterns of activity in the neuronal net woven by the synaptic connections of ten thousand million neurons, and even then only by operating on neurons that are momentarily poised close to a just threshold level of excitability. It would appear that it is the sort of machine a "ghost" could operate, if by ghost we mean in the first place an "agent" whose action has escaped detection even by the most delicate physical instruments.[8]*

Eccles postulated a two-way interaction between brain and mind, with "brain receiving from conscious mind in a willed action and in turn transmitting to mind in a conscious experience."[9] It is not clear whether Eccles was convinced of the existence of an afterlife, but he did write, "At

---

*Along with the mechanists, Eccles seems to think that organisms can be thought of as "machines," but the accuracy of this comparison is highly questionable. The brain and nervous system appear to be highly dynamic, in contrast to the static structure of machines. For instance, studies of the brains of canaries, especially those parts involved in the learning of song, have shown that not only do many new connections between nerve cells continue to develop but many new nerve cells also appear, especially in males as mating season approaches. Experiments with monkeys have shown that sensory areas of the brain that map different parts of the body are not hardwired; amputation of fingers, for example, resulted in shifting of function into now unused areas of the brain, with greater acuity of sensation in the remaining fingers. And damage to parts of the cortex resulted in a shift of the map to regions surrounding the lost area, with some loss of acuity (Sheldrake 1990, 114–15).

In addition, astronomer V. A. Firsoff wrote, "Structure is fundamental to machines, whatever emergent characteristics these may display, inasmuch as the performance of a machine is the direct outcome of its structure. The concept of structure is essentially static. A machine can perform if actuated, but it need not perform. This does perhaps resemble the behavior of a virus, whose true aliveness is in doubt on this score. An organism, however, is no machine, not even one operated by a ghost: It is an event propagated by continuous change in the four dimensions of space-time. Its 'structure' is like that of a river, which is never the same and cannot be stepped into twice, in the words of Heraclitus. The real essence lies in the process, seen in time cross section, like a snapshot" (Firsoff 1975, 117).

least I would maintain that this possibility of a future existence cannot be denied on scientific grounds."[10]*

It needs to be stressed that the findings of modern neuroscience do not alter the argument one bit, as they are equally compatible with both production and transmission. Gary Schwartz, professor of psychology, neurology, psychiatry, medicine, and surgery at the University of Arizona, points out that among neuroscientists with a materialist bent, the belief that consciousness arises from physical processes in the brain is based on three kinds of investigation:

1. Correlation studies (e.g., electroencephalogram, or EEG, correlates of visual perception)
2. Stimulation studies (e.g., electrical or magnetic stimulation)
3. Ablation studies (e.g., the effect of brain lesions).

However, analogous methods are applied during television repair with parallel results, yet no one comes to the conclusion that pictures on the screen are created inside the television. Schwartz describes the brain as the "antenna-receiver" for the mind and points out that the evidence from neuroscience, like the evidence from television repair, is just as compatible with the hypothesis of reception-transmission as it is with the hypothesis of production.

Like Penfield and Eccles before him, Schwartz has also come to the conclusion that the mind is a separate entity from the brain, and that mental processes cannot be reduced to neurochemical brain processes but on the contrary direct them. Like Penfield and Eccles, he also thinks that a mind may conceivably exist without a brain. Since Edwards has not suc-

---

*Compare the following statement of Eccles, given in the introduction of his book, with the statement of McGinn provided earlier by Edwards: "There need be no fear that this attempt to understand the brain scientifically will lead to the removal of the 'final illusions of man about his own spiritual existence,' which would be the claim of some positivist scientists as well as philosophers. On the contrary, the framework of a quite inadequate and primitive concept of the brain provides the medium in which flourish the materialistic, mechanistic, behaviouristic, and cybernetic concepts of man, which at present dominate research" (Eccles 1970, 6).

ceeded in showing that the possibility of survival is inconsistent with the facts of neurology, and since we have seen that three prominent neuroscientists do not share Edwards' opinion that the transmission theory is "absurd," we can now clearly see Edwards dismissal as what it is: dogmatic prejudice against an empirical possibility that does not coincide with his materialistic faith.*

---

*Consider this recent remark from Sam Parnia, physician and biochemist: "In the scientific community it is generally thought that the mind is a product of brain cell (neuronal) activity. This is based upon a number of studies including those with a technique known as functional MRI which have shown that certain sets of brain cells (neurones) in various areas of the brain become metabolically (chemically) active in response to a particular thought or feeling. This has led to a common view that the particular area of the brain that has been observed to change metabolically equates with the production of a particular thought. However, when examined critically, this observation only implies the role of such cells as a mediator in expressing those thoughts and does not necessarily imply an origin to the thought itself. What is not known and what is currently an issue causing great debate in the field of neuroscience is how brain cells (neurones) which like other cells in the body produce molecular products such as proteins can lead to the subjective experience of the mind and thought. Although the conventional scientific view is that the mind is the product of complex chemical processes in groups of brain cells (neural networks) there are others who disagree. In a lecture at the Royal College of Physicians in London a few years ago, entitled 'Brains and minds: a brief history of neuromythology' to my surprise, the lecturer; a well respected professor of medicine discussed the mind/brain topic and concluded that the belief held by some neuroscientists that some day the discovery of more complicated molecular pathways would lead to an understanding of the mind is more compatible with 'neuromythology' than neuroscience" (S Parnia and P Fenwick 2002).

FOUR

PHYSICS AND CONSCIOUSNESS

The stream of knowledge is heading toward a non-mechanical reality; the universe begins to look more like a great thought than like a machine. Mind no longer appears to be an accidental intruder into the realm of matter; we ought rather hail it as the governor of the realm of matter.

PHYSICIST JAMES JEANS

What many people believe to be our "modern, scientific worldview" is in fact a legacy of classical, Newtonian physics, which has been known to be fundamentally flawed since the early years of the twentieth century. As we will see, many of the arguments of the materialists are based on classical physics and the worldview it spawned. However, many physicists now believe that modern physics supports a dualistic model of mind-brain interaction. It is to this issue we now turn.

THE ANCIENT AND MEDIEVAL WORLDVIEW

The philosophers of ancient Greece set the scene for science by seeing nature as explicable. When their writings were rediscovered in the late

Middle Ages, setting the stage for the Renaissance, they were considered to be the wisdom of a lost golden age; and none of these ancient philosophers had a greater impact on the Middle Ages than Aristotle.

Aristotle realized that the physical events we observe are essentially the motion of matter. He therefore sought to explain the motion of objects using a few fundamental principles, which is the way we do physics today; but his method was to derive these principles as intuitively self-evident truths. For instance, Aristotle stated that an object sought rest with respect to the cosmic center, which seemed clearly to be Earth. An object fell to Earth because of its desire to be at the cosmic center. Hence, a heavier object will "obviously" fall faster than a lighter object because of the former's greater desire to unite with the center. And in the perfect heavens above, heavenly objects moved in perfect spheres around the cosmic center, Earth.

Greek philosophers would argue over conflicting theories of nature indefinitely, much as they would argue over theories of politics or esthetics. Aristotle did not propose to *test* his theories, and so progress was impossible; science had been conceived, but had not yet been born.

In the second century CE, Ptolemy of Alexandria developed an astronomical system based on the idea that the planets moved in perfect circles around a stationary Earth. More precisely, to explain the back and forth "wandering" motion of the planets (*planet* means "wanderer" in Greek), Ptolemy had the planets move in epicycles, complicated motions of circles rolling on circles. However, the system was in fact so accurate that calendars based on his model worked very well, as did predictions of the positions of the planets.

During the late Middle Ages, the views of Aristotle and Ptolemy became official Catholic Church dogma, mostly through the work of Thomas Aquinas. Combining Aristotle's natural philosophy with the moral and spiritual teachings of the Church, Aquinas created a compelling synthesis. Earth, to which things fell, was the home of "fallen" man; the perfect heavens above, where objects moved in perfect spheres around Earth, was the realm of God and his angels; and the center of Earth, the lowest point to which things could fall, was hell, the abode of Lucifer, the fallen angel. The physics of Aristotle and the astronomy of Ptolemy became not only practical truth but also religious doctrine, enforced brutally by the Inquisition.

In the sixteenth century, Copernicus devised an alternative to Ptolemy's model by suggesting that Earth and the planets orbit the sun. In this model, Earth became the third planet from the sun. The model was simpler, but seemed to be in conflict with both common sense (after all, no one *feels* the Earth move) and with official Church doctrine. Fearful of provoking the authorities, Copernicus was careful to describe his model as only a mathematical convenience, not actual fact.

Galileo lacked the humility and tact of Copernicus. Convinced the Copernican system was true, Galileo argued for a new worldview and eventually came to the attention of the Holy Inquisition. In 1600, Giordano Bruno had been burned at the stake for, among other things, the heresy of expressing belief in the heliocentric theory of Copernicus.* It is therefore not surprising that when Galileo fell into the hands of the Inquisition sixteen years later, he played it safe and recanted.†

Galileo also contradicted Aristotle's claims, arguing, for instance, that in the absence of air resistance, heavy and light objects will fall at the same rate. These assertions also met with stiff resistance, particularly from the lower levels of the clergy and the Aristotelians in the universities.[1] Aristotle's system was an all-encompassing worldview, and rejecting

---

*Bruno is sometimes presented as a martyr to the cause of science, but his execution had more do to with his religious heresies than his scientific ones. Within some orders of the Church, such as the Jesuits, the Copernican system could be freely discussed and advocated, but only as a working hypothesis, because it seemed contrary to scripture. More definite proof was needed than was available at the time of Galileo before it could be presented as fact (which was how Galileo presented it).

†This review of Galileo's troubles is brief and so somewhat simplistic. His conflict with the Church was by no means inevitable and seems to have been provoked by his confrontational attitude with those he considered intellectually inferior. Many in the Church were sympathetic to his views. However, the Aristotelians in the universities had a vested interest in protecting their worldview and were hostile to Galileo for decades. An excellent and balanced review of this conflict can be found in Part Five of Arthur Koestler's book *The Sleepwalkers: A History of Man's Changing Vision of the Universe.*

any part of it would seem to imply the rejection of all of it. How could Galileo convince others that he was right and Aristotle was wrong?

His novel solution was to create special situations in which his ideas could be *tested,* that is, he invented experiments. Testing theoretical predictions with experiments seems obvious today, but in his time it was a new and profound idea. Galileo is said to have simultaneously dropped an iron ball and a wood ball from the Tower of Pisa, thus demonstrating that heavy and light objects fall at the same speed. Galileo argued that scientific claims should be based on observation and experimental demonstration, and not on the statements of authority. Within a few decades, Galileo's new method was widely accepted, and the scientific revolution was launched with a vengeance.

CLASSICAL PHYSICS

Classical physics is a set of theories of nature that originated with the work of Isaac Newton in the seventeenth century, was advanced by many scientists through the eighteenth and nineteenth centuries, and finally culminated in the relativity theories of Albert Einstein, the last great classical physicist. Building on the earlier work of Galileo and Johannes Kepler, Newton developed a theory of gravity and three simple laws of motion that accurately predicted the motions of the planets as well as that of terrestrial objects here on Earth, such as cannonballs, falling apples, and the tides.

Newton assumed that all physical objects were composed of tiny versions of large visible objects, which he described as "solid, massy, hard, impenetrable moveable particles."[2] These tiny objects were assumed to interact by means of direct contact, much like billiard balls. The only exception was the mysterious action at a distance called gravity: Newton's theory of gravity proposed that every tiny particle in the solar system attracted every other one with a force inversely proportional to the square of the distance between them. This deeply troubled Newton, who referred to this action at a distance as an "absurdity"; nevertheless, he formulated his theory of gravity as an equation and simply declined to speculate on how it was mediated, famously writing *"hypotheses non fingo"* ("I make no hypotheses").

It was Einstein who finally proposed a mediating agent for gravity: a distortion in space and time caused by the mass of objects, with more massive objects causing greater distortion. This contribution made classical physics a *local* theory: there is no action at a distance. All influence is transmitted locally along a force field, and no influence—including that of gravity—propagates faster than the speed of light. If, for instance, the sun were to be suddenly destroyed, Earth would drift out of its orbit about eight minutes later.

In classical physics, all interactions between particles are local and occur independent of anyone observing them. Moreover, the interactions are assumed to be deterministic: that is, the future state of the physical world is completely determined by the state at an earlier time. According to classical physics, the complete history of the physical world was determined for all time at the origin of the universe. The universe was now seen as a great machine. God may have created the machine and set it running—according to Newton, the planets were originally hurled by the hand of God—but once started, the solar system was kept going by its own momentum and operated as a self-regulating machine in accordance with inviolable laws.

Classical physics had two ways of dealing with the problem of consciousness and free will. The first, followed by Newton and René Descartes, was to assume that human consciousness and free will lay outside the domain of physics. Descartes taught that animals were mindless automatons, but humans had a soul and were thus the sole exceptions in an otherwise deterministic, mechanistic universe. The second way of dealing with free will, popularized by the eighteenth-century *philosophes* who were greatly inspired by Newton's work, was to argue that classical physics was a complete description of the entire world, including human beings, and that free will was therefore an illusion.

The ancient philosophy of materialism was now thought to have a scientific foundation. Scientists and philosophers now had good reasons to believe that the physical aspects of reality were causally closed: the physical could affect the mental via its affect on the brain, such as the experience of pain after touching a flame, but the mental could not affect the physical. Pulling one's hand away from the flame was now seen by the materialists as the predetermined response of an automaton. Thoughts, feelings, and intentions were now seen as causally redundant: it was now argued that consciousness serves no purpose and that our intuitive feeling of free will is only an illusion.

These views became prevalent in the eighteenth century, during what became known as the Enlightenment, which can be thought of as the ideological aftermath of the scientific revolution. Its most striking feature was the rejection of dogma and tradition in favor of the rule of reason in human affairs, and it was the precursor of modern secular humanism. Inspired by the dazzling success of the new physics, prominent spokesmen such as Denis Diderot and Voltaire argued for a new worldview based on an uncompromising mechanism and determinism that left no room for any intervention of mind in nature, whether human or divine.

In the eighteenth century, the horrors of the religious wars, the witch hunts, and the Inquisition were still fresh in peoples' minds, and the new scientific worldview, spread by men such as Diderot and Voltaire, can be seen partly as a reaction against the ecclesiastical domination over thought that the Church held for centuries. As we have seen, Bruno was burned at the stake for his opinions, and Galileo was persecuted for his but recanted. Yet Galileo's insistence that only observation and experimentation, not authority, were the arbiters of truth in science had launched a revolution in thinking. When Newton's *Principia* was published in 1687, it was not suppressed but instead reached a wide audience. The Newtonian system predicted the orbits of the planets with astonishing accuracy and even reduced comets from portents of disaster to phenomena whose appearance in the sky could be predicted like clockwork. The universe was now viewed as a gigantic clockwork mechanism. The so-called modern scientific worldview was thus born and has had enormous impact on philosophy for the last three hundred years.

For a philosopher whose thinking is tied to classical physics, there are two possible ways to understand the inability of the mental to influence the physical. The first is to consider thoughts, feelings, and intentions as epiphenomena, that is, useless by-products that are somehow produced by the brain, but in turn exert no causal influence on the brain. The second is to consider the mind as identical to the brain, that is, thoughts and feelings are the same thing as the motion of tiny particles inside the brain.

QUANTUM MECHANICS

Quantum mechanics was developed early in the twentieth century to explain the behavior of atoms. The energy of an atom was found to change, not continuously, but by a discrete amount called a quantum. "Quantum mechanics" is the term that includes both the experimental observations and the quantum theory that explains them.

In the closing years of the nineteenth century, physics was thought to be nearly complete. All the important discoveries had been made, many thought, and all that was left was to fill in some minor details. One of these "details" was the hot-body problem concerning the colors of light given off by hot bodies. Max Planck set about to solve it.

The problem was that classical physics gave the wrong answer: its predictions were wildly inaccurate. Planck found that when he assumed, as an act of desperation, that energy could only be released from an atom in discrete packets, his formula gave predictions that matched the data perfectly. Quantum theory was born.

Classical physics assumed that a charged particle, such as an electron, would lose energy gradually and continuously over time. Planck assumed that energy could only be radiated in discrete packets. Each of these packets of energy would have an energy level equal to a tiny number (now called Planck's constant) times the frequency of the vibration of the particle. Energy at the atomic level would be measured in quanta (the plural of "quantum"), with one quantum being the lowest energy level possible, above zero.

It was found that an electron would vibrate for a while at a constant energy level without losing energy to radiation. Then suddenly, unpredictably, *randomly*, it would jump to a lower energy level and in the process radiate a photon of light (the energy of the photon given by Planck's constant times its frequency of vibration). An electron could also gain energy by such "quantum jumps." A graph of an electron's energy level over time was now given by a stepped function, not a smooth curve.

It was later realized that quantum theory should apply to all objects, large and small. However, the reason we don't see children on swings suddenly change their energy level in quantum jumps is because Planck's constant is far too small. Quantum effects are just far too tiny for us to notice them at the macroscopic level.

Quantum theory was rapidly developed in the decades to follow, with Einstein, Niels Bohr, Louis de Broglie, Erwin Schrödinger, and many others making major contributions. Classical mechanics is now seen as only an excellent approximation for the behavior of objects at the macroscopic level we normally deal with. Quantum mechanics can account for everything that classical mechanics can account for, and also for data that classical mechanics neither predicts nor explains. Modern physics *is* quantum mechanics. It also has many practical applications, such as the transistor, the laser, and the florescent light bulb. It has been estimated that one-third of our economy depends on devices that operate on quantum mechanical principles. Trying to understand what quantum mechanics means, however, brings us face-to-face with some of the most baffling mysteries ever confronted, and must profoundly change our worldview.

Newtonian physics was based on the metaphysical assumptions of determinism, the assumption that an observer did not affect a system being observed, and localism. But classical physics has been superseded by quantum physics, as classical physics has clearly been shown to be false. This implies that the mechanistic worldview based on it must also be false.

DETERMINISM AND THE ROLE OF THE OBSERVER

Quantum mechanics replaces the deterministic universe described by classical physics with a probabilistic universe. This is the idea that the behavior and various properties of subatomic systems and particles cannot be predicted precisely, that only a range of probable values can be specified. If you roll a series of marbles at a hill at less than a certain critical velocity, all the marbles will roll back down, and if you roll the marbles at more than the critical velocity, all the marbles will make it over the hill. In our classical macroscopic world, either they all get over or they all fall back. Things are not so simple at the quantum level.*

For instance, if subatomic particles such as electrons are fired at a potential barrier at a given velocity, it may not be possible to say with certainty whether an individual electron will pass through the barrier. Fire the electrons at a low enough velocity and most will be reflected, although a minority will pass through; at a high enough velocity most will pass through; and at some intermediate velocity about half will pass through and half will be reflected. But for any individual electron (out of a group of apparently identical electrons), all we can specify is the *probability* that the electron will pass through.

Another example of quantum randomness is radioactive decay. Say we have radioactive uranium isotope A that decays into isotope B with a half-life of one hour. One hour later, half of the uranium atoms will have decayed into isotope B. By all the known methods of physics, all of the uranium isotope A atoms appeared to be identical, yet one hour later, half have decayed and half are unchanged. The half-life of isotope A is highly predictable in a statistical sense, yet the precise time at which any individual atom decays is completely unpredictable.

Probability enters here for a different reason than it does in the tossing of a coin, the throw of dice, or a horse race: in these cases probability enters because of our lack of precise knowledge of the original state of the system. But in quantum theory, even if we have complete knowledge of the original state, the outcome would still be uncertain and only expressible as a probability. (Philosophers refer to these two sources of uncertainty as subjective and objective probability. Quantum mechanics suggests that in some situations probability has an objective status.)

---

*Those encountering quantum theory here for the first time may wish to bear in mind the words of physicist Niels Bohr: *"If a person does not feel shocked when he first encounters quantum theory, he has not understood a word of it."*

Another surprising proposition was that subatomic particles do not have definite properties for certain attributes, such as position, momentum, or direction of spin, until they are measured. It is not simply that these properties are unknown until they are observed, instead, they do not *exist* in any definite state until they are measured.

This conclusion is based, in part, on the famous "two-slit" experiment, in which electrons are fired one at a time at a barrier with two slits. Measuring devices on a screen behind the barrier indicate the electrons seem to behave as waves, going through both slits simultaneously, with patterns of interference typical of wave phenomena: wave crests arriving simultaneously at the same place in time will reinforce each other, but waves and troughs arriving simultaneously at the same place will cancel each other (interference patterns result when two wave fronts meet, for instance, after dropping two stones into a pond). These waves are only thought of as *probability* waves, or wave functions, as they do not carry any energy, and so cannot be directly detected. Only individual electrons are detected by the measuring device on the screen behind the barrier, but the distribution of numerous electrons shows the interference patterns typical of waves. It is as though each unobserved electron exists as a wave until it arrives at the screen to be detected, at which time its actual location (the place at which the particle is actually observed on the screen) can only be predicted statistically according to the interference pattern of its wave function.

If, however, a measuring device is placed at the slits, then each electron is observed to pass through only one slit and no interference pattern in the distribution of electrons is observed. In other words, electrons behave as waves when not observed, but as particles in a definite location when observed!* All quantum entities—electrons, protons, photons, and so on—display this wave-particle duality, behaving as wave or particle depending on whether they are directly observed.

A variation of this experiment by physicists Bruce Rosenblum and Fred

---

*A very clear description of this experiment can be found in "The Philosophy of Karl Popper Part II" by W. W. Bartley, pages 679 to 683. Note that when it was written in 1978, it was still only a thought experiment, but has since been performed.

Kuttner[3] makes this bizarre point even more clearly. If a wave corresponding to a single atom encounters a semitransparent reflecting surface (such as a thin film), it can be split into two equal parts, much as a light wave both going through and reflecting from a windowpane. The two parts of the wave can then be trapped in two boxes, as shown in figure 4.1.

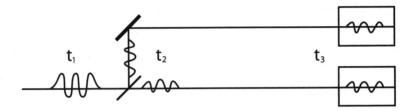

Figure 4.1. The wave function at three successive times: t_1, t_2, and t_3.

Since the wave was split equally, if you repeated this process many times, then each time you looked into the boxes you would find a whole atom in box A about half the time and in box B about half the time. But according to quantum theory, before you looked the atom was not in any particular box. The position of the atom is thus an observer-created reality. Its position will also be the same for all subsequent observers, so it is a reality that depends on an initial observation only.

You may be tempted to think that the atom really was in one box or the other before you looked, but it can be demonstrated that before observation the atom as a wave was in a "superposition state," a state in which it was simultaneously in both box A *and* box B. Take a pair of boxes that have not been looked into and cut narrow slits at one end, allowing the waves to simultaneously leak out and impinge on a photographic film. At points where wave crests from box A and box B arrive together, they reinforce each other to give a maximum amplitude of the wave function at that point—a maximum of "waviness." At some points higher or lower, crests from box A arrive simultaneously with troughs from box B. The two waves are of opposite signs at these positions and therefore cancel to give zero amplitude for the wave function at these points.

Since the amplitude of an atom's wave function at a particular place determines the probability for the atom to be found there when observed, the atom emerging from the box-pair is more likely to appear on the film at places where the amplitude of the wave function is large, but can never appear where it is zero. If we repeat this process with a large number of box-pairs and the same film, many atoms land to cause darkening of the film near positions of wave function amplitude maximums, but none appear at wave function minimums. The distribution of darker and lighter areas on the film forms the interference pattern.

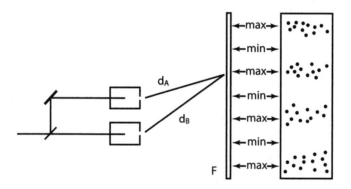

Figure 4.2. The box-pair experiment: (a) waves emanating from slits in the two boxes travel distances da and db and impinge on a film at F; (b) the resulting pattern formed on the film from many box pairs.

The distribution of electrons on the film will show the interference patterns typical of two waves, which overlap to cancel each other at some places. To form the interference pattern, the wave function of each atom had to leak out of both boxes since each and every atom avoids appearing in regions of the film where the waves from the two boxes cancel. Each and every atom therefore had to obey a geometrical rule that depends on the relative position of both boxes. So, the argument goes, the atom had to equally be in *both* boxes, as an extended wave. If instead of doing this interference experiment you looked into the pair of boxes, you would have found a whole atom in a particular box, as a particle. Before you looked, it was in both boxes; after you looked, it was only in one.

Rosenblum and Kuttner sum up the puzzle:

Quantum mechanics is the most battle-tested theory in science. Not a single violation of its predictions has ever been demonstrated, no matter how preposterous the predictions might seem. However, anyone concerned with what the theory *means* faces a philosophical enigma: the so-called measurement problem, or the problem of observation . . . before you look we could have proven—with an interference experiment—that each atom was a wave equally in both boxes. After you look it was in a single box. It was thus your observation that created the reality of each atom's existence in a particular box. Before your observation only probability existed. But it was not the probability that an actual object existed in a particular place (as in the classical shell game)—it was just the probability of a future *observation* of such an object, which does *not* include the assumption that the object existed there prior to its observation. This hard-to-accept observer-created reality is the measurement problem in quantum mechanics.[4]

Up until the moment of measurement, certain properties of quantum phenomena, such as location, momentum, and direction of spin, simply exist as a collection of probabilities, known as the wave function, or state vector. The wave function can be thought of as the probability distribution of all possible states, such as, for instance, the probability distribution of all possible locations for an electron.*

But this is not the probability that the electron is actually *at* certain locations, instead, it is the probability that the electron *will be found* at certain locations. The electron does not have a definite location until it is observed. Upon measurement, this collection of all possible locations "collapses" to a single value—the location of the particle that is actually observed.

Physicist Nick Herbert expresses it this way:

The quantum physicist treats the atom as a wave of oscillating possibilities as long as it is not observed. But whenever it is looked at, the atom stops vibrating and objectifies one of its many possibilities.

---

*Technically, the probability distribution is the absolute square of the wave function.

Whenever someone chooses to look at it, the atom ceases its fuzzy dance and seems to "freeze" into a tiny object with definite attributes, only to dissolve once more into a quivering pool of possibilities as soon as the observer withdraws his attention from it. The apparent observer-induced change in an atom's mode of existence is called the *collapse of the wave function.*[5]

Measurements thus play a more positive role in quantum mechanics than in classical physics, because here they are not merely observations of something already present but actually help produce it. According to one interpretation of quantum mechanics popular among many theorists, it is the existence of consciousness that introduces intrinsic probability into the quantum world.

This interpretation owes its origin to mathematician John von Neumann, one of the most important intellectual figures of the twentieth century. In addition to his contributions to pure mathematics, von Neumann also invented game theory, which models economic and social behavior as rational games, and made fundamental contributions to the development of the early computers. In the 1930s, von Neumann turned his restless mind to the task of expressing the newly developed theories of quantum mechanics in rigorous mathematical form, and the result was his classic book *The Mathematical Foundations of Quantum Mechanics.* In it he tackled the measurement problem head on and rejected the Copenhagen interpretation of quantum theory, which was becoming the orthodox position among physicists. Although it is somewhat vague, the central tenets of the Copenhagen interpretation seem to be (1) that all we have access to are the results of observations, and so it is simply pointless to ask questions about the quantum reality behind those observations, and (2) that although observation is necessary for establishing the reality of quantum phenomena, no form of consciousness, human or otherwise, is necessary for making an observation. Rather, an observer is anything that makes a record of an event, and so it is at the level of macroscopic measuring instruments (such as Geiger counters) that the actual values of quantum phenomena are randomly set from a range of statistical possibilities.

Von Neumann objected to the Copenhagen interpretation practice of dividing the world in two parts: indefinite quantum entities on the one side, and measuring instruments that obey the laws of classical mechanics on the other. He considered a measuring apparatus, a Geiger counter for example, in a room isolated from the rest of the world but in contact with a quantum system, such as an atom simultaneously in two boxes. The Geiger counter is set to fire if the atom is found in one box, but to remain unfired if it is found in the other. This Geiger counter is a physical instrument, hence subject to the rules of quantum mechanics. Therefore, it should be expected to enter into a superposition state along with the atom, a state in which it is simultaneously fired and unfired.

Should the Geiger counter be in contact with a device that records whether the counter has fired, then logically, it too should enter a superposition state that records both situations as existing simultaneously. Should an observer walk into the room and examine the recording device, this logic can be continued up the "von Neumann chain" from the recording device, to photons, to the eyes and brain of the observer, which are also physical instruments that we have no reason to suppose are exempt from the rules of quantum mechanics. The only peculiar link in the von Neumann chain is the process by which electrical signals in the brain of the observer become a conscious experience.

Von Neumann argued that the entire physical world is quantum mechanical, so the process that collapses the wave functions into actual facts cannot be a physical process; instead, the intervention of something from outside of physics is required. Something nonphysical, not subject to the laws of quantum mechanics, must account for the collapse of the wave function: the only nonphysical entity in the observation process that von Neumann could think of was the consciousness of the observer. He reluctantly concluded that this outside entity had to be consciousness and that prior to observation, even measuring instruments interacting with a quantum system must exist in an indefinite state.

Von Neumann extended the Copenhagen interpretation by requiring the measurement process to take place in a mind. He was reluctantly driven to this conclusion by his relentless logic: the only process in the von Neumann chain that is not merely the motion of molecules is the consciousness of the observer. His arguments were developed more completely by his illustrious followers, most notably Fritz London, Edmond Bauer, and Eugene Wigner. Wigner, who went on to win the Nobel Prize in physics, wrote, "When the province of physical theory was extended to encompass microscopic phenomena, through the creation of quantum mechanics, the concept of consciousness came to the fore again; it was not possible to formulate the laws of quantum mechanics in a fully consistent way without reference to the consciousness."[6]

The box-pair experiment also bears on the role of consciousness and free will. After all, you can choose to look in one of the boxes or to do an interference experiment, and you will get different "realities," one being particle-like, the other wavelike. But your choice of which experiment to do is not determined, even statistically, by anything in the physical theory. Nothing in quantum mechanics says you must choose one experiment rather than the other. If you deny that consciousness collapses the wave function, then this means atoms *prior to observation* existed as either particle or wave. Somehow you chose to only look in those boxes that contained particle atoms and you chose to only do an interference experiment with wave-form atoms. This would also deny free will, because then your illusion of choice is determined by a *conspiracy* of the physical universe with the state of your brain and your perceived choice. This replaces the deterministic universe with one that is deterministic and *conspiratorial*.

This is how von Neumann, Wigner, and others brought mind back into nature and made a strong case against the causal closure of the physical. As we will see, the case gets even stronger.

At this point, it should be stressed that this is only one interpretation of the facts of quantum mechanics: in addition to the Copenhagen interpretation, there are several other speculations about what is really happening when quantum possibilities settle down into one actuality. Most attempt to rescue the determinism and observer independence of classical physics.

For instance, the hidden variable theory holds that the indeterminacy of quantum physics is an illusion due to our ignorance: if we knew more about the system in question—that is, if we knew the value of some "hidden variables"—then the indeterminacy would vanish. However, there are several reasons why the general community of quantum physicists never held the hidden-variable theory in high regard.

One reason, according to quantum physicist Euan Squires, is that the hidden variable theory is "extremely complicated and messy. We *know* the answers from quantum theory and then we construct a hidden-variable, deterministic theory specifically to give these answers. The resulting theory appears contrived and unnatural." Squires points out that the hidden variable theory never gained widespread acceptance because "the elegance, simplicity and economy of quantum theory contrasted sharply with the contrived nature of a hidden-variable theory which gave no new predictions in return for its increased complexity; the whole hidden-variable enterprise was easily dismissed as arising from a desire, in the minds of those too conservative to accept change, to return to the determinism of classical physics."[7] Another reason the general community of quantum physicists consider the hidden variable theory highly implausible is that it explains away indeterminacy by postulating the existence of an ad hoc quantum force that, unlike any of the other four forces in nature, behaves in a manner completely unaffected by distance.

The many worlds hypothesis is perhaps the strangest of all. It is the only one that denies the existence of nonlocality, but it does so by postulating that *all* possible values of a measured property exist simultaneously in coexisting universes. When a measurement is made, we are told, the universe we are in splits into multiple universes, with one of the possible results in each of them. For instance, if a measurement may yield two possible results, then at the instant of measurement the entire universe splits in two, with each possible result realized in each universe. If a measurement may yield a continuum of possible states—such as the position of an electron—then the instant such a measurement occurs, it is proposed that the universe splits into an *infinite number* of universes! Since it is further assumed that these parallel universes cannot interact with each other, this hypothesis is completely untestable. Entities are being multiplied with incredible profusion. William of Occam must be spinning in his grave.

In the opinion of many physicists, the last two interpretations are simply desperate, last-ditch attempts to rescue the classical assumptions of determinism and observer independence that have been abandoned by quantum mechanics. For instance, one interpretation salvages determinism from classical physics by postulating hidden variables and the other by speculating that everything that can happen does in fact happen in an infinite number of constantly splitting parallel universes, regardless of the way things may appear to any particular version of our constantly splitting selves.

At any rate, these four interpretations are all consistent with the observed facts. They are attempts to describe what reality is really like between observations, to account for the seemingly bizarre behavior of matter predicted so accurately by the theory of quantum physics. They are not usually considered to be *scientific* theories about the nature of reality, but rather *metaphysical* theories, as within quantum mechanics there does not currently seem to be any obvious experiment that one could perform in order to choose between them.*

Physicist J. C. Polkinghorne sums up the metaphysical confusion many quantum theorists feel when he writes:

> It is a curious tale. All over the world measurements are continually being made on quantum mechanical systems. The theory triumphantly

---

*It should be pointed out that the average quantum mechanic is about as interested in philosophy as the average garage mechanic. In *Hyperspace,* theoretical physicist Michio Kaku writes, "When confronted with sticky philosophical questions, such as the role of 'consciousness' in performing quantum measurement, most physicists shrug their shoulders. As long as they can calculate the outcome of an experiment, they really don't care about its philosophical implications. . . . Nevertheless, although the average physicist is not bothered by philosophical questions, the greatest of them were. Einstein, Heisenberg, and Bohr spent long hours in heated discussions, wrestling late into the night with the meaning of measurement, the problems of consciousness, and the meaning of probability in their work" (Kaku 1995, 317).[8]

predicts, within its probabilistic limits, what their outcomes will be. It is all a great success. Yet we do not understand what is going on. Does the fixity on a particular occasion set in as a purely mental act of knowledge? At a transition from small to large physical systems? At the interface of matter and mind that we call consciousness? In one of the many subsequent worlds into which the universe has divided itself?[9]*

Perhaps one interpretation is simpler or more logically consistent, or perhaps one of the interpretations is more aesthetically pleasing than the others. These considerations may provide philosophical reasons for preferring one over the others, but such reasons can hardly be considered decisive. However, a fascinating set of experiments performed by physicist Helmut Schmidt and others appears to show that conscious intent can affect the behavior of otherwise purely random quantum phenomena. Could an experiment be designed to test the von Neumann interpretation?

Consciousness is central to the von Neumann interpretation of quantum mechanics. According to this interpretation, some properties of quantum phenomena do not exist in any definite state except through the intervention of a conscious mind, at which point the wave function of possibilities collapses into a single state. The usual form of this interpretation allows the observer to collapse the wave function to a unique outcome but not to have any effect on what outcome actually occurs: the actual outcome is assumed to be randomly chosen by nature from the range of values provided by the wave function. But the experiments of German physicist Helmut Schmidt and other physicists indicate that the consciousness of the observer may not only collapse the wave function to a single outcome but may also help specify what outcome occurs by *shifting the odds in a desired direction*.

---

*For excellent discussions of these matters aimed at the layperson, I refer the reader to *The Mystery of the Quantum World* by quantum theorist Euan Squires, to *The Quantum World* by physicist J. C. Polkinghorne, and to *Quantum Reality: Beyond the New Physics* by physicist Nick Herbert.

PSYCHOKINESIS AND THE AGE OF ELECTRONICS

Psychokinesis (PK) refers to the direct action of mind on matter, independent of muscles and limbs. When most people think of PK, they think of claims of spoon bending or levitation of objects. Most modern PK research is of phenomena far less dramatic and impressive, although the evidence for these less impressive phenomena is considered much sounder.

Schmidt is the world's leading exponent of modern PK research. After earning his doctorate from the University of Cologne, Schmidt settled in the United States, where from 1965 to 1969 he worked as senior research scientist at the Boeing research laboratory in Seattle. Since then, however, he has been fully committed to PK research.

It was Schmidt who first introduced automated electronic testing devices into PK research. A random event generator (REG) developed by Schmidt employs an extremely rapid clock that is stopped at random intervals by the emission of electrons as radioactive strontium 90 decays. What is so unusual about Schmidt's REGs is that the precise rate of radioactive decay is theoretically unpredictable, and so his experiments are essentially tests to see if human intention can influence random events at the quantum level.

To test this microscopic psychokinesis (called micro-PK), Schmidt employed a binary counter, one that flipped back and forth between two positions. This electronic coin flipper would be stopped in one of its two positions by the emission of an electron from the radioactive material. Since it is theoretically impossible to predict when an electron will be emitted, in the absence of mental influence the behavior of the REG should be completely random and an approximately equal number of 0's and 1's should be recorded.

The 0's and 1's generated by the REG were usually presented to the subject in one of two ways: either as a series of clicks in the left or right earpiece of a set of headphones or as a display of lights arranged in a circle. If the headphone device was employed, the goal of the subject was to produce more clicks in one earpiece than in the other. With the display of lights, the situation was a bit more complicated. If the oscillating device stopped in one position, the light moved one step clockwise; if it stopped in the other, it moved one step counterclockwise. If only chance was operating, the lights should then be expected to make a random walk around the circle, with about an equal number of clockwise and counterclockwise moves. The goal of the subject was to "will" the lights in one direction around the circle.

The absolute deviation from chance with Schmidt's experiments was slight, but because the experimental design allows enormous numbers of trials to be collected in a short space of time, highly significant results can be obtained. Most modern REG experiments are based on Schmidt's original design, and by 1987 an enormous database of results had been accumulated. In that year, Dean Radin and Roger Nelson at Princeton University searched the literature and found 832 PK studies conducted by sixty-eight different investigators between 1959 and 1987. These experiments all involved the use of true REGs (as described above) or else electronic pseudorandom number generators. Radin and Nelson subjected the database to meta-analysis, and their results, published in the prominent journal *Foundations of Physics,* showed an overall hit rate of about 51 percent, when 50 percent was expected by chance. Because of the size of the database, the odds against chance were beyond a trillion to one. They also assigned each study a quality score derived from many published criticisms of PK experiments and concluded, "This meta-analysis shows that effects are not a function of experimental quality, and that the replication rate is as good as that found in exemplary experiments in psychology and physics. . . . Skeptics often assert that only 'believers' obtain positive results in such experiments. However, a thorough literature search finds not a single attempted replication of the RNG experiment by a publicly proclaimed skeptic."[10]

IMPLICATIONS FOR PHYSICS AND CONSCIOUSNESS

The REG devices pioneered by Schmidt are driven by purely random events at the quantum level. So the subjects in these experiments are not really shifting matter around, but rather shifting probabilities of events in desired directions. As we have seen, the role that consciousness plays in quantum mechanics is one of the burning issues in modern physics. And as we will see, one of Schmidt's experiments may be able to settle this controversy.

If the observer can affect the outcome of the collapse, it should be possible to design an experiment to test at which point the wave function collapses. The following paragraphs explain the variation of Schmidt's standard experiment that is directly relevant to the choice between the von Neumann and Copenhagen interpretations.

First of all, Schmidt recorded signals (0's and 1's) from a binary REG simultaneously on two cassette tapes, without anyone listening to the signals or otherwise knowing the output of the REG. One tape was kept in a secure location, the other was given to a subject with instructions to produce more 0's or 1's, usually distinguished as clicks in the left or right speaker of stereophonic headphones. Results from these time-displaced PK experiments indicated that PK still operated and that the two records still agreed after the PK effort.

Some theorists have speculated that the PK effort reached back in time to when the random events were generated, but of course there is another possibility, one more consistent with the von Neumann/Wigner interpretation of quantum physics. As Schmidt, Robert Morris, and Lou Rudolph point out,

> Perhaps events are not physically real until there has been an observation. From this viewpoint, the PK effort would not have to reach into the past because nature had not yet decided on the outcome before the PK subject, the first observer, saw the result. Then, the PK effort should no longer succeed if we have some other observer look at the prerecorded data previous to the PK subject's attempt. [An] experiment to study this situation . . . has, indeed, reported a blocking of the PK effect by a previous observation."[11]

It appears that von Neumann, Wigner, and the others were right: prior to observation, *even measuring instruments interacting with a quantum system must exist in an indefinite state.*

Could Schmidt's results be the result of fraud? Well, Schmidt has even used this time-independence feature of PK to design a fraud-proof experiment involving skeptics. Essentially, it works like this: one of the unobserved tapes is sent to an outside observer and the other is sent to a subject. The outside observer decides whether she wants to see more 0's or 1's, and this decision is communicated to the subject, who then listens to the tape and attempts to exert an influence in the desired direction. The observer then examines her copy of the tape and counts the number of 0's and 1's to see if the experiment was a success. Obviously, there can be no possibility of fraud on the part of subject or experimenter, unless of course the skeptics are also in on the trick! Schmidt, Morris, and Rudolph performed this experiment: Morris is an active parapsychology researcher and Rudolph is a communications engineer, and both were skeptical with regard to PK effects on prerecorded events. But the experiment was a success, with odds against chance of one hundred to one.[12]

Quantum mechanics brings mind back into nature and eliminates the causal closure of the physical. Conscious observation seems required to collapse the wave function; the choice of what type of observation to make determines what form a part of reality will take (wave or particle), and according to the experiments of Schmidt and others, conscious intent may bias in a desired direction the otherwise random collapse of the wave function.

The von Neumann/Wigner interpretation of quantum physics, supported now by the experiments of Schmidt and others, may bring to mind the idealism of Bishop Berkeley, who thought that ordinary objects such as trees and furniture did not exist unless observed. But this interpretation does not deny that an external reality exists independent of anyone observing it. Properties of quantum phenomena are divided into static and dynamic properties, with the former, such as mass and charge, having definite and constant values for any observation. It is the dynamic properties, those that do not have constant values—such as position, momentum, and direction of spin—that are thought to exist as potentialities that become actualities only when observed.

But as Squires points out, this raises a very strange question:

> The assumption we are considering appears even more weird when we realize that throughout much of the universe, and indeed throughout all of it in early times, there were presumably no con-

scious observers. . . . Even worse are the problems we meet if we accept the modern ideas on the early universe in which quantum decays (of the 'vacuum,' but this need not trouble us here) were necessary in order to obtain the conditions in which conscious observers could exist. Who, or what, did the observations necessary to create the observers?[13]

Squires enters the realm of theology with great trepidation and considers what seems to be the only possibility under this interpretation—that conscious observations can be made by minds outside of the physical universe. This of course is one of the traditional roles of God, or of the gods.

Whether expressed in theological terms or not, the suggestion that conscious minds are in some way connected and that they might even be connected to a form of universal, collective consciousness appears to be a possible solution to the problem of quantum theory. It is not easy to see what it might mean, as we understand so little about consciousness. That there are "connections" of some sort between conscious minds and physical matter is surely implied by the fact that conscious decisions have effects on matter. Thus there are links between conscious minds that go through the medium of physical systems. Whether there are others, that exploit the non-physical and presumably non-localised nature of consciousness, it is not possible to say. Some people might wish to mention here the "evidence" for telepathy and similar extra-sensory effects.[14]

Squires concludes his discussion on the role of consciousness in physics with this remark:

It is remarkable that such ideas should arise from a study of the behavior of the most elementary of systems. That such systems point to a world beyond themselves is a fact that will be loved by all who believe that there are truths of which we know little, that there are mysteries seen only by mystics, and that there are phenomena inexplicable within our normal view of what is possible. There is no harm in this—physics indeed points to the unknown. The emphasis, however, must be on the unknown, on the mystery, on the truths dimly glimpsed, on things inexpressible except in the language of poetry, or religion, or metaphor.[15]

LOCALISM

All interactions in classical physics are explicitly local. Interactions between a body at location A and another body at location B must be mediated by a force field that traverses the distance between A and B at a speed not exceeding that of light. Body A causes a change in the force field, and this change in the field is propagated at or below light speed to body B. For instance, the gravitational field of the sun exerts an influence on Earth: if the sun were to be pulled out of its orbit, the orbit of Earth would be affected about eight minutes later.

Localism implies that any information exchange must be mediated by a signal, and relativity implies that no such signal can travel faster than the speed of light. But experiments in quantum mechanics strongly suggest that we can in fact have instantaneous action at a distance, with no signal required to transmit information.

This is one example of such an experiment. Suppose a pair of electrons is split off from an atom. Quantum theory tells us that when the spin of the electrons is measured along a chosen axis, they will be found to spin in opposite directions. This does not mean that they started off spinning in opposite directions: direction of spin is a dynamic property, and according to quantum theory, dynamic properties do not exist with any definite value until they are measured. The electrons are in a state of opposite direction of spin, but both are without any particular direction of spin until the spin of one is measured.

Let the electrons travel light years apart and measure the spin of one. If it is found to be clockwise, then according to quantum theory the other electron is instantaneously determined to spin in the opposite direction, despite the lack of any force or signal linking them. The observation of the spin of one of the electrons instantaneously collapses the wave functions of *both* electrons to actual, opposite spins. If the spin of the second is measured before there is any time for a signal from the first to reach it, it will be found to spin in the opposite direction. Einstein called this "spooky action at a distance" and rejected this on the grounds that there could be no harmony without some signal passing between the distant particles, a signal that in this case would have to travel faster than the speed of light, which his theory of relativity did not allow.

For years David Bohm and other physicists tried to determine whether the adjustment was truly instantaneous. These experiments are difficult to do with sufficient accuracy, but a series of early experiments, with two exceptions in the early 1970s, supported nonlocality. With progress in technology, more sophisticated experiments have become possible, usually using photons instead of electrons and measuring polarization (the direction of vibration of the electric field, which is totally polarized when it vibrates in only one direction) instead of spin. In the 1980s, a French team headed by Alain Aspect of the Institut d' Optique Theorique et Appliqué added to Bohm's experiment an ultrafast switch to eliminate the possibility of any light-speed signal between the paired photons and found the nonlocal prediction of quantum mechanics to hold.[16]

> *Einstein said that if quantum mechanics was correct, then the world would be crazy. Einstein was right—the world is crazy.*
>
> PHYSICIST DANIEL GREENBERGER

Several points about nonlocality are worth noting. First of all, nonlocality does not seem to violate special relativity's prohibition of faster-than-light signals, as no signals are sent. The four known forces of nature are thought to operate with the exchange of particles, all of which obey the cosmic speed limit. In the cases discussed above, a change in the state at location A (due to measurement) *instantaneously* causes a change at location B, regardless of distance or barriers. Since no signal is sent through space, the quantum connection is immediate and is unaffected by barriers and distance. Another important point is that nonlocality appears to have been established by arithmetic and experiment, and is thus a fact about the universe, independent of quantum mechanical theory. This means that any theory that eventually supersedes quantum mechanics will have to incorporate nonlocality.* Finally, it is worth noting that the quantum connection differs from ordinary forces in that it is very discriminating. Ordinary forces reach out and affect every particle of a certain kind in the immediate vicinity. For instance, gravity affects all particles, electromagnetism all charged particles. In contrast, the quantum connection only affects those systems that have interacted with each other since they were last measured (such systems are called "phase-entangled").

NONMECHANICAL CAUSATION

In classical physics, all causation is by mechanical means, that is, by contact interactions between neighboring entities or neighboring regions of a field, analogous to the interaction of billiard balls or the motion of a wave in the ocean. By contrast, quantum physics allows nonmechanical

---

*In the 1960s, Irish physicist John Bell derived a formula known as the Bell inequality, which basically states that if reality is really local, then changing the angles of measurements taken at distant locations should affect results only at those locations; so if we start out with angles of measurement giving perfect correlation, changing both angles of measurement should result in a change in correlation not exceeding what we would expect from sheer chance (assuming that a change in angle of measurement at location A does not affect the result at location B). The Bell inequality has been violated by a number of experiments, indicating that reality is in fact nonlocal. In his book *Quantum Reality,* physicist Nick Herbert writes, "Bell's theorem has since been proved entirely in terms of quantum facts; no reference to quantum theory is necessary. In its most up-to-date version Bell's theorem reads: The quantum facts plus a bit of arithmetic require that reality be non-local. In a local reality, influences cannot travel faster than light. Bell's theorem says that in any reality of this sort, information does not get around fast enough to explain the quantum facts: reality must be non-local. . . . Bell's discovery of the necessary non-locality of deep reality is the most important achievement in reality research since the invention of quantum theory" (Herbert 1985, 51–52). A clear description of Bell's theorem and the experiments that demonstrate violations of the testable part (that is, Bell's inequality) can be found in chapter 12 of *Quantum Reality.*

causation. The nonlocal, instantaneous influence discussed above is one example.

A second example would be the collapse of the wave function by an act of conscious observation. In the orthodox von Neumann interpretation, the actual outcome was assumed to be randomly determined from a range of values, but the experiments of Schmidt and others indicate that consciousness may in fact bias the outcome in a desired direction. This obviously adds another level of nonmechanical causation to conscious observation.

A third example would be the so-called quantum Zeno effect (named after the philosopher Zeno of Elea). Physicists have found that if they continuously observe an unstable particle in its original state, it will never decay. That is, physicists can "freeze" the decay of the unstable system by measuring it frequently enough in its initial state.

This is what these phenomena led physicist John Wheeler to imagine when he looked to the future: "There may be no such thing as the 'glittering central mechanism of the universe' to be seen behind a glass wall at the end of the trail. Not machinery but magic may be the better description of the treasure that is waiting."[17]

A NEW CONCEPTION OF MATTER

One of the most striking differences between classical physics and quantum mechanics is the changed conception of matter. Atoms are no longer thought of as tiny billiard balls that have definite properties, regardless of whether they are observed. Physicist Werner Heisenberg expressed it this way:

Atoms are not *things*. The electrons which form an atom's shells are no longer things in the sense of classical physics, things which could be unambiguously described by concepts like location, velocity, energy, size. When we get down to the atomic level, the objective world in space and time no longer exists, and the mathematical symbols of theoretical physics refer merely to possibilities, not to facts.[18]

Atoms are no longer thought of as "solid, massy, hard, impenetrable moveable particles," as Newton described them, but rather as potentialities, possibilities with a wavelike structure that can interfere like waves. Their dynamic properties are intrinsically linked to the mental. Possibilities that become fully real only when observed are more like ideas than like tiny, observer-independent billiard balls. Quantum theorist Henry Stapp has remarked on how the purely physical aspects of reality are no longer thought of as having the qualities assigned to rocks by classical physics: "In quantum theory the purely physically described aspects are mere potentialities for real events to occur. A potentiality is more like an idea than a persisting material substance, and is treated in the theory as 'an idea of what might happen.'"[19]

This new conception of matter, along with nonmechanical causation, is what physicist James Jeans was referring to when he wrote that "the universe begins to look more like a great thought than like a machine."[20]

QUANTUM MECHANICAL THEORIES OF MIND

Free will is permitted in classical physics only by excluding the mind from the realm of physics. But this leads to certain difficulties: the brain is a physical instrument, and the state of the brain does seem to affect the mind. If we do not exclude the brain and the mind from the realm of physics, then free will is ruled out in classical physics by the hypothesis that the state of the brain (and thus of the mind) is driven from the bottom up by the deterministic motion of elementary particles in the brain. Of course, this assumes that classical physics is applicable at the microscopic level, which we now know is grossly incorrect.

In the nineteenth century, when classical physics was widely assumed to be absolutely correct, William James questioned the idea that consciousness was causally irrelevant. If the consciousness of men and animals was useless, he asked, why then did it exist and fool us with the illusion of effectiveness? He recognized the incompatibility of his theories of consciousness with the physics of his day and realized that a new type of physics would have to be invented to help explain the interaction between mind and body. Referring to the future scientists who would one day illuminate the mind-body problem, James wrote, "The best way in which we can facilitate their advent is to understand how great is the darkness in which we grope, and never forget that the natural-science assumptions with which we started are provisional and revisable things."[21]

Henry Stapp is one of the scientists whose advent James appears to have foreseen. Stapp has pointed out how, even today, the thinking of many philosophers, psychologists, and neuroscientists remains locked in the grip of classical physics. Stapp writes, "It is testimony to the power of the grip of old ideas on the minds of scientists and philosophers alike that what was apparently evident to William James already in 1892—namely that a revision of the mechanical precepts of nineteenth century physics would be needed to accommodate the structural features of our conscious experiences—still fails to be recognized by many of the affected professionals even today, more than three-quarters of a century after the downfall of classical physics, apparently foreseen by James, has come, much-heralded, to pass."[22]

Various modern neuroscientists and physicists have proposed theories of mind-body interaction based on quantum mechanics. The most detailed of these theories so far has been the result of work done by theoretical physicist Evan Harris Walker, but we will first review the theories of neuroscientist John Eccles and of physicist Henry Stapp.

All of these theories follow the von Neumann/Wigner interpretation of quantum mechanics. The brain is a physical entity, and we have no reason to suppose that it evades the rules of quantum physics. In 1924, when quantum theory was still in its infancy, biologist Alfred Lotkas proposed the daring conjecture that mind exerts control over the brain by modulating the occurrence of otherwise random quantum events. Since then, our knowledge of both quantum mechanics and the brain has increased immeasurably, and today most quantum models of consciousness place the mechanism of mind-matter interaction at the level of the neural synapse—the tiny gap between the electric tentacles of the nerve cells.

In 1963, Eccles received the Nobel Prize in Medicine and Physiology for discovering how nerve cells communicate with each other: they do it with drugs. The synaptic gap is too wide to be bridged by electrical signals: instead, when a nerve cell is excited, its extremities emit tiny packets of chemicals called neurotransmitters that quickly transverse the gap and cause or inhibit the firing of adjacent nerve cells. Herbert writes that "to handle the fine details of its vast informational traffic, the human brain employs a veritable pharmacy of exotic transmitter substances."[23] Most mind-altering drugs achieve their effects by altering the transmission of neurotransmitters, which gives us important clues about the consciousness-sensitive areas of the brain.

Eccles has written about how the firing of just one "critically-poised neuron" could have a cascading effect on activity in the brain, and he speculates that consciousness affects brain activity by manipulating the way chemicals are released into the synaptic gap. The neural sites where packets of chemicals are released are so tiny that quantum uncertainty may govern whether the release mechanisms are activated. Eccles speculates that an immaterial mind controls these microsites in one particular part of the brain—the premotor cortex—in order to produce voluntary behavior.

We should expect quantum uncertainty to play an even larger role in systems smaller than this, and so other quantum theories of consciousness place the mind's role in controlling matter at smaller locations near the synaptic gap.

Stapp has developed a model similar to Eccles's, but he places the critical juncture between mind and matter at the level of the calcium ion, which is about a million times smaller than Eccles's synaptic microsites and is essential for the operation of the synapse. A synapse will "fire" when it emits molecules of neurotransmitters from synaptic vesicles (small containers of drugs) into the synaptic gap, across which they drift to the adjacent nerve cell to stimulate or inhibit its activity. Research in neuroscience has demonstrated that the release of neurotransmitters into the synaptic gap is triggered by the migration of calcium ions (electrically charged calcium atoms) from the interior of the cell's terminal to special sites in the synapse. Calcium ions are certainly small enough to demonstrate quantum effects.

Certain states of the brain, if maintained long enough, will produce certain effects on the body, such as voluntary motion. Stapp refers to these brain states as "templates for action." A simple example would be the template for raising one's arm, and we all have memories of these templates. According to Stapp's model, if we intend to raise our arm, conscious observation collapses the wave functions of the calcium ions in our brains that are responsible for initiating the template to raise our arm.* However, Stapp adheres to the orthodox von Neumann interpretation, which holds that the outcome of the collapse will be completely random: that is, nature decides the actual outcome and that outcome may be raising the arm or not raising the arm. So as Stapp writes, "The effectiveness of conscious intent would appear to be diluted by the entry of quantum randomness in the choice (on the part of nature) of the outcome of the posed question."[24] Stapp's solution to this problem is the quantum Zeno effect. If the answer to the question posed is not the desired one, the question is rapidly posed again at another nerve terminal within the appropriate part of the brain. When the desired result is achieved, the template for action is initiated and then held in place by conscious attention via the Zeno effect. When it is no longer needed, attention is removed and the template rapidly decays.

Stapp argues that the Zeno effect can hold the template for action in place in the face of strong mechanical forces that would otherwise disturb it, and so these quantum effects will not be wiped out in a warm, wet brain. Thus, animals whose mental efforts can sustain a template for action more effectively would enjoy a survival advantage over their competitors, and therefore "the rules of quantum mechanics can endow conscious effort with the causal efficacy needed to permit its evolution and deployment via natural selection."[25]

Stapp offers various data from psychology in support of his theory, such as the puzzling phenomena that mental distraction reduces the amount of physical force a person can apply (which will be familiar to anyone who has tried pumping iron while someone distracts them with conversation). Stapp argues that the distraction withdraws attention

---

*This model is similar to deciding to look into one particular box out of thousands of box-pairs each containing an atom to see if that particular box will contain an atom, or not.

(continuous observation) from the quantum template for action, allowing it to decay. That is why physical force requires a mental effort that
opposes the natural tendency for the template to dissipate.[26]

Now we come to quantum theorist Evan Harris Walker, who has
developed the most detailed, comprehensive model of quantum consciousness so far. Walker places the interaction between mind and matter at the
level of the electron, which is almost one hundred thousand times less
massive than the calcium ions.

According to Walker's model, when a synapse is excited, electrons may
"tunnel" across the synaptic gap connecting an initiating neuron with its
neighbor, a feat not possible in classical physics. In this model, electrons
not only tunnel across the synaptic gap between adjacent neurons but may
also influence the firing of distant synapses by tunneling to far-away synapses via a series of stepping-stone molecules. This network of quantum-
tunneling electrons connecting distant synapses is postulated by Walker
to compose a second nervous system, operating by completely quantum
rules and acting in parallel with the conventional nervous system. The
conventional nervous system handles unconscious data processing, while
the secondary nervous system allows an immaterial mind to interact with
matter by selecting which second-system quantum possibilities become
actualized. Walker's model explains this interaction between mind and
matter by incorporating Schmidt's experimental results indicating that
the conscious mind may bias the collapse of state vectors of quantum phenomena within the brain in such a way as to influence brain activity in a
desired manner. In turn, these actualized possibilities act on the conventional nervous system to produce voluntary action.

Using a mathematical model, Walker shows that when the activity of
the conventional nervous system is low, the activity of the second nervous
system is sporadic and uncoordinated. However, once a critical mass of
activity of the conventional nervous system is reached, the second system's
tunneling electrons "form a unified self-sustaining system of excitation
similar to the self-sustaining activity of a nuclear power plant."[27] Walker
identifies this process of reaching a critical mass of activity with the sleep-
to-waking transition. Another advantage of his model is that it helps

account for the unity of conscious experience we observe, despite the fact that the brain activity associated with even simple perception is spread out over different parts of the brain.

Brain scientists have generally ignored Walker's model of consciousness because it contains what are considered by some to be rather unreasonable neurological assumptions.* Nevertheless, it is the most ambitious and detailed attempt so far to relate quantum mechanics to the mind-body problem. Walker has also developed a theory of psychic ability based on his theory of consciousness, and in a nutshell it is this: consciousness can collapse state vectors to a single desired outcome inside a person's own brain, and because of the nonlocal property of quantum phenomena, it can on occasion instantaneously affect the state of another person's brain (telepathy), another person's body (psychic healing), or a distant physical process (PK).†

Walker's theory is thus an extension of the original formulation of von Neumann's interpretation, in which observation collapses state vectors. Von Neumann's original formulation implicitly assumed that conscious observation has no effect on *which specific value* the quantum phenomena actually take upon observation; the actual outcome was assumed to be purely random. But we have seen that the experiments of Schmidt apparently demonstrate that human consciousness can bias the collapse of random quantum systems in a desired direction.‡ Yet we have also seen that the effect with REGs appears to be weak. Walker must therefore postulate that either a weak bias in a desired direction somehow has a greater macroscopic impact inside the brain, or that consciousness may exert a stronger influence on quantum events within the brain because of its close and intimate link with this sensitive instrument. Both of these ideas seem reasonable. After all, it is hardly surprising that the effect of mind

---

*Concerning the strength of electrical barriers in the synapses; for more information see pages 260 and 261 of *Elemental Mind* by Nick Herbert.

†Walker comprehensively defended his model against criticisms in nontechnical language in an article titled "A Review of Criticisms of the Quantum Mechanical Theory of Psi Phenomena" in the December 1984 issue of *Journal of Parapsychology*.

‡Walker's model apparently predicted Schmidt's retro-PK results (on tape recorded data). See Walker's previously cited 1984 article, page 321.

on the fission of atoms in the REG experiments is very weak; we should rather wonder why there should be any effect at all. Any such effect must inevitably be greater on the brains of animals and men, which have presumably evolved to respond to mental influence.

> *If mind exerts its power over nature by selecting which quantum outcome actually occurs, then our perceived freedom of action is not illusory, for physics as currently conceived regards quantum events as essentially uncaused, unrestrained by prior physical events.*
>
> PHYSICIST NICK HERBERT

These three theories differ regarding the precise location of mind-matter interaction, but it should be noted that they are all clearly dualistic in the sense that they postulate a nonphysical mind that also exerts a real influence in the physical world.* As an adherent of the von Neumann interpretation, Walker believes,

> Duality is already a part of physics. . . . The dualism enters because "observation" as it is used in quantum theory must have properties that go beyond those that can be represented in terms of material objects interacting by way of force fields (which is the way all of physics describes physical processes). The reason is that the observer is introduced in QM as a way to account for state vector collapse.[28]

Stapp agrees, noting, "In view of the turmoil that has engulfed philosophy during the three centuries since Newton's successors cut the bond between mind and matter, the re-bonding achieved by physicists during the first half of the twentieth century must be seen as a momentous development."[29] Stapp continues:

---

*Quantum theories of the mind do not necessarily imply that the mind can exist without a brain to express itself with. This is a separate issue.

The only objections I know to applying the basic principles of orthodox contemporary physics to brain dynamics are, first, the forcefully expressed opinions of some non-physicists that the classical approximation provides an entirely adequate foundation for understanding mind-brain dynamics, in spite of quantum calculations that indicate just the opposite; and second, the opinions of some conservative physicists, who, apparently for philosophical reasons, contend that the successful orthodox quantum theory, which is intrinsically dualistic, should be replaced by a theory that re-converts human consciousness into a causally inert witness to the mindless dance of atoms, as it was in 1900. Neither of these opinions has any rational basis in contemporary science.[30]

PHENOMENA QUANTUM MECHANICAL MODELS OF MIND CAN EXPLAIN

Does a dualistic, nonmaterialistic model of mind-brain interaction account for the observed facts better than a materialistic model? The answer is clearly yes: such a model can account for several phenomena that remain utterly inexplicable by materialism. These would include:

- The placebo effect
- Cognitive behavioral therapy
- Psychic abilities, also known as psi
- The NDE

The placebo effect is well known in medicine. It refers to the healing effect created by a sick person's belief that a powerful remedy has been applied when the improvement could not have been the physical result of the remedy. It should not be confused with the body's natural healing process, as it depends specifically on the patient's mental belief that a specific remedy will work. Neuroscientist Mario Beauregard describes the well-known effectiveness of placebos:

Since the 1970's, a proposed new drug's effectiveness is routinely tested in controlled studies against placebos, *not* because placebos are useless but precisely because they are so useful. Placebos usually help a percentage of patients enrolled in the control group of a study, perhaps 35 to 45 percent. Thus, in recent decades, if a drug's effect is statistically significant, which means that it is at least 5 percent better than a placebo, it can be licensed for use.

In 2005, *New Scientist,* hardly known for its support of nonmaterialist neural theory, listed "13 Things That Don't Make Sense," and the placebo effect was number one on the list. Of course, the placebo effect "doesn't make sense" if you assume that the mind either does not exist or is powerless.[31]

A nonmaterialist approach to the mind has also been instrumental in developing treatments for various psychiatric disorders. Cognitive behavioral therapy is based on the assumption that directed, willed mental effort can reorganize a disordered brain and has been used to treat obsessive-compulsive disorder and various phobias. Jeffrey Schwartz, a nonmaterialist neuropsychiatrist at the University of California, Los Angeles, routinely treats obsessive-compulsive disorder as a case of an intact mind troubled by a malfunctioning brain. Schwartz has developed a treatment designed to help patients realize that faulty brain messages cause the problem and to help the patients actually rewire their brains to bypass the problem. PET scans of the patients' brains before and after treatment showed that the patients really had changed their brains.[32] Schwartz writes, "The time has come for science to confront the serious implications of the fact that directed, willed mental activity can clearly and systematically alter brain function."[33]*

Reports of demonstrated psychic abilities are a persistent embarrassment to materialism. Considered as a scientific hypothesis, materialism makes a bold and admirable prediction: psychic abilities such as telepa-

---

*Contrast Schwartz's statement with that of materialist philosopher Daniel Dennett, who writes, "A brain was always going to do what it was caused to do by local mechanical disturbances" (Daniel Dennett, *A Companion to the Philosophy of Mind,* Samuel Guttenplan, ed. [Oxford: Blackwell, 1994], 237).

thy simply do not exist. If they are shown to exist, then materialism is clearly refuted. But psychic abilities—or psi as they are called—have been demonstrated again and again under the most rigorously controlled experimental conditions.* However, as I have shown in my previous book, *Parapsychology and the Skeptics,* the materialists have gone to extraordinary lengths to try to dismiss, explain away, and even suppress the data.[34]† In any other field of inquiry, the collective evidence would have been considered extremely compelling decades ago.‡ However, parapsychology is *not* like any other field of inquiry. The data of parapsychology challenge deeply held worldviews, worldviews that are concerned not only with science but also with religious and philosophical issues. As such, the data arouse strong passions and, for many, a strong desire to dismiss them.

Refusing to accept data that proves a scientific theory false turns the theory into an ideology, a belief held as an article of faith; in other words, a belief that simply *must* be true, because it is considered so important. Concerning this point, Beauregard writes,

> Materialists have conducted a running war against psi research for decades, because *any* evidence of psi's validity, no matter how minor, is fatal to their ideological system. Recently, for example, self-professed skeptics have attacked atheist neuroscience grad student Sam Harris for having proposed, in his book titled *The End of Faith* (2004), that psi research has validity. Harris is only following the

---

*Dean Radin's excellent and entertaining book *The Conscious Universe* summarizes the results of thousands of psi experiments.

†A particularly shameful episode was the National Research Council report meant to evaluate the psi research performed by the U.S. Army. Colonel John Alexander (chief, U.S. Army Intelligence, 1982–1984, retired) responded to the council's report, writing in part, "It seems clear that Hyman and James Alcock proceeded on an intentional path to discredit the work in parapsychology. . . . What, we may ask, are they afraid of? Is protecting scientific orthodoxy so vital that they must deny evidence and suppress contrary opinion?"

‡In *Parapsychology and the Skeptics,* I quote articles from the 1950s written by academic skeptics, in which they freely admitted that if this were any other field of inquiry, the debate would be settled by the quality of the data then available. See pages 85 and 86, and pages 127 and 128.

evidence. But in doing so, he is clearly violating an important tenet of materialism: materialist ideology trumps evidence.[35]

The NDE, in which people have reported clear memories of conscious experience at times when their brains did not seem to be functioning, also strongly challenges materialism. As you read through this book, you may come to realize that many of the arguments challenging a transcendental interpretation of these experiences are motivated by an a priori commitment to a materialist worldview.

MATERIALIST THEORIES OF MIND

The doctrine of materialism is one of the implications of taking classical physics to be a complete description of all of nature, including human beings.* It is essentially the idea that all events have a physical cause; in other words, that all events are caused by the interaction between particles of matter and force fields. It follows from this that mind has no causal role in nature but is at most merely a useless by-product produced by the brain, and so in short, all that matters is matter.

There are three basic materialist approaches: the mind does not exist, the mind is identical to the brain, or the mind is a useless by-product produced by the brain.

The eliminative materialists seriously argue that consciousness and the self do not exist, but that children are indoctrinated by "folk psychology" into believing that they exist as conscious, thinking beings. For instance, journalist Michael Lemonick writes, "Despite our every instinct to the contrary, there is one thing that consciousness is not: some entity deep inside the brain that corresponds to the 'self,' some kernel of awareness that runs the show, as the 'man behind the curtain' manipulated the illusion of a powerful magician in *The Wizard of Oz*. After more than a century of looking for it, brain researchers have long since concluded that

---

*As mentioned above, Newton did not subscribe to this view, but instead followed Descartes on this matter. This doctrine was popularized by Newton's followers, such as Voltaire and Diderot, both of whom were strongly motivated by opposition to religion and superstition.

there is no conceivable place for such a self to be located in the physical brain, and that it simply doesn't exist."[36]

This may sound bizarre, but since materialism cannot account for consciousness, some materialists simply deny their own existence as conscious beings. They are driven to this act of desperation by their conviction that science, which they understand as applied materialism, supports them. Note the self-refuting nature of this position: If I believe that consciousness does not exist, then how could my belief exist? If my consciousness does not exist, then neither does my belief. And if my professed belief is nothing more than a machine going through its motions, then you have no reason to accept it as correct.

The identity theory holds great attraction for many philosophers, as it seems to offer a simple and easy solution to the problem. It says, for instance, that the subjective awareness of a red patch is objectively the movement of particles taking place in one's brain. Some identity theorists hope that neuroscience will one day be able to map out the brain states that correspond to mental states, so that we will be able to simply describe mental activity as the activity of the brain. But Beauregard points out why this is a false hope:

> Every human mind and brain moves through life differently, changing as it goes, so the information obtained for his brain would not apply to anyone else's—or even to his *own* brain at a later time! This point bears repeating because it is so contrary to materialist hopes that it is often ignored in public discussions. One outcome, for example, is that [Jean-Peirre] Changeux's view that mind states and brain states are completely identical is untestable and lacks predictive value.[37]

Any theory that is untestable and lacks predictive value does not belong to science, but rather to philosophy at best, ideology at worse. And it does get worse. How are we even to understand the assertion that thoughts and brain states are really one and the same? If they are the same, then every characteristic of one must be a characteristic of the other; but this leads to nonsense, as physicist and philosopher C. D. Broad pointed out.

There are some questions which can be raised about the characteristics of being a molecular movement, which it is nonsensical to raise about the characteristics of being an awareness of a red patch; and conversely. About a molecular movement it is perfectly reasonable to raise the question: Is it swift or slow, straight or circular, and so on? About the awareness of a red patch it is nonsensical to ask whether it is a swift or slow awareness, a straight or a circular awareness, and so on. Conversely, it is reasonable to ask about an awareness of a red patch whether it is a clear or a confused awareness; but it is nonsense to ask of a molecular movement whether it is a clear or a confused movement. Thus the attempt to argue that "being a sensation of so and so" and "being a bit of bodily behavior of such and such a kind" are just two names for the same characteristic is evidently hopeless.[38]

Eliminative materialism and identity theory are varieties of monism, the idea that only one kind of substance exists in the universe. A materialist monist believes that matter is all that exists, in contrast to a dualist, who believes that reality contains two sorts of essences: psychical and physical. The materialist believes that the full authority of science supports his position and that dualism is an outmoded legacy of a prescientific era, but many modern scientists disagree. Astronomer V. A. Firsoff writes, "To assert there is *only matter* and no mind is the most illogical of propositions, quite apart from the findings of modern physics, which show that there is no matter in the traditional meaning of the term."[39] As we saw earlier, many quantum theorists were driven to the conclusion that prior to conscious observation, matter exists only in a half-real state as possibility waves, without definite values for dynamic attributes such as position or velocity. Hence Walker's remark that "duality is already a part of physics."

Wolfgang Pauli, one of the major contributors to quantum theory, concluded, "The only acceptable point of view appears to be the one that recognizes *both* sides of reality—the quantitative and the qualitative, the physical and the psychical—as compatible with each other, and can embrace them simultaneously."[40]

Epiphenomenalism does not deny the existence of consciousness, but holds that the interaction between the brain and mind runs strictly one way, from brain to mind. This view was popularized by Darwin's friend and colleague Thomas Huxley, who described the mind as a mere epiphenomena—a useless by-product of brain activity. According to this theory, free will and intent are only illusions.

Although Darwin liked and admired Huxley, he would have none of this. Supporting Huxley's opinion would have contradicted his life's work, as Karl Popper rightly pointed out.

> The theory of natural selection constitutes a strong argument against Huxley's theory of the one-sided action of body on mind and for the mutual interaction of mind and body. Not only does the body act on the mind—for example, in perception, or in sickness—but our thoughts, our expectations, and our feelings may lead to useful actions in the physical world. If Huxley had been right, mind would be useless. But then it could not have evolved . . . by natural selection.[41]

So from a strictly Darwinian approach, the mental powers of animals and men should be expected to lead to useful actions and should therefore be a causal influence in nature. According to this account, perceptions, emotions, judgments, and thoughts all have a real effect. And the more highly developed the mental powers, the more causal impact they should be expected to have.

However, Darwin's viewpoint was thought to conflict with the physics of his time, which could specify no mechanism by which the mental could influence the physical. Arguments based on physics, being a more "basic" science than biology, were thought to trump arguments based on evolutionary theory. However, as we have seen, modern physics allows nonmechanical causation and has eliminated the causal closure of the physical.

Harold Morowitz, professor of molecular biophysics and biochemistry at Yale University, pointed out that while biologists have been relentlessly moving toward the hard-core materialism that characterized nineteenth-century physics, "at the same time, physicists, faced with compelling experimental evidence, have been moving away from strictly mechanical models of the universe to a view that sees the mind as playing an integral role in all physical events. It is as if the two disciplines were on fast-moving trains, going in opposite directions and not noticing what is happening across the tracks."[42] For Beauregard, this raises questions: "If physics fails to support biology, which discipline should rethink its position—physics or biology? On a practical note, can we reasonably expect much progress in neuroscience, given the problems, if we do not begin by reassessing the materialism that has characterized our hypotheses for decades?"[43]

Materialist theories of mind are based on the assumption that brain activity, and hence mental activity, is driven from below by the deterministic, observer-independent motions of elementary particles in the brain, as described by classical physics. But we have known since the early years of the twentieth century that classical physics fails drastically at the atomic and subatomic levels, and that the behavior of such particles is indeterministic and observer dependent. The irony here is that while materialists often describe themselves as promoting a scientific outlook, it is possible to be a materialist only by ignoring the most successful scientific theory of matter the world has yet seen. The materialist believes that consciousness is created by matter, yet the best theory we have about the nature of matter seems to require that consciousness exists independently of matter. And materialist models of mind utterly fail to answer the hard problem: why should consciousness exist in the first place and then constantly deceive us as to its function?

Materialist philosopher of mind John Searle has lamented the bankruptcy of most work in the philosophy of mind and has candidly suggested that the motivation behind acceptance of materialist views is more emotional than rational.

Acceptance of the current views is motivated not so much by an independent conviction of their truth as by a terror of what are apparently the only alternatives. That is, the choice we are tacitly presented with is between a 'scientific' approach, as represented by one or another of the current versions of 'materialism,' and an 'antiscientific' approach, as represented by Cartesianism or some other traditional religious conception of the mind.[44]

THE DREADED INTERACTION PROBLEM

Critics of dualism often question how two fundamentally different properties such as mind and matter could possibly interact (materialist philosopher William Lycan calls this the "dreaded" interaction problem).[45] How can something nonspatial, with no mass, location, or physical dimensions, possibly influence spatially bound matter? As K. R. Rao writes,

> The main problem with such dualism is the problem of interaction. How does unextended mind interact with the extended body? Any kind of causal interaction between them, which is presumed by most dualist theories, comes into conflict with the physical theory that the universe is a closed system and that every physical event is linked with an antecedent physical event. This assumption preempts any possibility that a mental act can cause a physical event.[46]

Of course, we know now that the universe is *not* a closed system and that the collapse of the wave function—a physical event—is linked with an antecedent mental event. The objection Rao describes is of course based on classical physics.

By asking "How does unextended mind interact with the extended body?" Rao is making the implicit assumption that phenomena that exist as cause and effect *must* have something in common in order to exist as cause and effect. So is this a logical necessity or is it rather an empirical truth, a fact about nature? As philosopher and historian David Hume pointed out long ago, we form our idea of causation from observations of constant correlation; and since anything in principle could correlate with anything else, only observation can establish what causes what. Parapsychologist John Beloff considers the issue logically:

> If an event A never occurred without being preceded by some other

event B, we would surely want to say that the second event was a necessary condition or cause of the first event, *whether or not* the two had anything else in common. As for such a principle being an empirical truth, how could it be since there are here only two known independent substances, i.e. mind and matter, as candidates on which to base a generalization? To argue that they cannot interact *because* they are independent is to beg the question. . . . It says something about the desperation of those who want to dismiss radical dualism that such phony arguments should repeatedly be invoked by highly reputable philosophers who should know better.[47]*

Popper also rejects completely the idea that only like can act upon like, describing this as resting on obsolete notions of physics. For an example of unlikes acting on one another, we have interaction between the four known and very different forces, and between forces and physical bodies. Popper considers the issue empirically:

In the present state of physics we are faced, not with a plurality of substances, but with a plurality of different kinds of forces, and thus with a pluralism of different interacting explanatory principles. Perhaps the clearest physical example against the thesis that only like things can act upon each other is this: In modern physics, the action of bodies upon bodies is mediated by fields—by gravitational and electrical fields. Thus like does not act upon like, but bodies act first upon fields, which they modify, and then the modified field acts upon another body.[48]

---

*Beloff considers this argument along with the other objection that if we require a self to scan the perceptual field, then we also need a second self to monitor the experiences of the other, and so on, ad infinitum. He correctly views this objection as ridiculous, as a two-term relationship between object and subject does not lead to infinite regress any more than any other two-term relationship. Just because a ticket needs to be stamped to be validated does not imply that the stamp in turn needs to be validated by another stamp, and so on, ad infinitum.

THE OBJECTIONS OF DANIEL DENNETT

Daniel Dennett's book *Consciousness Explained* has a chapter titled "Why Dualism is Forlorn," which begins with the following words: "The idea of mind as distinct from the brain, composed not of ordinary matter but of some other kind of stuff, is dualism, and it is deservedly in disrepute today. . . . The prevailing wisdom, variously expressed and argued for is materialism: there is one sort of stuff, namely matter—the physical stuff of physics, chemistry, and physiology—and the mind is somehow nothing but a physical phenomenon. In short, the mind is the brain."[49]

Dennett then asks, "What, then, is so wrong with dualism? Why is it in such disfavor?" His answer:

> A fundamental principle of physics is that any change in the trajectory of a particle is an acceleration requiring the expenditure of energy . . . this principle of conservation of energy . . . is apparently violated by dualism. This confrontation between standard physics and dualism has been endlessly discussed since Descartes's own day, and is widely regarded as the inescapable flaw in dualism.[50]

Shortly after this, he writes: "This fundamentally antiscientific stance of dualism is, to my mind, it most disqualifying feature, and is the reason why in this book I adopt the apparently dogmatic rule that dualism is to be avoided *at all costs*."[51]

Commenting on the argument Dennett presents, Stapp writes,

> The argument depends on identifying 'standard physics' with classical physics. The argument collapses when one goes over to contemporary physics, in which trajectories of particles are replaced by cloud-like structures, and in which conscious choices can influence physically described activity without violating the conservation laws or any other laws of quantum mechanics. *Contemporary physical theory allows, and its orthodox von Neumann form entails, an interactive dualism that is fully in accord with all the laws of physics.*[52] (emphasis in original)

Rosenblum and Kuttner also reject Dennett's arguments:

> Some theorists deny the possibility of duality by arguing that a signal from a non-material mind could not carry energy and thus could not influence material brain cells. Because of this inability of a mind to supply energy to influence the neurons of the brain, it is claimed that physics demonstrates an inescapable flaw of dualism. However, no energy need be involved in determining to *which particular* situation a wave function collapses. Thus the determination of which of the physically possible conscious experiences becomes the actual experience is a process that need not involve energy transfer. Quantum mechanics therefore allows an escape from the supposed fatal flaw of dualism. It is a mistake to think that dualism can be ruled out on the basis of physics.[53]

Finally, as Broad pointed out decades ago, at a time when quantum mechanics was still in its infancy, even if all physical-to-physical causation involves transfer of energy, we have no reason to think that such transfer would also be required in mental-to-physical or physical-to-mental causation.[54] This, of course, is completely consistent with the point made above by Rosenblum and Kuttner.*

CONCLUDING REMARKS

Cognitive scientist Roger Sperry has proposed that consciousness is an emergent property of the brain. A simple example of an emergent property is the fluidity of water, which is nothing like any property of hydrogen and oxygen. Another example is the geometrical and optical properties of crystals, properties that the molecules that compose them do not possess. Sperry proposes that consciousness emerges from the configuration of the brain in

---

*Despite giving his book the rather pompous title *Consciousness Explained,* Dennett of course does no such thing: he ends up simply denying the existence of conscious experience (presumably because of his inability to explain it). The fallacies in Dennett's philosophical arguments are listed in chapter 5 of *The Mystery of Consciousness* by John R. Searle.

the way that fluidity emerges from combining hydrogen and oxygen.

This is different from the materialist production theory, according to which the brain produces consciousness the way the liver produces bile. It is a temporal distinction: in the production theory, brain states precede the conscious states they produce, but if conscious states are emergent properties of brain states, then they occur simultaneously with them.

However, as philosopher of mind B. Alan Wallace notes,

> A genuine emergent property of the cells of the brain is the brain's semi-solid consistency, and that is something that objective, physical science can well comprehend . . . but they do not understand how the brain produces any state of consciousness. *In other words, if mental phenomena are in fact nothing more than emergent properties and functions of the brain, their relation to the brain is fundamentally unlike every other emergent property and function found in nature.*[55] (emphasis in original)

The von Neumann interpretation of reality leaves open the possibility that the mind is not an emergent but rather an elemental property, that is, a basic constituent of the universe as elemental as energy and force fields. This idea is seriously entertained by physicists such as Herbert, and in its favor we should note that it would resolve the paradox that is raised by the von Neumann interpretation: if consciousness depends on the physical world and if the value of many quantum physical properties depends on consciousness, then how did the physical world ever bring about consciousness in the first place? The solution to this puzzle is apparently what Jeans means when he writes, "Mind no longer appears to be an accidental intruder into the realm of matter; we ought rather hail it as the governor of the realm of matter."[56]*

Quantum mechanics can thereby be considered as supporting an

---

*Under this account, the origins of consciousness may lie outside of the evolutionary story; however, once primitive brains evolved to the required complexity, consciousness may have emerged into the physical world and provided conscious organisms with a survival advantage. Locked in a symbiotic union, the psychical and biological may have coevolved.

interactive dualism similar to that of Descartes. Cartesian dualism holds that there are two kinds of entirely separate substances: mind and matter. This theory fell into disrepute among many philosophers because classical physics provided no mechanism by which mind could influence material substance.

The classical idea of substance—self-sufficient, unchanging, with definite location, motion, and extension in space—has been replaced by the idea that physical reality is not made out of any material substance, but rather out of events and possibilities for those events to occur. These possibilities, or potentials, for events to occur have a wavelike structure and can interfere with each other. They are not substance-like, that is, static or persisting in time. Rather than being concerned with "substances" in the classical sense of the term, modern interactive dualism conceives of two differently described aspects of reality: the psychical and the physical.

Stapp sums up how a modern interactive dualism based on quantum mechanics simplifies the conceptual relationship between the two aspects of reality.

> This solution is in line with Descartes' idea of two "substances," that can interact in our brains, provided "substance" means merely a carrier of "essences." The essence of the inhabitants of res cogitans is "felt experience." They are thoughts, ideas, and feelings: the realities that hang together to form our streams of conscious experiences. But the essence of the inhabitants of res extensa is not at all that sort of persisting stuff that classical physicists imagined the physical world to be made of . . . their essential nature is that of "potentialities for the psychophysical events to occur." Those events occur at the interface between the psychologically described and physically described aspects of nature. The causal connections between "potentialities for psychologically described events to occur" and the actual occurrence of such events are easier to comprehend and describe than causal connections between the mental and physical features of classical physics. For, both sides of the quantum duality are conceptually more like "ideas" than like "rocks."[57]

FIVE

ARE MEMORIES STORED IN THE BRAIN?

We have seen that some skeptics of the idea of survival of bodily death have argued that memory is bound up with the structure of the brain, and so when the brain is destroyed then memories must also cease to exist. If memories are stored in the brain, and only in the brain, then it is indeed hard to imagine how personal identity could survive the dissolution of the brain.

Edwards tells us that "brain physiology supplies us with evidence against the existence of extra-cerebral memories."[1] He offers no detailed account of this evidence, but instead refers to a debate between psychiatrist Ian Stevenson, best known for his research on reincarnation, and two skeptics, mathematician John Taylor and psychologist John Cohen, that took place on a BBC program in 1976.

Cohen: . . . memories are tied to a particular brain tissue. If you take away the brain, there is no memory.

Stevenson: I think that's an assumption. Memories may exist in the brain and exist elsewhere also.

Cohen: But we have not the slightest evidence, even a single case, of a memory existing without a brain. We have plenty of slight damage to a brain, which destroys memory, but not the other way around.

Stevenson: I feel that's one of the issues here—whether memories can, in fact, survive the destruction of the brain.

Taylor: Professor Stevenson, do you have any evidence, other than these reincarnation cases, that memories can survive the destruction of physical tissue?

Stevenson: No. I think the best evidence comes from the reincarnation cases.

Taylor then brought up the well-known cases of people who lose all or most of their memory as a result of brain injuries. Stevenson was not fazed.

Stevenson: Well, it's possible that what is affected is his ability to express memories that he may still have.

Taylor: But are you suggesting, in fact, that memories are in some way nonphysically bound up, and can be stored in a nonphysical manner?

Stevenson: Yes, I'm suggesting that there might be a nonphysical process of storage.

Taylor: What does that mean? Nonphysical storage of what?

Stevenson: The potentiality for the reproduction of an image memory.

Taylor: But information itself involves energy. Is there such a thing as nonphysical energy?

Stevenson: I think there may be, yes.

Taylor: How can you define it? Nonphysical energy, to me, is a complete contradiction in terms. I can't conceive how on earth you could ever conceive of such a quantity. . . .

Stevenson: Well, it might be in some dimension of which we are just beginning to form crude ideas. . . . We are making an assumption of some kind of process that is not, and maybe cannot be, understood in terms of current physical concepts.[2]

Edwards remarks, "These exchanges bring out very clearly what is at issue between those who accept the body-mind dependence argument and the supporters of the instrument theory." Later Edwards recalls the debate and reminds us, "Professors Cohen and Taylor regarded the notion of extra-cerebral memories as totally absurd." As his last words on the subject, he concludes, "As for Stevenson's nonphysical storage depot of extra-cerebral memories—'the dimension which cannot be understood in terms of current physical concepts'—it must surely be dismissed as nothing but a vague picture which is of no scientific value whatsoever."[3]

REMARKS ON THE DEBATE

A televised debate is hardly the best place to attempt to settle a subtle problem philosophers have wrestled with for centuries, but some comments on the remarks from the debate quoted above seem to be in order at this point.

By "nonphysical," Stevenson seems to be referring to something "not . . . understood in terms of current physical concepts," which seems to be the right usage in this context.

With regard to Taylor's objection to the notion of "nonphysical energy," our notion of energy started with the idea of mechanical energy, which was changed when electrical energy was discovered, a discovery that violated Newtonian mechanics. This led to a reconstruction of physics in which electricity became basic and mechanics derivative with respect to electricity. But then other forms of energy were discovered, such as light, chemical, and nuclear energy, and the law of the conservation of energy had to be generalized whenever the physical world was enlarged. Remarking on this point and its relevance to the mind-body problem, Popper commented that the history of the conservation law "makes it very much easier to assume the possibility of interference from outside—from something as yet unknown which, if we want physics to be complete, would have to be added to the physical world."[4] So to rule out the idea of forms of energy "not . . . understood in terms of current physical concepts" as "a complete contradiction in terms" is to adhere to the old fallacy that our current understanding of physics is complete.*

After taking these considerations into account, is the notion of extra-cerebral memories "totally absurd?" Should it be dismissed as "nothing but a vague picture which is of no scientific value whatsoever?"

THE EVIDENCE FROM NEUROPHYSIOLOGY

It is commonly assumed today that memories are somehow stored in the brain, and this belief goes back to ancient times. Aristotle, for instance, compared memories with impressions left by seals in wax. As time has passed, the analogies have been updated—most recently in terms of tape recordings or computer memory stores—yet the basic idea has remained the same. But how well does the neurophysiological evidence support the belief that memories are stored somehow as traces within the brain?

Neuroscientists have tried for decades to locate the sites of memory traces within the brain, and an enormous number of animals have been expended in the attempt. The usual process has been to train the animals to perform some task and then cut out parts of their brains to find out where the memories are stored. But even after large chunks of their brains have been removed—in some experiments up to 60 percent—the unfortunate animals can often remember what they were trained to do. Even experiments on invertebrates such as the octopus have failed to locate specific memory traces, leading one researcher to conclude that "memory seems to be both everywhere and nowhere in particular."[5]

There is, however, much evidence that changes can occur in the brains of animals as a consequence of the way they grow up. Experiments with rats have shown that animals raised in an environment with plenty of stimulation and activity have bigger brains than those raised in solitary confinement. The nervous system is dynamic in its structure, and its development is influenced by its activity.

---

*An example of a form of energy not understood in terms of current physical concepts would be dark energy, the energy in empty space that is apparently causing the expansion of the universe to accelerate.

This consideration has been used in an experiment with chicks in an attempt to localize memory traces in the brain laid down during the learning process. A day after hatching, they were trained to perform a simple task, the effects of which were studied by injecting radioactive substances. Greater amounts of these substances were incorporated into nerve cells in a particular region of the left hemisphere of the forebrain in those chicks than in chicks that did not undergo the training.[6] In other words, nerve cells in a particular region of the brain showed greater growth and development in chicks that had learned to perform the simple task, but when the region of the forebrain associated with the learning process was removed a day after they were trained, the chicks could still remember what they had learned. The cells that had experienced greater growth and development during the learning process were not necessary for the memory retention. Once again, the hypothetical memory traces have proved to be elusive.

There is another empirical consideration that causes great difficulty for the trace theory of memory. If memories are somehow stored in brain cells or as modifications of the synaptic connections between them, then the structure of the synapses and the nervous system must remain stable over long periods of time. After all, the time span of human memory is often decades. Yet as Francis Crick writes, "It is believed that almost all the molecules in our bodies, with the exception of DNA, turn over in a matter of days, weeks, or at the most a few months. How then is memory stored in the brain so that its trace is relatively immune to molecular turnover?"[7]

Crick's "solution" is to postulate a mechanism whereby "molecules in the synapse interact in such a way that they can be replaced by new material, one at a time, without altering the overall state of the structure." His hypothesis involves protein molecules that he endows with a number of unusual properties, but there is no evidence yet that such molecules exist.

We can see from these considerations that the conventional theory of memory traces stored in the brain is in fact an assumption, one that follows from the currently orthodox theory of life, the mechanistic theory, according to which all aspects of life and mind are ultimately explicable in terms of the known laws of physics and chemistry. Results from the experiments mentioned above have not usually called this assumption into question. As one maverick biologist has pointed out,

> The conventional response to such findings is that there must be multiple or redundant memory-storage systems distributed throughout various regions of the brain: if some are lost, back-up systems can take over. This hypothesis, invented to account for the failure of attempts to find localized memory traces, follows naturally from the assumption that memories *must* be stored somehow inside the brain; but in the continuing absence of any direct evidence, it remains more a matter of faith than of fact.[8]

Since the assumption that memories must be stored in the brain follows directly from the mechanistic theory of life, the validity of this theory must be examined and the implications of alternative theories of life for the noncerebral storage of memories must be clearly set forth.

SIX

THEORIES OF LIFE

The starting point for speculation about the nature of life is death. At death, something seems to have left the body: it no longer moves and it starts to decay. All over the world, people have come to the conclusion that some life force, some vital factor, is necessary to animate living organisms.

In terms of modern science, this vital force is energy. Living systems draw energy from their environment and convert energy from one form to another as they carry out essential functions of growth, maintenance, and reproduction. The ultimate source of most of this energy on Earth is the sun: plants take energy from sunlight in photosynthesis, and in turn animals take chemical energy from their food in digestion.* When organisms die, the energy from their body is released to continue on its way in other forms.

But the flow of energy can only be one of the aspects of life. The fact that these flows of energy take so many different forms means that there must be some formative principle in operation over and above the flows themselves. Ever since the scientific revolution of the seventeenth century, the nature of this formative principle has been the subject of an intense and often bitter debate.

---

*The only known exception to solar-powered life on Earth appears to be certain deep-sea marine ecosystems that receive no sunlight, but instead thrive off the heat from thermal vents at the bottom of the sea.

One school of thought, vitalism, holds that living organisms are truly alive and are organized by immaterial souls or vital factors. The old animistic theories held that all of nature was alive to some degree, but since the seventeenth century, vitalism has confined life to biological organisms and has left the rest of nature to be explained by a science of physics that has so far restricted itself to a study of the inanimate.*

By contrast, the mechanistic theory of life denies there is any essential difference between living and inanimate matter, and regards organisms as inanimate machines, governed by the ordinary laws of physics and chemistry. Although the laws of physics have changed greatly since the seventeenth century and although modern physics has become increasingly removed from mechanistic explanations, the essence of the mechanistic theory of life remains the same: the organization of living organisms does not depend on any principles over and above those that apply to nonliving organisms. Rather, the mechanistic theory holds that the organization of life somehow emerges from complex physiochemical interactions in a manner that remains obscure.

The mechanistic approach to biology has been at its most successful in its accounts of the physiology of adult organisms. It regards them as machines and regards the various organs as parts of the machines. This analogy has some plausibility when accounting for adult organisms: some machines, especially those with automatic feedback mechanisms, do seem to resemble organisms or organs—pumps are like hearts, cameras are like eyes, computers are like brains, and so forth. No one denies that some machines are something like artificial organisms; the question is whether organisms are nothing but machines.

The machine analogy breaks down when it comes to understanding the growth and development of organisms, their morphogenesis

---

*Wigner believes that an extension of physics to deal with life would require radical changes: "It will have to be replaced by new laws, based on new concepts, if organisms with consciousness are to be described . . . in order to deal with the phenomenon of life, the laws of physics will have to be changed, not only reinterpreted." See his chapter, "Remarks on the Mind-Body Problem," in *Quantum Theory and Measurements,* edited by John Wheeler and Wojciech Zurek.

(from the Greek words *morphe* and *genesis,* meaning "form" and "coming into being"). Plants grow from seeds, and animals grow from tiny fertilized eggs, but machines do not grow spontaneously from machine eggs. Machines do not grow from small parts from other machines, nor do they regenerate themselves after damage. By contrast, cuttings made from a willow tree can develop into new complete trees, and cutting a flatworm into pieces will result in the formation of several new complete flatworms.

Vitalists have maintained that morphogenesis cannot be explained mechanistically, that there is some organizing principle or force directing the development of organisms. The mechanistic school of biology has always rejected vitalistic explanations as a matter of principle and has been forced to reinvent vital forces in mechanistic guises, most recently in the form of genetic programs written in the chemistry of DNA molecules. The problem with this idea is that the DNA molecules are the same in all the cells of the body; they are all genetically identical. In other words, all the cells have the same genetic program, yet they somehow behave differently and have formed tissues and organs of different structures.* Clearly some formative influence other than DNA is responsible for the growth and development of organisms in all their complexity.

In the 1920s, a number of biologists first proposed a new way of conceptualizing the development of organisms, in terms of morphogenetic fields. The idea of morphogenetic fields has been widely adopted in biology, but the nature of these fields has remained obscure. Some biologists consider them to be only convenient labels representing complex physiochemical interactions that remain obscure. However, other biologists seriously consider the open possibility that the phenomena of life may

---

*Many biologists realize that the concept of a genetic program is actually misleading. All that genes are recognized to actually do is code for the sequence of amino acids that are used to synthesize the more than thirty thousand different types of proteins found in the body. Different genes are expressed in different cells to produce different types of protein. An analogy would be the production of different types of building materials, but genes seem to have nothing to do with how those "building materials" are actually organized into different structures in the body. For a discussion of this, see chapters 5 and 8 of Rupert Sheldrake's *The Presence of the Past.*

depend on factors yet unrecognized by the physical sciences, and so consider them to be a new kind of field, one so far unknown to physics. Like the known fields of physics, they are thought of as invisible regions of influence, and like magnetic fields, they are thought to have a shape even though they are invisible. In terms of embryonic development, the development of an ear would be molded by an ear-shaped field, and a hand by a hand-shaped field. They are proposed to exist within and around organisms and to contain within themselves a nested hierarchy of fields within fields—organ fields, tissue fields, cell fields.

Firsoff has speculated on the possible connections between quantum physics and life, and at one point considers the concept of the morphogenetic field:

> The action for a morphogenetic field is poignantly exemplified by the experiments of Richard Sidman and G. R. Delong at Harvard, who had gently teased apart the cells in the developing brain tissue of a mouse embryo and placed these in test-tube cultures, where the cells rearranged themselves spontaneously in the correct original order. This is, indeed, a very strange field, because it is structured without obvious focal points, such as an attracting mass or charge. It recalls the immaterial spatio-temporal organization invoked by Sir John Eccles to explain the working of the brain. The organization appears to be largely independent from the material substratum of the cortex, and can migrate as it were "bodily" from one part to another, especially in cases of local injury. In fact, such morphogenetic and cerebral fields seem to resemble an "ethereal" or "astral" body. What kind of interactions, what kind of physics would be required to account for such behavior?[1]

One of the most daring theorists in biology in recent years has been Rupert Sheldrake, who in a number of works has proposed and developed the hypothesis of formative causation. This hypothesis was first introduced to the world in 1981 with the publication of Sheldrake's book *A New Science of Life*. Sheldrake's credentials as a biologist are impeccable, including degrees from Harvard and Cambridge. Yet shortly after its publication, *Nature,* one of Britain's leading scientific magazines, called the book "the best candidate for burning there has been for many years."* But not all reviewers were so hostile. The equally distinguished *New Scientist* stated, "It is quite clear that one is dealing here with an important scientific inquiry into the nature of biological and physical reality." A reviewer in the *Brain/Mind Bulletin* wrote that Sheldrake's hypothesis of formative causation was "as far-reaching in its implications as Darwin's theory of evolution."†

Sheldrake's theory is essentially an extension of the theory of morphogenetic fields. Like the known fields of physics, morphogenetic fields are thought to be invisible regions of influence that connect similar things across space, but Sheldrake postulates that they also connect similar things across time. They are thus considered to have an evolutionary nature, and so the fields of any given species are thought to be inherited from one generation to the next. The morphogenetic fields are thought to be a sort of collective memory that each member of a species draws on, and the more often a pattern of development is repeated, the more probable it is that it will be repeated again.

The process in which morphogenetic fields are influenced by the previous forms of organisms is what Sheldrake calls morphic resonance, that is, the influence of similar fields on each other through space and time, analogous to the acoustic resonance of similar tuning forks. However, unlike the more familiar forms of resonance, Sheldrake proposes that

---

*This quote was taken from the back cover of *A New Science of Life*. Most of the hostility toward Sheldrake's theories has come from fellow biologists, most of whom are still wedded to a mechanistic theory of life. As they are no longer bound to mechanistic explanations, physicists have been more ready to entertain Sheldrake's ideas, and quantum physicists such as Brian Josephson and David Bohm have expressed support for Sheldrake's hypothesis.

†Suitbert Ertel contributed a chapter titled "Testing Sheldrake's Claims of Morphogenetic Fields" to Cook and Delanoy's book *Research in Parapsychology 1991*. On page 183, he mentions one of his own tests of morphic resonance, the influence of similar fields on each other through space and time: "I set out with two students to show that Sheldrake's resonance claim would not be supported by empirical data. To my surprise, the data resisted, and my skepticism changed from a negative to a positive tone."

morphic resonance is not affected by distance, as "it does not involve a transfer of energy but of information."[2] The hypothesis of formative causation also suggests that self-organizing systems at *all* levels of complexity—molecules, crystals, cells, organisms, instinctive patterns of behavior—are organized by morphic fields subject to morphic resonance. Morphogenetic fields are considered just one type of morphic field, those concerned with the development and maintenance of the bodies of organisms.

This hypothesis is controversial, but is also readily testable. There does seem to be considerable circumstantial evidence in its favor. It is accepted, for instance, that new compounds are generally difficult to crystallize, but that as time passes they tend to form crystals more easily. The conventional explanation is that tiny fragments of crystals are carried from laboratory to laboratory on the clothing of migrant chemists and then serve as nuclei for new crystals of the same type. But the hypothesis of formative causation would suggest that this effect would persist even if migrant chemists were kept away and dust particles filtered from the air.

The theory also predicts that once animals in one part of the world learn a new trick, animals of the same type should learn the same trick more easily, even in the absence of any known connection. As evidence of this, Sheldrake discusses a long series of experiments with rats carried out in the United States, Scotland, and Australia, in which the rate of learning how to escape from a water maze increased in successive batches of rats, whether or not they were descended from trained parents. This increased rate of learning was found in laboratories separated by thousands of miles.[3]

In addition to these *ex post facto* interpretations of previous studies, there have been several attempts to directly test Sheldrake's hypotheses of morphic resonance. Fourteen of these studies were critically examined by skeptical psychologist Suitbert Ertel in 1991. In all of the studies except one, the researchers concluded that the results support Sheldrake's resonance claim. Ertel disputed these findings, pointing out that there were methodological problems with all but three of the studies. However, after writing that "morphic resonance has not been substantiated beyond all doubt," Ertel concluded that the data at hand nonetheless suggest that morphic resonance should be taken into account as a serious explanatory candidate rivaling vigorously what present-day ordinary theories are providing . . . if a large body of consistent data can be obtained, we might have accumulated sufficient evidence either to dismiss Sheldrake's theory as a disturbing intrusion into our ordinary world views or to accept it as the germ of a scientific revolution. Should the latter happen, most of the conflicts with our present world views created by Sheldrake's theory so far are bound to disappear, probably without much effort.[4]*

The theory of formative causation introduces a new twist to evolutionary biology, as it implies that living organisms inherit not only genes but also morphic fields. The genes are passed on materially from ancestors, but morphic fields are inherited nonmaterially, not just from direct ancestors but also from other members of the species. Genetic mutations may affect the ability of the organism to tune into the morphic fields of its species, just as changes in the components of a TV can affect its ability to tune into particular channels or the reception of programs. Forms and behaviors do not need to be programmed in the genes, any more than TV programs need to be programmed and generated inside the set.

IMPLICATIONS FOR MEMORY

This theory has direct relevance to our earlier discussion of experimental attempts to locate memory traces within the brain. Sheldrake explains:

There may be a ridiculously simple reason for these recurrent failures to find memory traces in brains: They may not exist. A search inside your TV set for traces of the programs you watched last week would be doomed to failure for the same reason: The set tunes in to TV transmissions but does not store them.

---

*The clearest exposition of Sheldrake's theories is in his comprehensive book *The Presence of the Past.*

The hypothesis of formative causation suggests that memory depends on morphic resonance rather than material memory stores. Morphic resonance depends on similarity. It involves an effect of like on like. The more similar an organism is to an organism in the past, the more specific and effective the morphic resonance. In general, any given organism is more like *itself* in the past and hence subject to highly specific morphic resonance from its own past. For instance, you are more like you were a year ago than like I was. This self-resonance helps to maintain an organism's form, in spite of the continuous turnover of its material constituents. Likewise, in the realm of behavior, it tunes in an organism specifically to its own past patterns of activity. Neither your habits of behavior, speech, and thought, nor your memories of particular facts and past events need be stored as material traces in your brain.

But what about the fact that memories can be lost as a result of brain damage? Some types of damage in specific areas of the brain can result in specific kinds of impairment: for example, the loss of the ability to recognize faces after damage to the secondary visual cortex of the right hemisphere. A sufferer may fail to recognize the faces even of his wife and children, even though he can still recognize them by their voices and in other ways. Does this not prove that the relevant memories were stored inside the damaged tissues? By no means. Think again of the TV analogy. Damage to some parts of the circuitry can lead to loss or distortion of picture; damage to other parts can make the set lose the ability to produce sound; damage to the tuning circuit can lead to loss of the ability to receive one or more channels. But this does not prove that the pictures, sounds, and entire programs are stored inside the damaged components.[5]

Sheldrake discusses the effects of other types of specific brain damage on memories and other abilities and argues that "the effects of brain damage on loss of memory provide no persuasive evidence in favour of the materialist theory, as they are usually assumed to do. The hypothesis of formative causation fits the facts just as well, if not better."[6]

For instance, some individuals after head injury have difficulty turning short-term memories into long-term memories, and this condition often persists for some time after the concussed patient has recovered consciousness. From the conventional point of view, this failure is due to the inability to lay down long-term memory traces; from the hypothesis of formative causation, it is due to the inability to establish new morphic fields.

There are various memory defects characteristic of damage to the cortex due to strokes, accidental injury, or surgery. Lesions of the frontal lobes affect the ability to concentrate, and other forms of injury have specific effects on the ability to recognize and recall. The same is true of other forms of disorder, such as disorders of language use due to lesions in various parts of the cortex in the left hemisphere. The mechanistic explanations for these effects have included destruction of memory traces, disruptions of organized patterns of activity in the brain, and disconnections between intact areas of the brain such as the language and visual regions of the cortex. The hypothesis of formative causation offers an alternative explanation. Sheldrake writes:

> On the present hypothesis, these abilities are lost because the brain damage affects parts of the brain with which the morphic fields are normally associated. If an appropriate pattern of brain activity is no longer present, the fields cannot be tuned in to or bring about their organizing effects.
>
> This interpretation makes it much easier to understand the fact that lost abilities often return; patients often recover partially or completely from brain damage even though the damaged regions of the brain do not regenerate. The appropriate patterns of activity come into operation somewhere else in the brain. This is almost impossible to understand if programs are "hard-wired" into the nervous system; but fields can move their regions of activity and reorganize themselves in a way that fixed material structures cannot. Such recoveries are reminiscent of the regenerative abilities of plants and

animals, and they pose the same kind of problem for mechanistic explanation.[7]*

Hans-Lukas Teuber, a cognitive psychologist who has extensively analyzed brain damage in war veterans, writes that "one is struck, before anything else, with the enormous resiliency of cerebral functions in the majority of instances. This far-reaching restitution of function remains, in my view, essentially unexplained."[8]

Finally, Penfield's experiments, in which he invoked vivid memories by electrically stimulating the temporal cortex of patients, are sometimes considered as evidence in support of the trace theory of memory. But Sheldrake points out that "here again, this need not mean that the memories are actually stored inside the nerve tissue. If one stimulates the tuning circuit of a radio or a TV set, the tuning may be changed such that transmissions from a different station are picked up; but this would of course not mean that these new programs are stored inside the components of the tuning circuits that were stimulated."[9] Penfield himself, on further reflection, abandoned his original conclusion; he writes, "In 1951, I had proposed that certain parts of the temporal cortex should be called 'memory cortex,' and suggested that the neuronal record was located here in the cortex near the points at which the stimulating electrode may call forth an experiential response. This was a mistake. . . . The record is *not* in the cortex."[10]

Like several researchers before him, Penfield gave up the idea of localized memory traces in the cortex in favor of the idea that they were distributed in other parts of brain instead, or as well. This hypothesis also explains the recurrent failure to find local memory traces, but unlike the hypothesis of formative causation, it is an untestable idea, one not

---

*On page 219 of in *The Presence of the Past,* Sheldrake includes a quote from neuroscientist E. R. John, who writes that in general, after traumatic head injury, "memories and skills return at a rapid rate during the first six months, with recovery sustained at a lower rate for up to four months. Defects in sensory, motor, and cognitive functions caused by brain injury due to penetrating wounds are characterized by an enormous resiliency of function in the great majority of cases, ultimately leading to little or no detectable defect."

capable of being proved false in practice, and therefore not a scientific hypothesis.*

So the upshot from this long-winded discussion is that the notion of extracerebral memories is by no means "totally absurd." We can now see—contrary to Edwards' assertion that "it must surely be dismissed as nothing but a vague picture which is of no scientific value whatsoever"—that the theory of extracerebral memories can be considered more scientific than the mechanistic alternative. One prediction of the theory of memory traces—that they can be localized in the brain—has been convincingly proved false, and the theory is now left with the unfalsifiable ad hoc explanation that memory is stored in several places in the brain. Yet we have seen that the theory of formative causation not only has prima facie support from the available evidence but also entails several easily testable predictions. In Popper's terms, the theory of memory traces has become a metaphysical theory, and the theory of formative causation, with its notion of extracerebral memories, is the remaining scientific alternative!

IMPLICATIONS FOR SURVIVAL

If memories are not stored within the brain, then of course they should not be expected to decay when the brain decays. Of course, this hypothesis does not automatically lead to the conclusion that survival is a fact. Sheldrake has considered the implications of his theories for the survival of bodily death and realizes that the crucial issue is the relationship of the mind to the body.

> On the one hand, this hypothesis can be interpreted within the framework of a sophisticated and updated philosophy of materialism. If the conscious self is nothing but an aspect of the functioning of the brain and its associated fields, then the brain would still be

---

*The brilliant philosopher of science Karl Popper has argued that the difference between scientific and metaphysical theories is that scientific theories are capable of being tested and proved false. Chapter 15 of my previous book, *Parapsychology and the Skeptics,* is devoted to explaining Popper's philosophy of science.

essential for the process of tuning in to memories, even if they are not stored inside the brain. In this case, the decay of the brain would still result in the extinction of consciousness.

On the other hand, if the conscious self is not identical with the function of the brain, but rather *interacts* with the brain through morphic fields, then it is possible that the conscious self could continue to be associated with these fields even after the death of the brain, and retain the ability to tune in to its own past states. Both the self and its memories could survive the death of the body.[11]

It should be clear from the above that a consideration of only the neurophysiological evidence leaves us at an impasse with regard to the question of whether consciousness continues to exist after the death of the material brain. Both possibilities are fully consistent with the neurophysiological evidence considered alone, and so there is really no antecedent improbability of survival (or any antecedent probability, either). The question can only be resolved in a rational manner by a consideration of other forms of evidence.

OTHER LINES OF EVIDENCE

Although it does not bear directly on the issue of survival, one line of evidence that seems to support the idea that the role of the brain is to transmit and limit consciousness is the evidence that has been gathered on the effects of certain mind-altering drugs on the nature of consciousness.

In Aldous Huxley's book *The Doors of Perception,* Huxley describes and reflects on his experiences with the drug mescaline, experiences that led him to the view that the role of the brain and nervous system is eliminative rather than productive. Like Bergson and Schiller before him, Huxley came to accept the theory that the brain functions as a sort of two-way filter, normally shutting out perceptions, memories, and thoughts not necessary for the survival and reproduction of the organism. Huxley writes, "According to such a theory, each one of us is potentially Mind at Large. But in so far as we are animals, our business at all costs is to survive. To make biological survival possible, Mind at Large has to be funneled through the reducing valve of the brain and nervous system. What comes out at the other end is a measly trickle of the kind of consciousness which will help us to stay alive on the surface of this particular planet."[12]

Most people, most of the time, know only what comes through the reducing valve, but certain people, such as mystics and visionaries, seem to be born with a kind of bypass that circumvents the reducing valve. Huxley writes that others may acquire temporary bypasses spontaneously, through practices such as meditation or hypnosis, or by ingesting certain drugs. One such drug appears to be mescaline, a drug he suggests has the power to impair the efficiency of the cerebral reducing valve and thereby create a temporary bypass. Huxley explains that mescaline inhibits the production of enzymes that regulate the supply of glucose to the brain cells and thus reduces the brain's ration of sugar. Although the intellect remains unimpaired and perception is enormously improved, mescaline takers find ordinary concerns completely uninteresting, as they now have better things to think about. Huxley goes on to explain how these facts support the idea that the brain functions as a sort of reducing valve.

These effects of mescalin are the sort of effects you could expect to follow the administration of a drug having the power to impair the efficiency of the cerebral reducing valve. When the brain runs out of sugar, the undernourished ego grows weak, can't be bothered to undertake the necessary chores, and loses all interest in those spatial and temporal relationships which mean so much to an organism bent on getting on in the world. As Mind at Large seeps past the no longer watertight valve, all kinds of biologically useless things start to happen. In some cases there may be extra-sensory perceptions. Other persons discover a world of visionary beauty. To others again is revealed the glory, the infinite value and meaningfulness of naked existence, of the given, unconceptualized event. In the final stage of egolessness there is an "obscure knowledge" that All is in all—that All is actually each. This is as near, I take it, as a finite mind can ever come to "perceiving everything that is happening everywhere in the universe."[13]

Huxley suggests that he experienced an expansion or enhancement of consciousness as a result of ingesting mescaline. These effects would not be expected if the brain functions as a generator of consciousness, as presumably the brain would use raw materials such as glucose and oxygen to fashion its product. On this account, reducing the supply of at least one of the raw materials should be expected to diminish the production of consciousness. On the other hand, if the brain functions as a selective inhibitor of consciousness, then an interference with its normal operation may be expected to result in an expansion or enhancement of consciousness, as nonutilitarian forms of consciousness are allowed to seep "past the no longer watertight valve."

Certain features of the NDE also support the hypothesis of selective transmission. As Schiller and Bergson pointed out earlier, those who are dying have often reported that their entire life histories flashed before their eyes in incredible detail, suggesting that one purpose of the brain is to filter out memories not necessary for day-to-day existence. More recently, Raymond Moody, Kenneth Ring, Michael Sabom, and many other researchers have described the experiences of people who underwent clinical death but were later revived. Instead of being unconscious, many of the individuals, in later interviews, remembered experiences they had while clinically dead, and several described their perceptions as being sharpened to an incredible degree and their thought process becoming unusually lucid and rapid.

In contrast to Moody and others, Erlunder Haraldsson and parapsychologist Karlis Osis conducted an extensive analysis of cases in which unusual experiences were reported on deathbeds shortly before death, cases in which the individuals involved did not recover. Several phenomena suggestive of survival were reported in many cases, but of direct relevance to the present discussion are cases in which individuals suffering from severe mental illness or a disease affecting the brain were reported as showing improvement just prior to death. Osis and Haraldsson reported two cases of chronic psychotics, both completely out of touch with reality, who seemed to the medical observers to be their normal selves again shortly before death. An even more interesting case is that of a woman dying from meningitis, a disease that is primarily destructive to the brain. She was severely disoriented almost until the end, but then "she cleared up, answered questions, smiled, was slightly elated and just a few minutes before death, came to herself. Before that she was disoriented, drowsy, and talked incoherently."[14]

These are not the sort of experiences one would expect dying individuals to report on the assumption that the brain generates consciousness, but they make perfect sense if the purpose of the brain is to selectively inhibit consciousness and memory to those thoughts and memories of utilitarian value to the organism. These experiences can be interpreted as the activity of mind disengaged, or in the process of disengaging, from the restrictions of a material brain.

Finally, the evidence for communication from deceased individuals is directly relevant to the hypothesis that consciousness can survive the death of the brain. This evidence will be discussed in great detail in the third book of this series, so I will say no more about it at this point, except to note that under the hypothesis of materialism, these reports must either remain completely inexplicable or be dismissed outright as due to some combination of hallucination, self-deception, and fraud.

CONCLUSIONS

We have seen from the above that survival is both a theoretical and an empirical possibility. The statement that consciousness may survive the death of the brain is not self-contradictory, nor is it in conflict with any of the laws or facts of science as currently understood.*

---

*Concerning the compatibility of quantum mechanics with survival, Henry Stapp has written: "Strong doubts about personality survival based *solely* on the belief that post-mortem survival is incompatible with the laws of physics are unfounded. Rational science-based opinion on this question must be based on the content and quality of the empirical data, not on a presumed incompatibility of such phenomena with our contemporary understanding of the workings of nature" (Stapp 2010).

A few words should perhaps be said here about complexity. Some have argued that the transmission theory is more complex than the production theory, and so this means the latter should be preferred. But a theory must accommodate all known facts, not merely those that we think support our pet theory. The quantum mechanical theory of matter is much more complex than the simple classical theory, but it is now known that the classical theory is fundamentally and grossly incorrect. We should not pretend the world is simpler than it is, just so we can go on believing whatever we like.

The issue of whether survival is a fact cannot be settled by declaring, as Lamont does, that the connection between mind and body "is so exceedingly intimate that it becomes inconceivable how one could function without the other," or that "man is a unified whole of mind-body or personality-body so closely and completely integrated that dividing him up into two separate and more or less independent parts becomes impermissible and unintelligible." Nor can it be decided, as Edwards does, by simply dismissing a crude caricature with the sneer that "the instrument theory is absurd." The issue can only be decided by conceiving of the various possible relationships between mind and body, by determining what sorts of evidence would tend to corroborate the various possibilities, and then by critically examining the evidence without prejudice one way or the other to decide which of the possibilities provides the best fit with all of the evidence. In the absence of such a careful inquiry as a basis for the conclusion that mind and body are in fact inseparable, these assertions of Lamont and Edwards are merely examples of pseudoscientific dogmatism. If we are to decide the issue on rational grounds as opposed to religious or materialistic faith, then we must carefully examine the empirical evidence with our minds both critical and open.

PART II

The Near-Death Experience

I approached the frontier of death
I saw the threshold of Persephone
I journeyed through all the elements and came back
I saw at midnight the sun, sparkling in white light
I came close to the gods of the upper and the netherworld
And adored them near at hand.

NEAR-DEATH EXPERIENCE
FROM ANCIENT GREECE

SEVEN

REPORTS FROM THE BRINK

One phenomenon that would seem to be able to shed light on the relationship between mind and body is the NDE. Many individuals, when faced with a life-threatening emergency, have reported strange experiences in which they claim to have left their bodies, entered a tunnel leading to another realm of existence, and there encountered deceased relatives or a mysterious "being of light." After being turned back—or deciding to go back—they suddenly find themselves back in their bodies, often with resuscitation efforts in full swing.

Reports of NDEs come from people who have survived life-threatening accidents or illnesses. NDEs have also occasionally been reported by those who only perceived their lives to be under threat, but there are also many reports from individuals who did not expect to die, either because the accident or illness was sudden and unexpected or because the NDE occurred during an operation they fully expected to survive.

How common is the NDE? The estimates vary widely. Kenneth Ring estimates that about 30 percent of those individuals who come close to death report an NDE,[1] and his estimate closely matches the 27 percent found in cardiologist Michael Sabom's sample.[2] But an English study of 63 survivors of cardiac arrest found that only about 10 percent experienced an NDE;[3] a larger Dutch study of 344 patients found that although 12 percent reported a deep NDE, after adjusting for multiple crisis events (several of the patients had experienced more than one cardiac arrest), the researchers estimated the true frequency of the reported experience to be about 5 percent.[4] The actual frequency of the remembered experience remains unknown and may depend on the nature of the life-threatening trauma.

Fragmentary accounts of the NDE have appeared in the art and literature from all ages,* but it is only recently that these reports have been gathered and analyzed in a systematic manner. Before turning to the contemporary reports, let us first examine an older case.

A. S. Wiltse, a physician, contracted typhoid fever in 1889 and was considered dead by everyone at the bedside, including a physician who failed to evoke a response by jabbing a needle into Wiltse's body.[5†] The case was investigated by Frederic Myers and Edmund Gurney of the British Society for Psychical Research. Myers and Gurney obtained sworn testimony on the events that occurred during the four-hour coma, during which Wiltse's body was without pulse or perceptible heartbeat. He recalls being about to emerge from the body and appearing to himself like a jellyfish in color and form. He had the sensation of floating up and down and laterally like a soap bubble attached to the end of a pipe until

> I at last broke free from the body . . . and fell lightly on the floor, where I slowly rose and expanded into the full stature of a man. I seemed to be translucent, of a bluish cast, and perfectly naked. As I turned, my elbow came into contact with the arm of one of two gentlemen who were standing in the door. To my surprise his arm passed right through mine without apparent resistance, the severed parts closing again without pain, as air reunites. I looked quickly up at his face to see whether he had noticed the contact but he gave me no sign. . . . I directed my gaze in the direction of his and saw my own dead body. It was lying just as I had taken so much pains to place it, partially on the right side, the feet close together, and the

---

*Examples would include Plato's legend of Er, written about 300 BCE, and Hieronymous Bosch's mysterious painting *Ascent into the Empyrean,* completed sometime around 1500.

†The case was originally reported by Wiltse in the *St. Louis Medical and Surgical Journal* and later republished by the Society for Psychical Research in 1892, along with depositions from the primary witnesses.

hands clasped across the breast. . . . I was surprised at the paleness of the face . . . and saw a number of persons sitting and standing about the body . . . and . . . attempted to gain the attention of the people with the object of comforting them as well as reassuring them of my own immortality. . . . I passed among them, but found they gave me no heed. Then the situation struck me as humorous and I laughed outright. . . . I concluded that they "are watching what they think is I, but they are mistaken." That is not I. This is I and I am as much alive as ever. How well I feel, I thought. Only a few minutes ago I was horribly sick and distressed. Then came the change called death which I have so much dreaded. This has passed now, and here I am still a man, alive and thinking, yes thinking as clearly as ever, and how well I feel; I shall never be sick again, I have no more to die.

Wiltse then describes his experiences in another world, in which he encounters a barrier, communicates with an unknown presence, and finally has to decide whether his task on Earth is finished. After deciding that it is not, he loses his awareness, and then, "Without previous thought and without apparent effort on my part, my eyes opened. I looked at my hands and then at the little white cot upon which I was lying and realizing that I was in the body, and in astonishment and disappointment, I exclaimed 'What in the world has happened to me? Must I die again?'"

Systematic study of the NDE began in the 1970s, starting with the publication of Moody's *Life after Life* in 1977. Moody's early work was criticized for lack of rigor, but it was soon followed by much more rigorous scientific investigations. The amount of data on the NDE continues to grow, and there is even an organization devoted exclusively to near-death research, the International Association of Near-Death Studies, with its own publication, *Journal of Near-Death Studies.*

Here is a much more recent example of an NDE, obtained by psychology student Norm McMaster from a man who had cardiac bypass surgery at age 55. When the patient regained consciousness after his operation, he was in a great deal of pain and then apparently passed out. He later said:

All of a sudden I was standing at the foot of the bed looking at my own body. I knew it was me in bed because there were certain features I could recognize easily. If felt no pain at all. I was a bit puzzled. I wasn't anxious or worried, I just didn't understand what I was doing at the foot of the bed. Then I was traveling. I was at the entrance of a tunnel. There was a light at the end of the tunnel just like sunlight. I had a feeling of comfort and all the pain was gone, and I had a desire to go toward the light. I seemed to float along in a [horizontal] position. When I reached the other end I was in a strange place. Everything was beautiful, yet it was more of a feeling rather than seeing. I could see other people. They ignored me completely and the next thing I heard a voice saying, "You must go back . . . it is not your time." Afterwards I seemed to think it was my father [speaking] but this may have been imagination. Then I was in my bed. There was no sensation of moving back. It was just as though I woke up and all the pain was back and [hospital staff] were working on me.[6]

There are obvious similarities between this report and the earlier one. At present, an enormous number of NDEs are on record, and although no two are exactly the same, there are several common features. A clear pattern has emerged, and several researchers have constructed a composite NDE. Here is the composite NDE constructed by Moody, the man largely responsible for the revival of interest in these reports.

A man is dying and, as he reaches the point of greatest physical distress, he hears himself pronounced dead by his doctor. He begins to hear an uncomfortable noise, a loud ringing or buzzing, and at the same time feels himself moving very rapidly through a long dark tunnel. After this, he suddenly finds himself outside of his own physical body, but still in the immediate physical environment, and he sees his own body from a distance, as though he is a spectator. He watches the resuscitation attempt from this unusual vantage point and is in a state of emotional upheaval.

After a while, he collects himself and becomes more accustomed to his odd condition. He notices that he still has a "body," but one of a very different nature and with very different powers from the physical body he has left behind. Soon other things begin to happen. Others come to meet and help him. He glimpses the spirits of relatives and friends who have already died, and a loving, warm spirit of a kind he never encountered before—a being of light—appears before him. This being asks him a question, nonverbally, to make him evaluate his life and helps him by showing him a panoramic, instantaneous playback of the major events of his life. At some point he finds himself approaching some sort of barrier or border, apparently representing the limit between earthly life and the next life. Yet, he finds that he must go back to Earth, that the time for his death has not yet come. At this point, he resists, for by now he is taken up with his experiences in the afterlife and does not want to return. He is overwhelmed by intense feelings of joy, love, and peace. Despite his attitude, though, he somehow reunites with his physical body and lives.

Later he tries to tell others, but he has trouble doing so. In the first place, he can find no human words adequate to describe these unearthly episodes. He also finds that others scoff, so he stops telling other people. Still, the experience affects his life profoundly, especially his views about death and its relationship to life.[7]

STAGES OF THE NEAR-DEATH EXPERIENCE

Other researchers have identified the common elements of the NDE, and most of them are found in Moody's composite account: the separation from the body, passage through a tunnel, feelings of peace and joy, encountering a presence, a life review, entering another realm, and meeting with deceased relatives. However, most NDEs do not include all of these features, and they do not always occur in a fixed order. Nevertheless, they have been described by Ring as "stages," and Ring has remarked in an interview, "In general, people who seem to be clinically dead longer have deeper experiences, but there are many exceptions to this generalization."[8]

The table on page 110 shows the frequency with which the various stages were reported in five independent studies of roughly the same size. The studies are not perfectly comparable, as they differ somewhat in the sampling method used. Nevertheless, the table and the chart below provide an indication of how often each stage is reported.

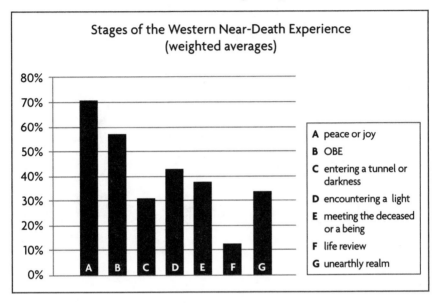

FEELINGS OF PEACE

The first stage of the NDE is usually a feeling of deep peace and well-being, including freedom from pain. This state is sometimes depicted as one of happiness and joy. Although there may be moments of sadness or anxiety, these tend to be transient, and the overall experience is almost always described as very enjoyable. Almost all studies report this as the most commonly found feature of the NDE, with estimates of the frequency ranging from about 56 to 100 percent of those reporting experiences while near death.

SEPARATION FROM THE BODY

The second stage of the NDE is the impression of having left one's body. This is usually the second most commonly reported experience, with a

NEAR-DEATH STAGES IN FIVE INDEPENDENT STUDIES

	Ring[a]	Evergreen Study[b]	Southern California Study[c]	Sabom[d]	Dutch Study[e]	Weighted Averages
Peace or joy	60%	75%	70%	100%	56%	71%
Out-of-body experience	37%	71%	66%	99%	24%	57%
Entering a tunnel/dark void	25%	38%	32%	23%	31%	30%
Encountering a light	33%	56%	56%	28%	N/A	44%
Meeting others or a being	25%	N/A	48%	48%	32%	38%
Life review	25%	9%	12%	3%	13%	13%
Entering the light	20%	34%	34%	54%	29%	33%
Sample size*	49	55	50	42	62	258

[a] Ring, *Life at Death*.

[b] Lindley, Bryan, and Conley, "Near-Death Experiences in a Pacific Northwest American Population: The Evergreen Study."

[c] Green, "Near-Death Experiences in a Southern California Population."

[d] Sabom, *Recollections of Death*.

[e] van Lommel et al., "Near-Death Experience in Survivors of Cardiac Arrest: A Prospective Study in the Netherlands."

* Where the information is provided, sample size refers to the number of NDEs, not the number of participants. Note that most participants reported a single NDE.

frequency ranging from about 24 to almost 100 percent of those who have reported NDEs.

The majority of those reporting an out-of-body experience (OBE) do not recall any sensation of leaving the physical body, only realizing their new state when they seem to see their own physical body from the outside. However, a substantial minority reports noises or other sensations during the separation. Afterward, some perceive themselves to exist as completely disembodied consciousness; others believe that while they were "outside" they had a new body-like form.

The unusual properties of this body are illustrated in the following account:

> People were walking up from all directions to get to the wreck. I could see them, and I was in the middle of a very narrow walkway. Anyway, as they came by they wouldn't seem to notice me. They would just keep walking with their eyes straight ahead. As they came real close, I would try to turn around, to get out of their way, but they would just walk *through* me.[9]

Those who experience the separation report that their mental processes are clear, sharp, and rational; if anything, they report being able to think faster and more clearly than ever. Vision and hearing are usually the only two senses reported, and these are often described as enhanced to an incredible degree. Panoramic, 360° vision is sometimes reported, and some individuals claim they could see through walls and other objects. The ability to read people's thoughts telepathically is sometimes mentioned. In movement, there seems to be weightlessness and an ability to project themselves wherever they want.

The following is an example of an OBE reported by a man who was pinned underneath a waterfall as a result of a rafting accident.

> All of a sudden, I noticed a floating sensation, as if I were rising. I was shocked to find that I was floating upwards into the open air above the river. I remember vividly the scene of the water level passing

before my eyes. Suddenly I could see and hear as never before. The sound of the waterfall was so crisp and clear that it just cannot be explained by words. Earlier that year, my right ear had been injured when somebody threw an M-80 into a bar where I was listening to a band, and it exploded right next to my head. But now I could hear perfectly clearly, better than I ever had before. My sight was even more beautiful. Sights that were close in distance were as clear as those far away, and this was at the same moment, which astounded me. There was no blurriness in my vision whatsoever. I felt as if I had been limited by my physical senses all these years, and that I had been looking at a distorted picture of reality.

As I floated there about six feet above the water, I gazed downward toward the falls. I knew that my physical body was eight feet below the surface of the water, but it did not seem to bother me. . . . Now, separated from my physical body, I found that I could survive without all the pain and suffering of physical existence. I had never thought of it as pain and suffering when I was in my physical body, but now, after experiencing such total bliss and harmony, it seemed like everything prior to this was like being in some sort of cage.[10]

Occasionally, a report of an NDE will include the claim that the experiencer observed something that she should not have been able to perceive in any normal fashion, either because she was unconscious or, more rarely, because her body was in a position that did not allow for the necessary sight lines. Here is an example of such a case. It is the report of a woman who described an OBE following postsurgical complications in 1974. In an interview with Ring, she described how she had gone into shock and heard her physician say, "This woman's dying." Suddenly,

Bang, I left! The next thing I was aware of was floating on the ceiling. . . . I'm very nearsighted, too, by the way, which was another of the startling things that happened when I left my body. I see at fifteen feet what most people see at four hundred. . . . They were hooking me up to a machine that was behind my head. And my very first thought was, "Jesus, I can see! I can't believe it, I can see!" I could read the numbers on the machine behind my head and I was just so thrilled. And I thought, "They gave me back my glasses."[11]

The woman later told Ring that after she recovered she asked permission to return to the operating room to determine whether the numbers she had seen on the machine were correct. Ring writes, "She claims that this was indeed so and that she told her anesthesiologist at the time, but since he is no longer practicing in Connecticut and she has lost track of him, it was not possible for me independently to corroborate her testimony."[12]

Unfortunately, this has almost always been the case concerning reports such as the one above. Many of these reports are gathered years after the experience, and by this time potential witnesses have moved away, changed their names, or are simply unavailable. Although many similar reports can be found in the literature, it is rare for investigators to provide corroborating evidence to support the claims of unusual perception.

From the perspective of a philosopher or scientist interested in the relationship between mind and body, the OBE is by far the most important aspect of the NDE. It is the only aspect of the NDE that is both frequently reported and capable of being independently corroborated. By contrast, the other stages of the NDE—a feeling of peace and joy, traveling through a tunnel, encountering a barrier over which another realm is glimpsed—are based only on first-person reports. These take the form of traveler's tales, told by those who claim to have traveled to the very edge of another world and to have there caught a brief glimpse of what lies beyond. The skeptic may concede that there is a great deal of similarity in these reports, but in the end dismiss them all as purely subjective experiences, corresponding to no objective reality.

But the OBE is different. Not only does it seem to provide evidence that the mind can function apart from and independent of the brain but it also is one of the few aspects of the NDE that is readily testable, at least in principle. As mentioned earlier, it has been rare for investigators to provide corroborating evidence to support claims that events or objects were seen in a way that defies normal explanation. However, as we shall see later, there are several notable exceptions to this rule.

PASSAGE THROUGH DARKNESS

The NDE is not always confined to the earthly environment. It may progress to or consist entirely of an experience in what seems to be an otherworldly realm. The transition to this realm is often experienced as a passage through darkness or through a tunnel. In studies involving Western subjects, the passage through darkness or a tunnel is reported about 30 percent of the time.

Moody's original work implied that this stage is usually experienced as traveling through a long dark tunnel, but some researchers have found that only a minority of those who entered a dark space described it as a tunnel. A few brief examples will suggest the nature of this passage.

The following is an interview with a woman who suffered a cerebral hemorrhage.

> I remember going through a tunnel, a very, very dark tunnel. . . . (*Did you feel the tunnel was vast?*) Yes, *very,* very. It started at a narrow point and became wider and wider. But I remember it being very, very black. But even though it was black, I wasn't afraid because I knew that there was something at the other end waiting for me that was good. . . . I found it very pleasant. I wasn't afraid or anything. There was no fear attached to it. I felt very light. I felt like I was floating.[13]

A victim of a cardiac arrest described something similar: "Well, it seemed at that particular time, when my heart died, I seemed to go up into a spiral in a deep black, pitch black tunnel. . . . I saw nothing. It was just *pitch* black. I mean, you never saw anything so dark in your life."[14]

Another man was resuscitated from three separate cardiac arrests within an hour of admission to a Florida hospital. He later described floating motionless, suspended in a dark void during the first two arrests.

The third cardiac arrest was more prolonged and was associated with a sense of movement through the void:

> [Arrest 1] Everything was black. Then a floating sensation, like spacelessness like they have in a space program. I wasn't floating in any direction, but it was like I was hanging there.
>
> [Arrest 2] Then I had the same feeling of floating, not upward or any direction, but just floating.
>
> [Arrest 3] I remember the black enfolding me again. . . . This time, instead of having the sensation of just hanging in space, I had the sensation of going up. Like I was lifting up. I had the sensation of going up.[15]

In some cases, people describe watching their resuscitation from within this region of darkness, as in the following two cases of cardiac arrest. The first case involves a sixty-year-old woman who described watching her resuscitation while surrounded by a region of darkness. She said that during the arrest, "I had left my body and was to the side in sort of like a tube. It was real dark in there, but I could see what they were doing. I could hear them. I saw them doing all this stuff to me. . . . Just like you would put a big tube off to the side of the bed, and I just slid from the bed right into that tube, just drifted in there. . . . Whatever I was in was black, but I could see out and watch everything."[16]

In the second case, a man described moving through a dark passage while observing the resuscitation attempts being performed on his unconscious body. He said, "I could see my body lying there. . . . I saw the whole show. . . . I was going up slowly, like floating in a dark or semidark corridor like. They were working the hell out of me. . . . And I kept thinking: What is this? What's happening? And I kept going up and up and up."[17]

As in some of the cases above, the darkness is sometimes described as a dark tunnel, a black tube, or a dark corridor. However, sometimes it is simply described as a black spaceless void. This description was made by a woman who reported recurrent near-death episodes, occurring as a child between the ages of nine and sixteen as a result of cardiac arrests during attacks of rheumatic fever. She described how during these attacks she would reach a point where she would seem to "descend into this feeling of soft velvet blackness. It wasn't like going into a tunnel [she had recently read Moody's first book]; I had no feeling of going into a tunnel. I just seemed to be surrounded by a velvet blackness and a softness and I would have absolutely no fear and the pain would disappear when I entered into this other state."[18]

An Englishwoman described a very similar experience, occurring to her while she was apparently unconscious during an operation. She said, "I realized I was looking at an immense space, black, velvety. . . . I looked at this blackness with some interest and noticed there were no stars. I didn't feel suffocated, as if this velvet was close to me or claustrophobic. Behind my right shoulder came a very gentle golden light (like old-fashioned oil lamplight) . . . I 'knew' I had to go through this blackness and I would know such joy unimaginable."[19]

There seem to be two major descriptions of this stage: a black, featureless void, or a dark tunnel, often with a light at the end. Could it be that some people interpret an image of traveling through darkness as a tunnel, especially if they see a distant light? There seems to be some support for this idea, coming from accounts such as the following. It was reported by a twenty-three-year-old woman after an episode of postoperative shock. She said, "There was total blackness around me. I want to say that it felt like I was moving very, very fast in time and space. I was traveling through a tunnel. It didn't look like a tunnel, but when you're in a tunnel, all you see is blackness around you. If you move very fast you can feel the sides moving in on you whether there are sides there or not because of the darkness."[20]

Sometimes, however, it is unmistakably a tunnel that is reported. The following case is unusual in that so many definite tunnel-like features are mentioned. It involves an Englishwoman, twelve weeks pregnant, in the hospital because of a threatened miscarriage. Shortly after being put on a saline drip, she lost all signs of blood pressure and pulse.

After that I faded out and found myself up at the top left-hand corner of the room against the ceiling, looking down in quite a detached way at all the people fussing around my body. I realized I must be dying and the odd thing was that I didn't mind in the least. . . .

Geographically, as I have said, I was up at the top corner of the room. There was a big sash window below me which was open at the top and through which the blazing light of the hot summer was coming in and I was vaguely surprised to discover that that was not the way out. Against the ceiling beside me was a wide-bore pipe or narrow tunnel through which I was obviously meant to make my exit and in the distance at the end of that it seemed to be even brighter. Bright light was nothing exceptional that summer, but this did seem to be actually like the sun itself up there. The pipe itself was corrugated or ridged in some way, rather like the sort of tube that you can attach to a tumble-drier to let the damp air out of a window.

I never actually went past the entrance to the pipe. I seemed to hover quite comfortably near the entrance for what seemed like a few minutes. . . . I was only a few feet away from the people round my body whom I could see were very busy. . . . The next thing I was aware of was that I was very much back in my body and being rushed along the covered ways that joined the building of the old hospital on my way to the theatre.[21]

SEEING A LIGHT

The transition to another realm is sometimes signaled by the appearance of a brilliant light, sometimes described as being seen at the end of the tunnel; however, it may often be experienced without passage through any sort of darkness. Although brilliant, the light is not blinding, and it seems to have an attractive, reassuring quality. Some experiencers report having felt a sense of homecoming as they approached the light. Roughly one-third to one-half of experiencers report seeing a light.

ENCOUNTERING THE DECEASED OR A PRESENCE

After entering the light, although sometimes before, the experiencer may encounter deceased friends or relatives, or a mysterious presence. The deceased are often described as looking younger and healthier than remembered, and the presence is sometimes described as a being of light. Communication with the deceased or the presence is usually described as telepathic, and it usually concerns the question of whether the individual is to return to the body. Sometimes the choice seems to be up to the individual; other times, the presence or a deceased relative orders the person to return.

Most studies have found no relationship between encountering the deceased or a presence and the individual's prior religious beliefs, although sometimes the presence may be identified as someone from the person's religion. These encounters are reported about 40 percent of the time.

Here is a woman's account of her experience, which included several of the features mentioned above: a tunnel, a light, an encounter with deceased relatives, and a command to return.

Fifteen years ago when I was fifty-nine I had a heart attack. An iron band around my chest was getting tighter and tighter. The doctor came, and when he left to ring for an ambulance he warned me not to move on any account. Then everything became warm and bright and light and beautiful. The iron band was gone and I was traveling along a tunnel. . . . Gradually there was a brilliant light at the end—really brilliant—and I knew I was going right into the glowing heart of that light, but then I saw a group of people between me and the light. I knew them; my brother, who had died a few years before, was gesticulating delightedly as I approached. Their faces were so happy and welcoming. Then somehow my mother became detached from the group. She shook her head and waved her hand (rather like a windscreen wiper) and I stopped, and I heard the doctor say, "She's coming round," and I was in my bed and the doctor and my husband were there. My first words to the doctor were, "Why did you bring me back?"[22]

Occasionally, encounters with unknown individuals are reported, individuals who are later identified. The following account concerns a man who passed out after recovering from an operation.

> I could see a wall and a gate, like an entrance. Behind the wall I could see my late grandparents on my father's side and an uncle who died before I was born, but the person with whom I seemed to be able to communicate I did not recognize. He was tall with fair hair, and his features were very clear. I felt I should know him, but did not. He asked if I really wanted to be there. It felt so good, no more pain, and so relaxed as I had never felt before. My grandmother held out her hand to draw me in, but the man told me that I had so much to give and live for. At this point I re-entered my body and sprang back up to a seated position . . . again I was sick, bringing up more clots of blood.
>
> I was afraid at that time to tell anyone. A while later I told my mother and father. My mother identified the man as her father, who had died when she was young, and can verify that I had at no time seen a picture of my grandfather.[23]

There are also cases in which experiencers report an encounter with a person whose death they are unaware of, such as the following case.

> I began bleeding badly after the birth of my daughter and I was instantly surrounded by medical staff who started working on me. I was in great pain. Then suddenly the pain was gone and I was looking down on them working on me. I heard one doctor say he couldn't find a pulse. Next I was traveling down a tunnel toward a bright light. But I never reached the end of the tunnel. A gentle voice told me I had to go back. Then I met a dear friend, a neighbor from a town that we had left. He also told me to go back. I hit the hospital bed with an electrifying jerk and the pain was back. I was being rushed into an operating theater for surgery to stop the bleeding. It was three weeks later that my husband decided I was well

enough to be told that my dear friend in that other town had died in an accident on the day my daughter was born.[24]

Reports such as these are rare, but they are of great importance to those who are interested in establishing whether the NDE is in any sense an objective phenomenon. Along with the OBE, claims of encountering the unknown dead provide the only components of the NDE that are capable of being independently corroborated. Unfortunately, the authors of the account given above do not mention if they made any effort to substantiate this woman's story.

LIFE REVIEW

At some stage of the NDE, often after encountering the being of light, the individual may experience a life review. This review is in the form of unusually vivid, almost instantaneous images of either the person's whole life or a few selected highlights. In many cases, the images may appear in an orderly, chronological sequence; in others, they seem to appear all at once. Sometimes individuals report re-experiencing a past event while feeling great empathy with others who were involved, sometimes even experiencing the event from the perspective of those they have hurt.

The life review, when it occurs, may be the only distressing part of the experience, depending on the memories evoked. More commonly, it is said to be experienced with a mixture of emotions, as in the following account from an English gentleman: "My life passed before me in a momentary flash but it was entire, even my thoughts were included. Some of the contents caused me to be ashamed but there were one or two I had forgotten about of which I felt quite pleased. All in all, I knew that I could have lived a much better life, but it could have been a lot worse. Be that as it may, I knew that it was all over now and there was no going back."[25]

The frequency of the life review varies between studies: Ring reported a life review in 25 percent of NDEs, yet Sabom found a life review reported in only 3 percent of his cases. Overall, in studies involving Western subjects, the life review seems to be reported about 13 percent of the time.

ENTERING THE LIGHT

In the deepest stage of the NDE, the experiencer *enters* the light. Many say it is like encountering a world of preternatural beauty, describing meadows or gardens with astounding colors; magnificent cities may be seen in the distance; wonderful, ethereal music may be heard. The overwhelming loveliness, color, and soft, diffuse lighting clearly set this world apart from any earthly scene.

The nature of this otherworld often does not correspond at all with the biblical stereotype of heaven. Reported contact with this environment also does not seem to be correlated with prior religious beliefs. About a third of NDEs include this final stage.

If the experience proceeds this far, then it is here that the person may encounter deceased relatives and friends, be forced to make a decision, or simply be ordered to return. The subject then usually finds himself back in the body instantaneously, sometimes experiencing the pain of drastic resuscitative measures. Occasionally individuals will experience a jolting sensation upon return, but the end of most NDEs is both abrupt and a blank.

AFTER EFFECTS:
THE IMPACT OF THE EXPERIENCE

Most of the individuals who have had an NDE feel that it has been the single most significant event of their lives. The nature of the NDE may be controversial, but there is little disagreement that the experience usually has profound, life-changing aftereffects. These typically include: a thirst for knowledge; increased compassion and tolerance for others; reduced competitiveness; reduced interest in material possessions; an increased interest in spirituality, coupled with a decreased interest in sectarian religion; a greater appreciation for life, coupled with a greatly reduced fear of death; and most strikingly, a greatly increased belief in an afterlife.

Are these changes due to the NDE or to simply coming close to death? An early study by Ring found that even people who recalled nothing from when they were close to death reported that their lives were altered in significant and drastic ways by the sheer fact of nearly dying. A statistical analysis showed that many personality and value changes were similar for both experiencers and nonexperiencers. There were more parallels than contrasts, but where there were differences, they tended to favor the experiencers. The main differences were that a higher percentage of experiencers tended to report an increased appreciation of life, a renewed sense of purpose, being a stronger person, being more patient and understanding, and an increased empathy for others. On ten other measures of change, the two groups were about the same.[26]

Sabom reported similar aftereffects in his study of mostly people who had cardiac arrest, but he performed statistical analysis comparing experiencers and nonexperiencers on only two measures: fear of death and belief in an afterlife. Here, however, his findings were completely in agreement with Ring's. Both studies found that experiencers had a significantly greater decrease in fear of death and a significantly greater increase in belief in an afterlife. Sabom's study found that these changes were by no means transitory, but persisted across time.

A more recent study of people who had cardiac arrest in the Netherlands came to very similar conclusions. Once again, those who had experienced an NDE reported an increase in appreciation of life, understanding, and empathy for others, all to a greater degree than those who had cardiac arrest who did not report an NDE. An eight-year follow-up showed that not only did these changes persist across time but they also were more apparent at eight years than at two.[27]

One of the most rigorous studies examining the impact of the NDE on the lives of experiencers was completed in 1998 by two clinical psychologists, Gary Groth-Marnat and Roger Summers. This study compared changes in fifty-three subjects who reported having had an NDE with a control group composed of twenty-seven individuals who reported having similar life-threatening incidents but without a corresponding NDE. The researchers concluded, "After the life-threatening situations, the areas of change indicated that persons having undergone NDEs became more concerned with the welfare of others; felt less anxiety regarding death with a strong belief in an afterlife; had more transcendental types of experiences; became less materialistic; and felt an increased sense of self-worth, a greater appreciation for nature, and an increase in awareness of paranormal phenomenon . . . the extent of changes found among NDErs was consistently and significantly greater than persons who had merely encountered life-threatening situations (non-NDE group)."[28]

The study also found that those who reported deeper experiences tended to have gone through more extensive changes than those who reported shallower experiences. This study was unusual for its rigorous design and in-depth comparison of near-death experiencers with a control group, and the researchers were unequivocal about their major conclusion. In short, they stated that "it is the actual NDE itself, rather than some other factor such as merely being exposed to a life-threatening situation, that is crucial in facilitating change."[29]

If there is any consistent message that is brought back by those who have a classic NDE, it is this: after death there is more, and the purpose of life is to grow in love and knowledge.

Critics have sometimes warned that publicizing the beautiful nature of the typical NDE will lead to a rash of suicides, but it has been found that depressed individuals who have an NDE after a suicide attempt report both a lifting of their depression and an end to suicidal thoughts.[30]* One set of researchers wrote that "several of our respondents stated that they would now be willing to counsel others *against* suicide despite (or, perhaps one should say, because of) having had a beautiful suicide-related NDE themselves."[31]

---

*The explanation for this seems to be the transcendental nature of the experience. Stanislav Grof and Joan Halifax, in *The Human Encounter with Death* (Plume, March 29, 1978) hypothesize that suicidal individuals are really seeking transcendence, not death. The implication is that when a transcendent experience is achieved, not only are suicidal tendencies diminished but positive appreciation of life also is enhanced. As Kenneth Ring and Stephen Franklin write, "When one has a subjectively undeniable view of the beauty of the cosmos and comes to understand that one is indissolubly a part of it, the means by which that insight is achieved becomes irrelevant. It only remains to return to physical life and to try to live in accordance with the knowledge one has gleaned while on the threshold of death."

Perhaps these positive changes can be best illustrated with a quote from a woman named Elizabeth Rogers, who, after suffering a heart attack, had a full-blown NDE in which she traveled along a tunnel toward a bright light, only to be stopped by her deceased brother and mother just before reviving. She said, "I now feel that every day is a new gift to me. Material things are not nearly as important as they used to be and I now look forward with peace and joy to the day of my death."[32]

But the aftereffects of the NDE are not always entirely positive. Many experiencers have difficulty integrating their NDE into their lives, especially if their experience conflicts with previously held beliefs. Longstanding relationships may be severely disrupted, sometimes to the breaking point. Depression and divorce plague some experiencers, and counseling may be required to help these individuals come to terms with what has happened to them. Some experiencers fear that their stories will be met with dismissal or even hostility from health care professionals; unfortunately, this is all too often the case.

FAITH AND THE NEAR-DEATH EXPERIENCE

As mentioned briefly above, the NDE also has an impact on the religious convictions of experiencers. British physician Peter Fenwick analyzed over three hundred NDEs, and wrote:

> For a few people, the NDE is a confirmation of a religious faith they already have. But for many, perhaps most, it is a spiritual awakening that may have very little to do with religion in the narrowest sense, and nothing to do with dogma. It seems to broaden religious faith rather than simply confirm it, leading to a recognition that many paths lead to the same truth. It certainly tends to confirm belief in some form of afterlife. But there is very seldom any sense of exclusivity in the experiences: when the presence of some higher "being" is felt, this is only seldom defined as, for example, a Catholic or a Jewish God. And Christian icons such as Jesus and Mary are notably absent except in very rare cases.

I found it interesting that, although most people's natural tendency is to try to interpret a new experience in the light of their existing belief system, experiencers tend not to do this with the NDE. They are more likely to try to modify their belief system if the experience does not seem to fit into it.[33]

One of the people he interviewed, a woman named Joan Hensley, expressed her transformation this way:

Certainly my life changed. I am less frightened of dying personally, and I do believe there is life after death. But it hasn't made me more "religious"; what I do feel is that there are so many religions in the world, why should our God be the only one or indeed the correct one? I feel my experience proved there is a God—before that I don't think I really believed in anything, just accepted what my parents believed in.[34]

FACTORS INFLUENCING THE NEAR-DEATH EXPERIENCE

Several studies have included details about the respondent's background with the intention of determining some factors that may influence the frequency or nature of the experience.

Within Western subjects, demographic factors such as age, gender, and marital status seem unrelated to the incidence of NDEs. Accounts of NDEs have even been gathered from children. Although children seem less likely to report a panoramic life review and may be more inclined to encounter deceased pets rather than deceased relatives, it does seem that children report experiences very similar to those of adults.[35]

Religious affiliation and degree of religious involvement seem to have no effect on the likelihood of an NDE or on the frequency with which the various elements occur, including encounters with the deceased or with a being of light.[36]

The type of medical emergency after which the NDE occurs does not seem to influence the nature of the experience: similar NDEs have been reported after cardiac arrests, drownings, automobile accidents, surgeries, childbirths, and suicide attempts.[37]*

Prior knowledge of the NDE does seem to be related to the likelihood of having one. Surprisingly, both Ring and Sabom found a lower incidence of prior knowledge among experiencers than among those who came close to death but did not report an NDE.[38]

While all elements of the classic NDE have been reported by individuals who merely perceived themselves to be near death, certain features, such as positive emotions, enhanced mental ability, and an encounter with a bright light, are significantly more common among individuals whose closeness to death can be corroborated by medical records.[39]

---

*In *Heading toward Omega,* Ring writes: "We now have cases on file of almost every mode of near-death circumstance that you can imagine: combat situations, attempted rape and murder, electrocution, near-drownings, hangings, etc., as well as a great range of strictly medical conditions—and none of these seems to influence the form and content of the NDE itself. Rather it appears that whatever the condition that brings a person close to death may be, once the NDE begins to unfold it is essentially invariant.

"Subsequent research on suicide-related NDEs by Stephen Franklin and myself and by Bruce Greyson has also confirmed my earlier tentative findings that NDEs following suicide attempts, however induced, conform to the classic prototype.

"In summary, so far at least, situations covering a wide range of near-death conditions appear to have a negligible effect on the experience" (Ring 1984, 44–45).

EIGHT

INTO THE ABYSS

Horrific Near-Death Experiences

In 1978, *Beyond Death's Door* by cardiologist Maurice Rawlings was published, and what made this book so unusual were several chilling testimonies that seemed to suggest that the NDE was not always the beautiful experience previously published reports would suggest.

Rawlings believes that his data provide evidence for the literal existence of hell. His first exposure to this evidence came when he was resuscitating a mail carrier who went into full cardiac arrest during a treadmill stress test. While Rawlings was frantically trying to revive him, the mailman started screaming that he was in hell. Each time the physician paused during the resuscitation attempt, the man would complain that he found himself slipping back into hell, with a look of abject terror on his face.

These visits to hell were not the end of the mailman's experience. He later experienced a more peaceful NDE during which he left his body and visited an otherworldly paradise where he met his deceased mother and stepmother. But when the Tennessee doctor interviewed the patient several days after the recovery, he was in for a surprise. Although he completely remembered his blissful experience, the mailman had completely forgotten his several close encounters with hell.

This man's experience led Rawlings to conclude that many people may experience hell while near death, but may forget about it later because of the shocking and horrific nature of the experience. He has suggested that this accounts for the rareness of such reports in the collections of other researchers. Rawlings believes these experiences are more common than other researchers believe and has collected several terrifying NDE accounts. However, not everyone in his accounts seems to experience hell in the same way; some of the accounts resemble the traditional Christian interpretation of hell with fire and brimstone, others describe a cold and dank realm, and yet others report scenes that seem to be straight out of Dante's *Inferno*. In other words, these reports lack the consistency found in the more classic NDEs.*

Here is an example of a surrealistic hell described to Rawlings by one of his patients who had a heart attack.

> I remember getting short of breath and then I must have blacked out. Then I saw that I was getting out of my body. The next thing I remember was entering this gloomy room where I saw in one of the windows this huge giant with a grotesque face that was watching me. Running around the windowsill were little imps or elves that seemed to be with the giant. The giant beckoned me to come with him. I didn't want to go, but I had to. Outside was darkness but I could hear people moaning all around me. I could feel things moving about my feet. As we moved on through this tunnel or cave, things were getting worse. I remember I was crying. Then, for some reason, the giant turned me loose and sent me back. I felt I was being spared, I don't know why.[1]

Rawlings has reported that over a quarter of his respondents have experienced negative or hellish NDEs, a figure far higher than that reported by any other researcher. His work has been roundly criticized for its lack of rigor and for its evangelical nature (Rawlings holds fundamentalist Christian beliefs). Sabom, who is also a cardiologist, is particularly criti-

---

*At least one NDE researcher considers hellish NDEs to resemble hallucinations more than they resemble pleasurable NDEs. Peter Fenwick writes, "In light of all the research we have done, I feel that distressing experiences are quite different. They have a strong confusional component seen much less often in the positive NDE" (Fenwick 2005, 135).

cal of Rawlings' claim that hellish NDEs are rarely reported because most researchers are not involved in medical resuscitations. Although Rawlings claims that those involved in resuscitations do confront hellish NDEs, Sabom points out that Rawlings has never provided any statistics to substantiate this claim. Sabom, who has never come across a case of a frightening NDE, has described Rawlings' research as "a curious combination of medical facts, religious opinions, and poorly documented near-death experiences."[2]

However, although comparatively rare, frightening NDEs do seem to occur, and reports of them have also been gathered by more objective researchers. Reliable statistics regarding their frequency are not available, although a nationwide survey by the Gallup Organization about NDEs in 1980 and 1981 found that 1 percent of their respondents experienced negative or hellish NDEs.[3] Other researchers have reported higher and lower figures, and so the true frequency of such NDEs remains unknown.

One of the most thorough investigations of frightening NDEs was completed by psychiatrist Bruce Greyson and counselor Nancy Evans Bush. These researchers summarized the results from a collection of fifty cases of frightening NDEs and distinguished three principal varieties: inverted NDEs, experiences of a meaningless void, and hellish NDEs.

INVERTED NEAR-DEATH EXPERIENCES

These experiences have the same form as the classic NDE—an OBE, seeing a light, and so on—but are accompanied not by feelings of peace and bliss, but by feelings of fear. These seem to be experienced by individuals who strenuously resist the process of dying rather than surrendering to the experience.

Ring described one such case, concerning a woman who had been living in Central America when she became ill. She was being driven to a local first-aid station when her experience began. She said, "As all of my energy started rolling inward, I was frantic. It was living hell and I never experienced such terror in my life. It was the death of my ego. It was accompanied by an incredible and totally consuming terror. . . . Most of my memories of this juncture are taken up with my struggle and terror. The image I retain is the simile of a small child being dragged somewhere against his will and kicking and screaming the whole way."[4]

However, she also became simultaneously aware of a detached part of herself that was dispassionately watching this struggle. This part of her realized that she was crossing over into death. She said, "Concurrent with this realization, I surrendered to the force and powers that be, I gave up and 'said' in effect, 'OK, I give up, I'll go quietly and peacefully . . .' I felt a loving presence surrounding me and in me. The space was composed of that presence of love and peace. . . . It was a lovely place to be; very peaceful, total harmony, everything was there."[5]

As soon as she let go, her NDE reverted to the classic form and went on to include a powerful life review. Ring concludes from this and other similar examples that "experiences of this type can be expected to convert themselves into the familiar classic form of the NDE if they persist long enough to allow the process of surrender to begin, or if the individual is simply overwhelmed by the intrinsic power of the NDE itself."[6]

THE MEANINGLESS VOID

In the second type of experience described by Greyson and Bush, the individual is drawn into a meaningless void, which sometimes includes a sense of despair that life as we know it not only no longer exists but in fact never did and was only a cruel joke, an illusion. The individual feels condemned to spend eternity in a meaningless void.

An example of this type of experience involved a woman giving birth to her second child. She described her state of mind after several hours of labor as "fearful, depressed, and panicky," and finally she was given nitrous oxide. She struggled against the mask but was restrained and eventually went under. She recalled traveling rapidly upward into darkness and then seeing a small group of black and white circles, clicking and alternating in color. In a mocking and mechanistic fashion, they jeered at her, "Your life never existed. Your family never existed. You were allowed to imagine it. . . . It was never there. . . . That's the joke—it was all a joke."[7]

A similar case involving a drug-addicted young man who suffered a seizure after an overdose was reported by physician Pamela Kircher.

> He found himself in an environment that he described as a "Void." As far as he could see, the atmosphere was entirely a dingy gray with no relief to its monotony. Nothing was visible at all except for a disc that was nearby. That disc was black on one side and white on the other. It turned back and forth very slowly. With each reversal, there was a clicking sound. That sound was the only sound, and the turning of the disc was the only movement in the environment. He felt totally isolated, totally alone in that heavy gray void. He felt that the same scene would go on for a very long time, perhaps even eternity.[8]

Greyson and Bush noted that "the majority of our cases . . . occurred during childbirth under anesthesia."[9] Ring has reviewed a collection of similar cases and concluded that the experience "is fairly typical of those reported by women in childbirth who have also been given nitrous oxide for anesthetic purposes."[10]* These existential nightmares resemble the "bad trips" sometimes experienced under hallucinogenic drugs such as LSD and mescaline, and so there seems to be little reason to regard them as anything but the unpleasant side effects of anesthetic or recreational drugs.

HELLISH NEAR-DEATH EXPERIENCES

Greyson and Bush reported that cases of this type formed the smallest of any of their three categories, although they do not specify exactly how many they found. Peter and Elizabeth Fenwick solicited over three hundred reports of NDEs in England, yet found, "Only two or three of the

---

*Ring further writes: "All in all, I believe the findings surveyed here bolster the argument that these frightening experiences are best understood as emergence reactions triggered by drugs, and not as true NDEs. This is not, however, to discount their capacity to instill the most soul-wrenching and long-lasting feelings of horror, or even necessarily to question their possible ontological significance. Instead, I merely want to make the claim that these experiences should not be indiscriminately lumped with NDEs, even those of a frightening cast" (Ring 1996, 19).

people who wrote to us described their experiences as 'hellish.'"[11] The drawback of their sample is that it was self-selected, so perhaps people who had a hellish experience were simply reluctant to write.

The idiosyncratic nature of the experiences is striking. One was reported by a man who suffered two cardiac arrests and had several experiences, most of which were positive, but he also had an experience of hell. He said:

> It was really like all the images I had ever had of Hell. I was being barbecued. I was wrapped in tinfoil, basted and roasted. Occasionally I was basted by people (devils) sticking their basting syringe with great needles into my flesh and injecting my flesh with the red-hot fat. I was also rolled from side to side with the long forks that the "devils" used to make sure that I was being well and truly roasted. I wanted to call out but no sound would come, it felt as if my brain or consciousness was buried deep within me and was too deeply embedded for either them to hear or for me even to make it work. I was overcome with the feeling of utter doom and helplessness.[12]

However, the man also wrote that "Hell has an easy explanation—I was wrapped in a tinfoil blanket, an electric heat cage was put over me and during that time I was turned several times and innumerable injections were given."[13] His hellish NDE does not include any of the familiar features found in the classic NDE; neither does the following case reported by Margot Grey.

> I was working in the nursing home where I have a part-time job. I am a partially trained nurse. I had spent the day on the beach. It was a glorious hot day, but I am used to the heat having lived in Khartoum for about sixteen years. I was in the kitchen supervising the evening suppers, when I was overcome by the heat from the aga cookers. I rushed outside the back door feeling faint and sick. I remember going down three or four steps. I don't remember falling, but the next thing that happened was that I had this experience. I found myself in a place surrounded by mist. I felt I was in hell.

There was a big pit with vapour coming out and there were arms and hands coming out trying to grab mine . . . I was terrified that these hands were going to claw hold of me and pull me into the pit with them. As I lay there worrying what would happen next, an enormous lion bounded toward me from the other side and I let out a scream. I was not afraid of the lion, but I felt somehow he would unsettle me and push me into that dreadful pit. I remained in a state of semi-consciousness for about three days.[14]

This case might be dismissed on the grounds that the heat from the pit could have been a vague awareness of the heatstroke the woman was suffering from. But it bears an eerie similarity to the following report, also gathered by Grey, which does include some of the elements found in the typical NDE.

I went into St Giles Hospital in London, to have an operation. Sometime while I was under the anesthetic I became aware that I was hovering above my body looking down at myself on the operating table. I felt very frightened and began to panic. I wondered why I was no longer in my body and thought I must be dead. I next found myself in a very frightening place, which I am sure, was hell. I was looking down into a large pit, which was full of swirling grey mist and there were all these hands and arms reaching up and trying to grab hold of me and drag me in there. There was a terrible wailing noise, full of desperation. Then suddenly I found myself rushing back through this dark tunnel and I found myself back in my body in the hospital bed. As I went back into my body it felt like an elastic cord, which had been stretched to its limit and then is let go. I sort of snapped back again and everything seemed to vibrate with the impact.[15]

Hellish experiences that appear to share parallels with the classic NDE seem to be the rarest of all, although again, reliable statistics on their frequency do not exist. Here is another case gathered by Grey, which occurred after a suicide attempt. The experiencer said:

I felt an inner struggle going on between myself and some evil force. At the last moment I suddenly felt an inner explosion and seemed to be enveloped in a blue flame which felt cold. At this point I found myself floating about six inches above my body. The next thing I remember is being sucked down a vast black vortex like a whirlpool and I found myself in a place that I can only describe like Dante's *Inferno*. I saw a lot of other people who seemed grey and dreary and there was a musty smell of decay. There was an overwhelming feeling of loneliness about the place.[16]

As in the case of positive experiences, a number of similar components can be found. There is the awareness of being out of the body, of traveling through a black space, and of finding oneself in another world. Grey sums up these parallels with positive NDEs.

1. Fear and a feeling of panic
2. Out-of-the body experience
3. Entering a black void
4. Sensing an evil force
5. Entering a hell-like environment[17]

Grey notes that people in this category also returned from their encounter with an increased belief that life continues after the death of the body and that they felt a strong urge to radically modify their former way of life.

Bush, who is a counselor, writes that on the basis of "many years" of personal observation, "It is my impression that among the people whose NDE was terrifying, those who heal most quickly and satisfactorily (in their terms) are likely to fit this model: people who interpret their NDE as a warning, who are able to connect it with previous behaviors they identify as unwise or downright wrong, and who then find avenues by which to modify their lives in satisfying ways."[18]

She also notes, "Not all such accounts are from people with a religious background. Some readily admit to earlier antisocial behaviors:

heavy drinking, drug use, violence, or trouble with the law; while others describe a more internalized history of quick temper, selfishness, or problems forming relationships."[19]

According to Bush, who herself had a frightening experience of the meaningless void variety while giving birth under the effects of nitrous oxide in her late twenties, those who have had the most difficulties with these experiences are those who "identified no comprehensible or acceptable meaning in the encounter. Especially following experiences of the Void but cutting across other types also, these are people who, years later, may still struggle with the existential implications of a frightening NDE."[20]

So what are we to think of frightening NDEs? If at least some NDEs are in fact what they appear to be, then perhaps the philosopher and mystic Emanuel Swedenborg was right when he argued in the eighteenth century that there is no single plane in the afterlife, but that the otherworld is composed of multiple levels, each different from the others. If this is the case, then different witnesses may simply be contacting different realms.

At present, there are no hard data indicating that only unethical or abusive individuals have had these unpleasant experiences. Some writers have even noted that frightening NDEs resemble the classic form of the hero's journey in which a descent is made into the underworld, where terrifying trials must be encountered and overcome before the hero can emerge, transformed, into the world of ordinary experience. Bush has noted that "holy figures in all traditions have endured similar experiences; not only Saint Teresa and other saints, but shamans, Krishna, and perhaps Jesus. The experience certainly did not keep them from being holy, so something must be going on other than damnation or being lost."[21]

She concludes her extensive article on the frightening NDEs by asking readers to reflect on some of the assumptions they may hold regarding the disturbing nature of these reports. She writes, "If there is a single conclusion to be drawn here, it may be that we are called to a higher level of understanding: to recast our assumption that pain is equivalent to punishment, that suffering is in itself malevolent, that there is no gift in the dark."[22]

NINE

NEAR-DEATH EXPERIENCES ACROSS CULTURES

The findings discussed up to this point have been gathered from Western accounts. If the NDE is a truly universal human experience, it should occur in all cultures. What about NDEs in non-Western cultures?

Most studies of the NDE have involved Western subjects, so perhaps the remarkable similarities found in the accounts are not surprising. Although comparatively few studies have involved non-Western subjects, enough data have been gathered to make some comparisons and to find out to what extent these experiences are culture bound.

CHINA

In 1976, an earthquake struck Tangshan, China. Eleven years later, two physicians, Feng Zhi-ying and Liu Jian-xun, interviewed eighty-one survivors and found that 40 percent reported NDEs.[1] Compared with Western accounts, this is an unusually large percentage, but we must remember that this sample was not randomly chosen and that all the subjects experienced a single disaster.

Similar to Western studies, the researchers found that age, gender, marital status, educational and occupational level, personality, brain trauma, and prior knowledge of NDEs and belief in spirits, ghosts, God, and destiny did not affect the contents of the NDE.

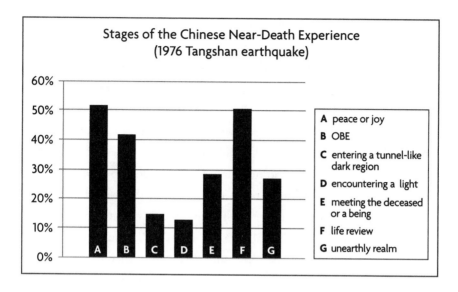

The main difference between the Chinese sample and Western reports seemed to be the frequency with which the various stages were reported. Fewer Chinese subjects reported feelings of peace or joy, an OBE, entering a tunnel-like dark region, and encountering a light. Many more Chinese subjects reported a life review. The percentage of experiencers who reported meeting deceased or religious figures or seeing an unearthly realm of existence was comparable with most Western studies.* The chart above summarizes the findings from this single Chinese sample.

INDIA

The first major report of NDEs from India was presented in 1977 by Osis and Haraldsson, who traveled to India to interview 704 Indian medical personnel about their experiences with the dying.[2] In this sample, they

---

*A major limitation of the Chinese study is that it used a questionnaire that simply asked subjects whether they experienced any of a list of 40 NDE phenomena "that we derived from previous reports in the literature." For instance, subjects were asked whether they experienced "an unearthly realm of existence" or "a tunnel-like dark region." The subjects were not free to describe the experience using their own terms and expressions, so it is not clear how their descriptions of these features may have differed from those of Western subjects.

found sixty-four reports of NDEs, which they were able to compare with reports of fifty-six American NDEs they had gathered earlier.

The experiences of the Indian patients were similar to those of the American patients. About 80 percent saw otherworldly apparitions, and about one-third of the Indians who reported apparitions also reported being explicitly sent back by the otherworldly figures. However, whereas the American patients were usually told something to the effect that it was not their time or that they had unfinished work to do, the manners of the Indian apparitions seemed more bureaucratic. Messengers would sometimes escort the dying patient to a clerk, who would then consult some records and announce that a mistake had been made! The bureaucratic bungling would be corrected, and the person would then be returned to his body.

A more recent systematic survey of sixteen NDEs in northern India was reported in 1986 by Satwant Pasricha and Ian Stevenson. In the majority of cases (ten), the experiencers were personally interviewed by the researchers, whereas for most of the other cases a "firsthand informant" was interviewed. Seven years later, Pasricha followed up this study with a survey of twelve NDEs in southern India, and in all twelve cases she was able to interview the subjects personally. Additional interviews with friends and relatives of the twelve subjects were conducted in five of these cases.

The findings of Pasricha and Stevenson were generally in agreement with the earlier findings of Osis and Haraldsson. Here is a sample report concerning a woman suffering from an abdominal ailment. After she fell unconscious, she said, "I saw three persons with curly hair coming. Then I found myself outside (on the threshold) of a door. Inside, a fat man was sitting on a bench and looking through some papers. He told those three persons: 'Why have you brought her? She still has [not completed her allotted] time' and he threw away my papers. After that I do not know how I came back."[3]

In several respects, it is apparent the Indian cases differ from the Western and Chinese ones. In all three studies, Indian accounts seem strongly influenced by Hindu religious beliefs. Yamaraj, the Hindu god of death, is a well-known figure in Indian mythology, as are his messengers, the yamadoots. So too is Chitragupta, the man with the book, who upon a person's death is said to consult the fabled Akashic Records, in which are inscribed all the deeds, good and bad, of a person's lifetime. The balance of positive and negative karma is said to determine to which heaven or hell the deceased is to be sent until her next incarnation on earth, as well as the nature of her next incarnation.

Several features typical of the Indian accounts can be seen in the following, given by a woman suffering from a fever for which she received no medical treatment. She recounted, "I was dragged 'up' by four yamadoots. I saw one door, and went inside. I saw my mother and father there. I also saw the Yama who was fat and had books in front of him. The Yama started beating the yamadoots for having taken me there instead of another person. . . . I was asked by my parents and the Yama to be sent back . . . and I was happy to be back so I could see my children."[4]

As in the account given above, the Indian subjects frequently report being taken to the "other realms" by some messengers, where a man with a book consults some records, decides a mistake has been made—that the subject's time has not yet come—and orders the subject's return. This contrasts especially with Western cases, in which the subjects are usually not escorted by messengers and no mistake accounts for their return. None of the Indian subjects reported a panoramic life review. Although Osis and Haraldsson found several OBEs in their reports, Pasricha and Stevenson found only one case out of twenty-eight that contained this feature. Also, descriptions of tunnels are conspicuous by their absence from the reports of Indian subjects; not a single informant in these studies reported the experience of a tunnel.

Nevertheless, we can also see that there are some striking similarities between Indian and Western accounts. In both cultures, experiencers frequently report meeting deceased acquaintances and otherworldly beings, usually in an unearthly realm. In both sets of reports, a decision is frequently made that it is not one's "time to go." Although the Indian reports lack a panoramic life review, the reading of Chitragupta's book can be considered a form of life review, although one that is thought to be postponed until the actual day of reckoning.

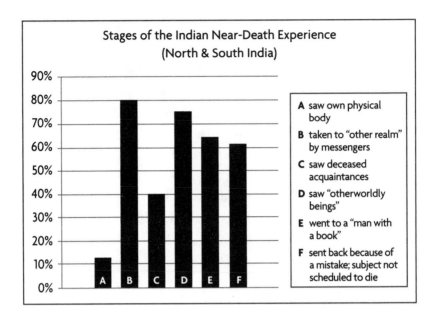

The chart above summarizes the main features of the Indian NDEs, taken from the two studies mentioned above by Pasricha and Stevenson, and Pasricha.

The most prominent features shared by the Indian and Western cases seem to be the perception of traveling to an unearthly realm and there meeting deceased acquaintances and otherworldly beings. Yet we also have seen that the otherworldly beings reported in the Indian experiences are those suggested by Indian mythology. However, as Pasricha and Stevenson point out, social variations in another realm, if another exists, should be expected, just as there are variations in features of our own world. The fact that different "inhabitants" are perceived by experiencers from different cultures could indicate the influence of culture on hallucination, but the same fact could just as easily be taken to indicate travels to different parts of the same world.

NATIVE AMERICA

There have been several stories of NDEs gathered from Native American accounts. H. R. Schoolcraft's 1825 work *Travels in the Central Portion of the Mississippi Valley* contains two such accounts. The first tale, "The Funeral Fire," tells of a Chippewa leader who was shot in battle. He saw his warriors mourn him, and as they left he leaped out of his body to follow his friends, trying without success to get their attention. Upon return to the camp, he also tried to get his wife's attention, but it was no use. Schoolcraft writes, "Foiled thus in every attempt to make himself known, the warrior-chief began to reflect upon what he had heard in his youth, that the spirit was sometimes permitted to leave the body and wander about. He reflected that possibly his body may have remained upon the field of battle, while his spirit only accompanied his returning friends."[5]

He then decided to return to his body and after a four-day journey came to the outskirts of the battlefield, where a moving fire continually blocked his path. After leaping through the fire he woke up alive. He told his story to his people upon his return to camp.

The second tale tells of a village chief who died and traveled through paradise, which had beautiful groves and numerous animals, to "the village of the dead." He returned to his grave to get his gun, and on his way met a large number of people carrying funeral paraphernalia—a procession of the recently deceased on their way to the land of the dead. When he reached his grave, he jumped through a line of fire blocking his way and in the effort came alive, and was thus able to relate his story.

In the 1930s, Black Elk, a shaman of the Sioux nation, related his life story to Nebraska poet John Neidhardt, who published it in his book *Black Elk Speaks*. In one chapter, Black Elk describes what appears to be an NDE that occurred to him in 1890 after he collapsed during a dance, although it is unclear if those around him thought that he was dead or dying.

> After awhile I began to feel very queer. First, my legs seemed to be full of ants. I was dancing with my eyes closed, as the others did. Suddenly it seemed that I was swinging off the ground and not touching it any longer. . . . There was no fear with this, just a growing happiness.
>
> I must have fallen down, but I felt as though I had fallen off

a swing when it was going forward, and I was floating head first through the air.

There was a ridge right in front of me, and I thought I was going to run into it, but I went right over it. On the other side of the ridge I could see a beautiful land where many, many people were camping in a great circle. I could see that they were happy and had plenty. The air was clear and beautiful with a living light that was everywhere.

I floated over the tepees and began to come down feet first at the center of the hoop where I could see a beautiful tree all green and full of flowers. When I touched the ground, two men were coming toward me, and they wore holy shirts made and painted in a certain way. They came to me and said: "It is not yet time to see your father, who is happy. You have work to do."

They told me to return at once, and then I was out in the air again, floating fast as before. When I came right over the dancing place, the people were still dancing, but it seemed they were not making any sound.

Then I fell back into my body, and as I did this I heard voices all around and above me, and I was sitting on the ground. Many were crowding around, asking me what vision I had seen.[6]

Shortly before he died in 1909, Apache war chief Geronimo dictated his memoirs through an interpreter to S. M. Barrett. In chapter 20, Geronimo relates this story:

Once when living in San Carlos Reservation an Indian told me that while lying unconscious on the battlefield he had actually been dead, and had passed into the spirit land.

First he came to a mulberry tree growing out from a cave in the ground. Before this cave a guard was stationed, but when he approached without fear the guard let him pass. He descended into the cave . . . sliding rapidly down its steep side into the darkness. He landed in a narrow passage running due westward through a canon [canyon] which gradually grew lighter and lighter until he could see as well as if it had been daylight; but there was no sun. Finally he came to a section of this passage that was wider for a short distance, and then closing abruptly continued in a narrow path. . . . He continued to follow the narrow passage . . . emerging into a section beyond which he could see nothing: the further walls of this section were clashing together at regular intervals with tremendous sounds, but when he approached they stood apart until he had passed. After this he seemed to be in a forest, and following the natural draws, which led westward, soon came into a green valley where there were many Indians camped and plenty of game. He said that he saw and recognized many whom he had known in this life, and that he was sorry when he was brought back to consciousness.[7]

In these Native American accounts, we find several of the components of the Western NDE, including OBEs, encountering a barrier, traveling to another world, and contact with the deceased, but no life review is mentioned in any of these accounts. With the possible exception of the story told by Geronimo, there is also no mention of a tunnel. In that case, descriptions of a tunnel are ambiguous, as a "narrow passage" is mentioned. Whether or not the narrow passage is interpreted as a tunnel of sorts, there does seem to be a passage through darkness and an emergence into light.

GUAM

Timothy Green reported learning of four NDEs among the native Chammorro people while working in Guam as a school psychologist. Two were told to him directly, and two were recorded by a local man interested in the subject.

In the first, a Chammorra woman "who had been pronounced dead four days after being hospitalized" reported traveling through the clouds and visiting relatives in America, where she claimed her granddaughter saw her. After leaving the scene, she reported meeting a man standing beside a road, who said to her in Chammorro, "You are not the one being called."[8]

The second concerns a Chammorra woman who had become ill and apparently had an allergic reaction to medication given to her by a physician. She also reported visiting relatives in America and provided a detailed description of what she believed she saw. She also reported visiting "the garden of paradise," which was surrounded by a fence. She said she longed to enter, but was told by a woman near the entrance, "You are not ready to enter that field."

The woman also said, "When I was in coma I saw my late husband, my father. When I saw my father he said, 'Don't touch me because we are not the same.' I saw my father and my grandfather and every time I want to go over and hug them and because you know I saw them and I know that I'm alive and I know that they're dead. . . . The only thing I saw when I saw my dead relatives was smoke, like they were walking in smoke."[9]

The third account came from a Chammorra woman who suffered a heart attack while being admitted to a hospital. She mentioned rising higher and higher, seeing children and adults, and hearing laughter and song. She said:

Such a nice song. I never heard those songs and then keep on going up and there's a trumpet there. And I look and there are people holding books, they are standing holding books and they were blowing the trumpet and it was very nice and I never heard that type of song here. . . . Then I am going up again and like there were steps but I'm not walking. . . . There was a door behind a man and it was open, but I didn't go in. It looked like a very nice place. The trumpet was long and skinny and beautiful music. I never hear music like that before.[10]

The last account was from a ninety-two-year-old man who reported that he had his experience at the age of ten, after falling out of a coconut tree. He reported walking down a road into a forest, where he met a Jesus-like figure surrounded by other children. He wanted to go further, to a hill that lay in the distance, but the figure ordered him back in the direction from which he came.

In these accounts, we find out-of-body travels, glimpses of an otherworldly realm, barriers such as fences and doors, ethereal music, meetings with deceased relatives and otherworldly beings, and orders to return. Absent from these accounts are life reviews and tunnels.

MAORI NEW ZEALAND

Historian Michael King has recounted the following story as told by Nga, a Maori woman thought to be over one hundred years old, who was a girl "just over school age" when she saw her first white men. She insisted to King that she had experienced little contact with Europeans until her recording sessions with him, as she had always lived in remote areas of New Zealand. As she spoke no English, she told her story through an interpreter.

> I became seriously ill for the only time in my life. I became so ill that my spirit actually passed out of my body. My family believed I was dead because my breathing stopped. They took me to the marae, laid out my body and began to call people for the tangi [funeral]. Meanwhile, in my spirit, I had hovered over my head then left the room and traveled northwards, toward the Tail of the Fish. I passed over the Waikato River, across the Manukau, over Ngati Whatua, Ngapuhi, Te Rarawa and Te Aupouri, until at last I came to Te Rerenga Wairua, the Leaping-Off Place of Spirits.
>
> I cleansed myself in the weeping spring and then ascended to a ledge from which hung Te Aka, the pohutukawa root. Here I crouched. Below me was Maurianuku, the entrance to the Underworld, covered by a curtain of seaweed. I began to karanga to let my tupuna know I had come. [She began to call to let her ancestors know she was ready to enter the land of the dead.] Then I prepared to grasp the root and slide down to the entrance. But a voice stopped me. It was Mahuta [Maori god of the forests]. "Who is it?" he asked. "Ko au," I said. "It is I, Ngakahikatea." "Whom do you seek?" he questioned me further. "My parents. My old people. I have come to be with my tupuna." "They are not here," said Mahuta. "They do not want you yet. Eat nothing and go back where you came from until they are ready. Then I shall send for you." So I did not

leap off. I rose and returned to my body and my people in Waikato. I passed over all the places and things I had seen on the way. My family and those who had assembled from Waahi for the tangi were most surprised when I breathed again and sat up. So it is that I live on. Because the spirits of my dead will not claim me. I shall not die until they do.[11]*

In this account, there is no mention of a tunnel; instead Nga flies to the land of the dead after leaving her body. However, she does encounter the entrance to a subterranean underworld, so passage through a tunnel of sorts may have been reported if her NDE had lasted longer. There are other features typical of Western accounts: a barrier is encountered, here in the form of "a curtain of seaweed"; there is an encounter with an otherworldly being—Mahuta—although dead acquaintances are only discussed, not seen. And of course, there is the order to return, on the grounds that it is not her time. However, as with the other reports from traditional societies, the life review is unequivocally missing in this account.

Although the accounts from Native Americans, the Chammorro in Guam, and the Maori in New Zealand are small in number, they may nevertheless represent important empirical evidence regarding the cross-cultural features of the NDE. Because of global Westernization, new accounts such as these from traditional hunter-gatherer and herding societies will become more and more difficult to find.

DISCUSSION

From the cases described above, the major cross-cultural features of the NDE appear to be OBEs and encounters with otherworldly realms and their inhabitants. The life review and the tunnel appear to be culture-specific features. Life reviews are found in Western, Chinese, and East Indian experiences; they are not reported in accounts from societies of hunter-gatherers

---

*King added in a footnote, "Nga eventually died on 1 June 1975. That same day a thick fog rolled off the Waikato River and covered the district for four days until she was buried on Taupiri Mountain" (King 1985, 87–88).

or herdsmen. With the possible exception of Chinese NDEs (which on the surface appear very similar to Western NDEs), travels through tunnels are either rare or nonexistent in non-Western accounts, although a period of darkness or a journey through a cave may be experienced.

Sociologist Allan Kellehear has carefully considered the cross-cultural accounts of the NDE and argues that certain cultural factors will strongly influence how the experience is described and what features of the experience are likely to be considered important (and therefore worth mentioning). He argues that in settled and developed societies a passage through darkness with a growing light in the distance is likely to be described in architectural terms as a tunnel, although we have seen that even in many Western accounts the transitional period is simply described as a passage through darkness. The manner in which we describe an unusual experience is obviously determined in large part by the experiences typical of our culture. If descriptions of the NDE are in largely metaphorical terms, we should not be surprised, especially given the fact that the NDE is often described as ineffable, that is, beyond words.

Kellehear also argues that there are cultural reasons for the absence of the life review in accounts from societies of hunter-gatherers and herdsmen. Historic religions, such as Christianity, Hinduism, and Buddhism, emphasize the development of the moral self. These religions actively appeal to notions of conscience, and conscience places great importance on past thought and action in the process of self-evaluation. But in the shamanistic religions of North America, Australia, and many Pacific islands, there is not such a sharp moral distinction between the self and the world. Kellehear points out that the psychology of the Australian aborigines, for example, is based on much less internalizing of social sanctions. They have very good opinions of themselves, are easygoing, and fear the social consequences of transgressions much more than private guilt or remorse. They obey their laws because they fear being caught.

In the following passage, Kellehear describes some of the early encounters between Westerners and aborigines. "When Christian missionaries began their proselytizing practices among the Arunda aborigines, these missionaries told the Arunda that they were all basically sinful and wicked and needed forgiveness before God. In response to this view, the Arunda retorted with great indignation "Arunda inkaraka mara"— the Arunda are all good. These were hardly a people who would seek a life review in evaluative terms, or indeed a cultural group that would be impressed by a moral review of their deeds."[12]

The fact that life reviews may be found in reports of Western, Chinese, and Hindu NDEs may be explained in terms of the broadly similar religious development of people in those cultures. Although a "tunnel-like dark region" was reported by 16 percent of the Chinese sample in response to a questionnaire, it is difficult to draw firm conclusions from this. This was only one sample from one area of China, and the respondents merely answered yes or no to questions that were derived from previous reports in the Western literature. So it is difficult to tell what percentage of respondents would have reported a "tunnel" and what percentage would have reported only a "dark region." Also, although both India and China obviously vary greatly in the development of their various regions, the people in the Chinese sample appear to have been much more urban and educated.* We may therefore reasonably expect them to have been much more familiar with architectural concepts like tunnels.

Journeys to other worlds, OBEs, and encounters with the deceased and otherworldly figures seem to be the most universal features of the NDE. Borders of some sort—doors, ridges, curtains, and so forth—are also found in accounts from different cultures. But, as Kellehear argues:

---

*Demographic details for the first Indian survey by Pasricha and Stevenson are sketchy. They only write, "All the subjects were Hindi-speaking persons of northern India from Uttar Pradesh and Rajasthan" (Pasricha and Stevenson 1986, 165). They also report that they learned of many of their cases "from a member of a crowd watching us. (Strangers coming into an Indian village, especially Westerners, nearly always attract a crowd of bystanders who observe the interviews)" (Pasricha and Stevenson, 169).

In the second Indian survey, Pasricha provides more detail of the respondents. She writes, "Four hundred and sixty (71%) were illiterate or functionally illiterate . . . and 47 (7%) had had education up to high-school or beyond" (Pasricha 1993, 163).

In contrast, in the Chinese sample, "Six subjects (7 percent) had no formal education . . . 18 (22 percent) had attended senior middle school or obtained secondary technical education; and 5 (6 percent) had higher education" (Ibid., 41).

Tunnel and life review experiences may be features of a certain type of human development and psyche. In Western reports of a tunnel experience when near death, this development materializes in the common shapes and symbols mentally associated with modernity and technology. In the case of life review, religions such as Hinduism, Buddhism, and Christianity have cultivated an ethic of personal responsibility and conscience. This may be the chief influence behind the evaluative style of mental process near death. Life review in people of this cultural orientation is part of the general social and psychological process of identity formation, a task of ongoing personal importance in cultures with little or no regard for tribe or totem.[13]

NEAR-DEATH RESEARCH TODAY

Today, most work on the NDE is not done by parapsychologists, but by medical personnel and psychologists in hospitals where data are easily gathered. Cardiologists in several countries seem to have taken a special interest in the phenomenon, and reports on NDE research have been published in prestigious medical journals such as *The Lancet* and *Resuscitation* as well as in the International Association of Near-Death Studies' *Journal of Near-Death Studies*.

The widespread interest in the NDE does not mean that a unanimous opinion exists among scientists and philosophers about what these experiences truly imply. Is the NDE actually what it at first appears to be, a literal separation of mind from body during the first stages of bodily death? Several researchers and philosophers think so, but this interpretation has met with stiff resistance. The NDE represents a challenge to the conventional idea that the mind is produced by the brain. In response to this challenge, several materialistic explanations for the NDE have been constructed and vigorously defended. According to the hypothesis of materialism, these experiences cannot be what they superficially appear to be. Several alternative explanations have been proposed, and it is to a consideration of these that we now turn. These alternative explanations fall into two main groups: the psychological and the physiological.

TEN

PROPOSED PSYCHOLOGICAL EXPLANATIONS

FANTASY AND WISHFUL THINKING

The simplest explanation proposed for the NDE is simply that it is fantasy, derived from wishful thinking. It is argued that the motivation is a dread or denial of death and that the content is derived from the person's belief system. In other words, NDEs are products of the imagination, constructed from our personal and cultural expectations to protect us from facing the threat of death.

However, this hypothesis is simply not supported by the empirical data. While we have seen that there are some cross-cultural variations in the content of NDEs, individuals sometimes report experiences that conflict with their religious and personal expectations of death.[1]*

---

*Henry Abramovitch describes the case of an Israeli man who had a remarkably rich NDE, including feelings of peace and joy, an OBE, passage through darkness, and travel to another world were he met with his deceased father and brother, who instructed him to return. Abramovitch writes, "Unknown to Ralbag, he had a fairly typical near-death experience, as described in the scientific literature. It is conceivable that the torment he described subsequent to his experience derived from his inability to integrate and/or relate this strange encounter with some pre-existing cultural form. Rather, I am suggesting his confusion was in part due to the lack of overall congruence between these near-death traditions of his native culture and what he actually experienced" (Abramovitch 1988, 183).

This theory should predict a strong correlation between the occurrence of NDEs and the strength of religious belief, yet as noted above, there is no such correlation. Furthermore, if NDEs are fantasies, then why are Western descriptions of "paradise" in NDEs so similar, yet so unlike the biblical stereotype?

Other consistencies in NDEs tend to refute this theory. People who have never heard or read of NDEs describe the same kinds of experiences as do people who are quite familiar with the reports. Similar NDEs are also reported by people who did not expect to die, either because the traumatic event happened too quickly for the person to be aware of what was happening or because it occurred during a medical procedure the person fully expected to survive. Finally, children too young to have received substantial cultural and religious training about death report NDEs similar to those of adults.

Tests have shown that there is a mild association between reporting an NDE and being fantasy prone. However, being fantasy prone is also associated with more intense sensory experiences, and individuals with a fantasy-prone personality do *not* commonly mistake fantasy for reality—a point specifically made by the psychologists who developed this concept. Psychologists Sheryl Wilson and Theodore Barber stated unequivocally that fantasy-prone people are as good at reality testing as anyone else.[2] Bruce Greyson, who is a clinical psychiatrist, writes, "There is absolutely no evidence that NDErs are fantasy-prone individuals. Although NDErs do score higher than nonNDErs on standard measures of fantasy-proneness, which may suggest nothing more than that their sensory perceptions of the outside world are much more vivid than those of nonNDErs, NDErs' scores do not come anywhere near the cut-off point on those measures for designation as a 'fantasy-prone personality.'"[3]

DISSOCIATED STATES

Dissociated states are defense mechanisms thought to be employed in times of great psychological stress. Three of the most common types of dissociated states are dissociation, derealization, and depersonalization.

Dissociation is a state in which emotions are separated and detached from distressing events to postpone having to emotionally deal with the trauma. Derealization refers to a state in which the environment feels unreal, as if the person were in a dreamworld. This state of mind could obviously be very comforting if the person were facing a threat she felt unable to deal with. Depersonalization involves a state of confusion over the reality of oneself. An individual who is depersonalized feels that he is not a real person.

The theory that dissociated states may explain the NDE is a somewhat more refined version of the motivated fantasy theory and has been popularized in the work of psychiatrist Russell Noyes. He has conducted extensive research into the subjective experiences reported by individuals who have suddenly faced the threat of imminent death, yet somehow survived. Many of these individuals reported strange experiences as they became aware that death was imminent and unavoidable.

One such experience was related to Noyes by a racecar driver who had been thrown thirty feet in the air after colliding with another car. At no time during the accident was the driver unconscious or physically near death.

> As soon as I saw him I knew I was going to hit him. I remember thinking that death or injury was coming but after that I didn't feel much at all. It seemed like the whole thing took forever. Everything was in slow motion and it seemed to me like I was a player on a stage and could see myself tumbling over and over in the car. It was as though I sat in the stands and saw it all happening . . . but I was not frightened. . . . Everything was so strange. . . . The whole experience was like a dream but at no time did I lose my sense of where I was. . . . I was like floating on air. . . . Finally, the car pancaked itself on the track and I was jolted back to reality.[4]

From experiences such as this, Noyes identified several characteristics of what he called "depersonalization in the face of life-threatening danger." These include an altered sense of time, increased speed of thought, a sense of detachment, a feeling of unreality, a lack of emotion, sharper vision or hearing, flashbacks of memories, and a sense of harmony or unity with the universe.

What is required for depersonalization to occur is the perception of imminent death. In other words, the person must clearly perceive the imminence of his own death before the syndrome can develop. As Noyes writes, "Subjective reports suggest that the chief prerequisite to their [NDEs] full development is the perception of imminent death. . . . [Otherwise] victims of cardiac arrest may not have such experiences unless convinced of their closeness to death."[5]

However, several researchers have found cases that involved a loss of consciousness so sudden the individuals simply had no time to perceive the threat to their lives. Cardiologist Michael Sabom, for instance, has encountered several such cases, one of which involved a middle-aged farmer who suffered from transient episodes of complete heart blockage, with total stopping of the heart. During some of these episodes, he would suddenly pass out in the middle of a sentence. Sabom interviewed the man after he had been fitted with a pacemaker and recorded the following account, which occurred before he was brought to the hospital.

> I was walking across the parking lot to get into my car. . . . I passed out. I don't recall hitting the ground. The next thing I do recall was that I was above the cars, floating. I had a real funny sensation, a floating sensation. I was actually looking down on my own body, with four or five men running toward me. I could hear and understand what these men were saying. To me, it was a real funny feeling. I had no pain whatsoever. I didn't feel any pain. Then the next thing, when I came back to my senses, I was in my body, and I had pain on the back of my head where I had hit the concrete.[6]

Although this man's experience clearly resembles the early stages on an NDE, according to this report he almost certainly had no time to appreciate the threat to his life.

A major difference between Noyes' study and most research studies of the NDE is that his study focused primarily on people who were not actually physically near death. However, he did interview a small number of individuals who both apprehended their own death and were in fact in serious danger. He found that the experiences of this group were clearly different from those who were never in any real danger, and so excluded them from his analysis. Emphasizing the differences between the two groups, Noyes writes, "It seems important to note that there are a great variety of near-death experiences. Those studies by the author [Noyes] were reported by persons who were psychologically—but not necessarily physically—close to death. A different kind of experience has been described by persons who narrowly escaped death from physical illness, cardiac arrest, and so forth."[7]

More recently, psychiatrists Glen Gabbard and Stuart Twemlow have noted that NDEs differ from depersonalization on a number of grounds.[8] They extracted several cases of depersonalization from the literature and broke down their characteristics, finding few similarities with the NDE. They point out that depersonalization usually does not include a sense of being outside of the body; is experienced as dreamlike; is usually unpleasant; and is often accompanied by feelings of anxiety, panic, or emptiness.

Psychologist Harvey Irwin conducted an empirical assessment of the tendency to dissociate and found no difference between those who have had an NDE and a control group. He concluded that those who have had an NDE are not habitually inclined to use dissociation to cope with trauma.[9]

Finally, we have some direct testimony that casts doubt on the theory that dissociated states may play a role in the classic NDE. Sabom gathered the following two accounts. In the first, the experiencer said, "I've had a lot of dreams and it wasn't like any dream that I had had. It was real. It was so real. And that peace, the peace made the difference from a dream, and I dream a lot."[10] The second experiencer noted, "That was real. . . . I've lived with this thing for three years now and I haven't told anyone because I don't want them putting the straitjacket on me. . . . It's real as hell."[11]

In their investigation of over three hundred English NDEs, Peter and Elizabeth Fenwick write:

This feeling that the "me" up there and out of the body is the real me, infinitely more real than the body it leaves behind, is described over and over again. Avon Pailthorpe . . . was surprised "how clearly I felt myself to *be* myself without my body."

Mrs Frances Barnshey: "I couldn't see any kind of body belonging to me. I seemed to be mind and emotions only, but I felt more vital, more myself than I've felt in my life at any time before or since."[12]

The accounts above illustrate why derealization and depersonalization as explanations will not work: experiencers almost unanimously report that the experience was real and that it happened to *them,* with their sense of self fully intact.

IMAGINATIVE RECONSTRUCTIONS

Some have raised the possibility that the accurate accounts given by cardiac arrest survivors of their resuscitations are really nothing more than imaginative reconstructions based on previous hospital experience and on documentaries and medical dramas. Many of us have seen resuscitations enacted on television, and it is argued that a patient with a history of heart disease may reasonably be expected to know even more about such procedures than someone with no such medical history. In other words, it is argued that the reports are in truth merely fantasies based on educated guesses about what goes on during resuscitations in an emergency room.

Cardiologist Michael Sabom set out to test this hypothesis. He interviewed thirty-two survivors of a nonsurgical crisis—mostly cardiac arrest—who claimed to have seen portions of their own resuscitation from a position outside of their bodies. He also interviewed twenty-five patients with a similar background—patients with heart disease—who had been admitted to a coronary care unit and had thus received considerable exposure to hospital routine. Four of these patients had experienced cardiac arrest without an NDE.

These twenty-five patients served as a control group. Sabom asked them to imagine standing in a corner of a hospital room watching a medical team revive a person whose heart had stopped beating. The patients were then asked to describe in visual detail what they would expect to see.

Eighty percent of these control patients made at least one major error in describing standard hospital resuscitation technique, despite being "reasonably confident" they were correct.

In contrast, not one of the thirty-two survivors who claimed to have witnessed their own resuscitations committed such an error when describing what happened to them. Twenty-six of the thirty-two could recall only general visual impressions, not specific verifiable details. This the patients attributed to being far more interested in an experience they found amazing than in what was being done to their bodies. However, six of the thirty-two survivors provided specific details of their own resuscitation, including details of their own resuscitation that did not occur in the other resuscitations.[13]

SEMICONSCIOUS PERCEPTION

While Sabom was conducting a medical grand rounds presentation on NDEs at the University of Florida in 1978, another professor of medicine raised the following point: "We have all resuscitated patients who have appeared dead at the time but who later could tell us of our conversation during the period of resuscitation. How do you know that these people who are describing an 'accurate' near-death experience are not just hearing the conversation while *semiconscious* at the time and later conjuring up a visual image in their mind of what went on?"[14]

Sabom has dealt extensively with this possibility. He has provided four reasons why it is highly unlikely that semiconscious aural perception can explain the visual descriptions of resuscitations and other details of the environment so often found in NDE accounts.

First, when patients who had been under general anesthesia during a major operation are later hypnotized and regressed back to the time of the operation, they can sometimes recall conversations among the physicians and nurses, but not visual impressions. Such recall, even when frightening, has been reported by these patients to be of an auditory nature, quite unlike the detailed visual impressions of an NDE.

Second, the experience of a semiconscious patient undergoing resuscitation can be compared with that of a semiconscious patient undergoing elective cardioversion. To correct abnormal heart rhythm, patients sometimes elect to undergo cardioversion, a procedure in which electric shocks are applied to the chest. This technique is also commonly used during cardiac resuscitations to correct life-threatening rhythmic disturbances of the heart. In the elective situation, the patient is commonly given a sedative to render him semiconscious and to minimize the pain of the shock. However, patients in this semiconscious state can sometimes hear nearby conversations and recall the sensations associated with the shock; for example, they have said it's like having everything torn out of your insides. If NDEs occur when individuals are merely semiconscious, then we should expect similar sensations to be remembered by those who report watching emergency cardioversion being performed on their bodies during an NDE. But the accounts are very different following an NDE, as excerpts from these three reports illustrate:

> I could see myself jolt, but again it didn't hurt like an electric shock should hurt. . . . I wasn't hurting, I wasn't anxious. . . . I had no pain.
>
> They were rubbing those things together and then I bounced off the table. . . . I came off the table about nine to ten inches, I seemed to arch. . . . [While watching] I seemed to be in a very peaceful state.
>
> I thought they had given my body too much voltage because my body jumped about two feet off the table. . . . [While watching, I felt] floating, soft, easy, comfortable, nothing wrong.[15]

Third, several people who had described an NDE to Sabom could distinguish between semiconscious auditory perception of nearby conversation and the subsequent occurrence of an NDE complete with visual perception. One man found his vision fading as he suffered a heart attack. He described what he experienced as medical assistance was rushed to his aid: "I was in total blackness and I didn't have any ability to move but I could hear well and understand. I heard them talk and I heard the guy say my pressure was zero and who it was and I heard Dr. J say, 'Shall we try to get a pulse?' And I wanted to answer and tried to answer but couldn't. . . . That's when I had the experience [NDE]—*After* sound and all had gone and I couldn't hear anymore."[16]

Another man who had experienced both the semiconscious state with auditory perception and unconsciousness associated with an NDE compared the two situations. He said, "I didn't see nothing. I just heard. This other time with the cardiac arrest [and NDE], I was looking down from the ceiling and there were no ifs, ands or buts about it."[17]

These reports show that individuals who have experienced both semiconscious hearing and visual perception during an NDE could clearly distinguish between the two.

Finally, Sabom points out that NDEs including visual perception of the environment have been reported by individuals who were unconscious and near death while no one else was present. Obviously, in these cases, semiconscious perception of verbal information would have been impossible, since no one was around to supply it.

MEMORIES OF BIRTH

Astronomer Carl Sagan, speculating on a field somewhat removed from his area of expertise, offers a novel explanation for the consistency and universality of the NDE.

> The only alternative, so far as I can see, is that every human being, without exception, has already shared an experience like that of those travelers who return from the land of death: the sensation of flight; the emergence from darkness into light; an experience, in which, at least sometimes, a heroic figure can be dimly perceived, bathed in radiance and glory. There is only one common experience that matches this description. It is called birth.[18]

Sagan's theory has been roundly criticized, as it can easily be shown to run into trouble on several grounds.

First of all, it is, at most, only an attempt to account for the tunnel, the light, the OBE, and the being of light. It does not account for other important aspects of the experience, such as visions of deceased friends and relatives or of glorious fields and gardens. Second, a study by psychologist Susan Blackmore comparing tunnel and OBE experiences of those born normally with those born via cesarean section found no significant difference in experiences between the two groups.[19]

Sagan suggests that the birth canal would look like a long dark tunnel with a light at the end, but philosopher Carl Becker has shown that "birth is more analogous to breaking through a membrane from a dark room into a lighter room or to surfacing from a muddy swimming hole."[20] The baby's head presses tightly against the lips of the uterus, and even if the opening did let light in, the baby would be unable to tilt his head upward to see it. For all these reasons, travel down the birth canal would not look anything like traveling forward, looking down a long tunnel with light at the end.

Also, the circumstances of birth show great variety, not great consistency: some babies are born in almost complete darkness, others under bright lights, some with eyes closed, others with eyes open. If birth experiences are played back near the moment of death, we should hardly expect the memories to resemble each other, except by coincidence.

And at any rate, studies have shown infant perception to be far too limited, blurry, and fragmentary to be able to account for the detailed perception found in most adult NDEs.[21] Finally, even if infants could remember details of their own births, the prevailing opinion is that the memories would be of traumatic expulsion from a place of peace and serenity and into a hellish world of pain, quite the opposite of the classical NDE. In this regard, is it is realistic to suppose that the delivering doctor or midwife would be perceived as a heroic figure? As Becker writes, "The figure would more likely seem like a clinical torturer, holding him upside down by the feet, spanking him, cutting his connection with his womb and food supply, putting silver nitrate in his eyes and strapping bands around his ankles."[22]

ELEVEN

PROPOSED PHYSIOLOGICAL EXPLANATIONS

ENDORPHINS

Morphine was first synthesized from opium in 1806 and was well received in medical circles as a great advance in pain relief. Lacking the unwanted side effects of opium, it could be injected into patients in controlled amounts. In the 1970s, it was discovered that the body produces its own natural painkillers, the endorphins—short for "endogenous morphine." They are similar to morphine, but produced by the body. The so-called runner's high experienced after vigorous exercise has been attributed to the production of endorphins, and it has been speculated that the pain or stress of dying may be expected to trigger the massive release of endorphins and other related painkilling neurotransmitters.

Since opiates—those derived from the poppy as well as those produced by the body—are not potent hallucinogens, the role of endorphins is usually limited to accounting for the first stage of the NDE: the feelings of peace and bliss. At first glance, this explanation seems plausible. For instance, one of the more powerful endorphins, known as beta-endorphin, has been synthesized and injected directly into the cerebrospinal fluid of volunteer patients with cancer who were suffering from intractable pain. One study of fourteen patients found that all fourteen reported complete relief from pain, with relief usually evident within one to five minutes.[1]

However, total pain relief lasted from twenty-two to seventy-three hours, a finding at variance with reports of NDEs, in which pain is only absent during the experience. When the experience ends, pain abruptly returns, as in the following account.

> I was hurting real bad. . . . But all of a sudden the pain completely stopped and I could feel my being rising out of the body. It seemed like I got up to the ceiling high and I could look back and see my body and I looked dead. I could see the attendant working on me. . . . Then I started floating back down to my body. As soon as I got down to my body, the pain came back.[2]

Endorphins have a sudden rise and a slow decay over several hours, as anyone who has experienced the feeling of well-being and euphoria induced by vigorous exercise will testify. This is the main problem with endorphins as an explanation of even the first and most common stage of the NDE, and it has led some to speculate the involvement of enkephalins, a neurotransmitter related to endorphins. These painkillers are thought to have a much more rapid offset of action, degrading within five to ten minutes.[3] However, this also seems much too slow to account for the *instantaneous* return of pain reported by many experiencers, and no reason is offered for the stress of dying triggering a massive release of enkephalins but not endorphins.

In addition to endorphins and enkephalins, there are dozens of other more mundane psychoactive neurotransmitters in the brain that could plausibly be released under stress, such as serotonin, epinephrine, dopamine, and so on. Several cases have been made for one or some combination of these being implicated in the production of various aspects of the NDE. But at this point, all theories involving neurotransmitters are little more than pure speculation, as they are all difficult to test directly. We cannot stick probes into numerous brain areas to take tissue samples from dying patients or of patients undergoing resuscitation. However, the indirect evidence that we do have would seem to rule out the morphinelike neurotransmitters as the causes of the peace and bliss so often found in the NDE.

OXYGEN STARVATION

One explanation that has frequently been proposed to account for the NDE is lack of oxygen (anoxia) in the brain. Normally, the brain receives an adequate supply of oxygen from the oxygen-rich blood delivered to it through the arteries. Total cessation of blood flow to the brain, as in cardiac arrest, causes unconsciousness in seconds. If blood flow is not restored, progressive brain damage will usually occur in three to five minutes. However, if the oxygen supply is not cut off but merely reduced (hypoxia), then prior to unconsciousness a series of subjective phenomena will be encountered by the individual with an increasingly hypoxic brain.

The effects of hypoxia are well known. In the 1930s, a physician named R. A. McFarland studied the effects of hypoxia on members of the International High Altitude Expedition to Chile. He found that mountain climbers exposed to the thin atmosphere found at extreme elevations reported mental laziness, heightened irritability, difficulty in concentrating, slowness in reasoning, and difficulty in remembering.[4]

Hypoxia has also been induced in laboratory experiments. Years ago, it was common practice for medical students to be shown the consequences of depriving their brains of oxygen. Students were told to breathe through a carbon dioxide absorber into and out of a spirometer filled with air (which is mostly nitrogen and oxygen). While doing this, they were given some simple task to perform. Since the carbon dioxide was not allowed to build up in the spirometer but was instead absorbed, the students would not become aware that they were slowly suffocating. They would continue to breathe normally, unaware that the air they were breathing contained less and less oxygen and more and more nitrogen. Their performance at the task would become increasingly inept, until eventually they would lose consciousness. In thousands of such experiments on thousands of people, no one ever reported an NDE.[5]

These studies show that as the brain becomes anoxic, it ceases to function. As the oxygen supply is reduced, the person becomes progressively more disoriented and confused. This is in sharp contrast to the clarity of thought and perception described over and over again in the reports of near-death experiencers.

Explanations for the NDE in terms of anoxia have also been dealt a blow by a medical study of the NDE occurring in patients whose blood gases were being monitored during the resuscitative effort. Four British physicians published their findings in a 2001 edition of *Resuscitation,* a prestigious medical journal. Over a one-year period, the authors interviewed all survivors from cardiac arrest in the medical, emergency, and coronary care units of a general hospital. Out of sixty-three patients interviewed, seven survivors (11%) reported memories and four of these patients had full-blown NDEs.* All four of these patients sensed a point of no return. Three of the four also experienced feelings of peace and joy, and of seeing a bright light. Two of the four saw deceased relatives and felt they had entered another world. None of the patients felt themselves to be out of their body yet within the hospital room,† and no tunnels or life reviews were reported. The researchers described the memories of those who recalled an NDE as "dissimilar to those of confusional hallucinations, as they were highly structured, narrative, easily recalled, and clear."[6]

The oxygen levels found in the patients' blood samples (obtained by the routine practice of drawing blood from the arteries during cardiac arrest) were obtained by the researchers from medical notes. This allowed a direct comparison of the oxygen levels found in the bloodstreams of patients who did and did not report an NDE. Although the sample of experiencers was too small to permit statistical significance testing, it is nevertheless interesting that patients in the group that reported an NDE had *higher* oxygen levels than those in the control group.[7]‡

---

*Of the three who did not have full-blown NDEs, two reported memories that had some features of an NDE (including feelings of peace or seeing deceased relatives). The third had a dreamlike experience with no NDE features ("Saw some unknown people jumping off a mountain").

†This was unfortunate, as the researchers had suspended boards from the ceiling of the wards, with various figures on the surface facing the ceiling that were not visible from the floor.

‡Carbon dioxide levels in the blood were also compared, and the authors also noted that there was "little difference between the mean CO_2 levels."

DOES ANOXIA PRODUCE THE TUNNEL?

These difficulties have led to the more modest claim that anoxia is only responsible for the tunnel and light experiences reported in some NDEs. The visual cortex of the brain is organized with many more cells devoted to the center than to the outside of the visual field (this is why whatever you are looking at directly appears much more focused and detailed than whatever is in your peripheral field of vision). Susan Blackmore and T. S. Troscianko[8] have argued that lack of oxygen will cause random activity throughout the visual system, giving the impression of bright lights flashing in the middle of the visual field, where there are lots of cells, but fading out toward the periphery, where there are fewer. This, it is argued, will give the impression of a bright light at the end of a dark tunnel. As the oxygen level continues to fall and the brain's random activity increases, the bright light in the middle will get bigger and bigger, giving the impression of rushing through a tunnel toward a light. Eventually the whole visual field will seem to be light, giving the impression of having entered the light. Although this light may seem very bright, it will not hurt your eyes, because it is not really seen with the eyes, but only that part of the brain responsible for seeing. As oxygen is restored to the brain, the random firing slows, the light dims, and the sensation is reversed so that the subject then feels that he is shooting backward down through the tunnel.

One obvious problem with this theory is that reports of a tunnel are conspicuously absent from most non-Western accounts of the NDE, as we have seen. If there is a physiological explanation for the tunnel in terms of anoxia, then reports of a tunnel should be commonly found in NDEs from across different cultures. Unless death is instantaneous—as for example, from a bullet into the base of the brain—the dying person's brain is almost always starved for oxygen as breathing and circulation are impaired. Yet we have seen that even in Western accounts a tunnel or passage through darkness is only found about 30 percent of the time and that even in many of these cases the experiencers only describe a passage through darkness.

Blackmore has challenged the view that tunnels are not universal NDE features with a study of her own. She placed an advertisement in the Indian newspaper *Times of India,* found eight near-death experiencers, and on the basis of these cases concluded that "the proportions experiencing tunnels, dark places, and lights are remarkably similar to those in previous studies."

Early in her article, Blackmore argues that random firing of cortical neurons should "produce a much brighter impression in the center of the field of view, fading out toward the periphery: in other words, a tunnel pattern."[9] What she actually found in this study was that two individuals reported passage through darkness ("I felt I was going through complete blackness" and "I seemed to be floating in a dark space") and one individual reported lights ("Below me, above me, surrounding me on all sides were lights of all colours—shining spots which were *not* moving with me"). In other words, not one individual in her sample reported a bright impression in the center of the visual field. These reports do not support Blackmore's own theory of tunnels.

This and other problems with the study led Kellehear, Stevenson, Pasrischa, and Cook to describe it as "an example of torturing data until they give you the answer you need." The authors added,

> Although Blackmore acknowledged that the readers of the *Times of India* are "not at all representative of Indians in general," she discussed her results as if they *were* representative. They most certainly are not. The *Times of India* is read only by a highly educated and English speaking readership. If Blackmore had wished to sample more widely, and more typically, she might have arranged for her notice to be published in a Hindi-medium newspaper, such as the *New Bharat.*[10]

The authors also reminded us that the cases investigated by Pasricha and Stevenson (see the "India" section of chapter 9) came from the heart of India, not from the Westernized readers of the *Times of India.*

Reports of tunnels seem to be found almost exclusively in Western accounts, but there are reasons to doubt that anoxia has anything to do with these reports. Sometimes, as in some of the accounts mentioned earlier, the inside of the tunnel is simply pitch black, with no flashing lights or even a light in the distance. Other times, the experience is simply too structured, too detailed, in other words, there is nothing random about the perception. In some of the accounts mentioned earlier, the individuals described watching their resuscitation from within this region of darkness. The Englishwoman whose report containing many tunnel-like features was quoted in the "Passage through Darkness" section of chapter 7 said, in part:

> I was up at the top corner of the room. There was a big sash window below me which was open at the top and through which the blazing light of the hot summer was coming in and I was vaguely surprised to discover that that was not the way out. Against the ceiling beside me was a wide-bore pipe or narrow tunnel through which I was obviously meant to make my exit and in the distance at the end of that it seemed to be even brighter. Bright light was nothing exceptional that summer, but this did seem to be actually like the sun itself up there. The pipe itself was corrugated or ridged in some way, rather like the sort of tube that you can attach to a tumble-drier to let the damp air out of a window.

She mentions seeing other features of the room besides the tunnel, including a window through which bright light was coming in, which she seems able to distinguish from the light seen at the end of the tunnel. She does not enter the tunnel and, like some of the others quoted above, reports watching the resuscitation attempts: "I seemed to hover quite comfortably near the entrance for what seemed like a few minutes. . . . I was only a few feet away from the people round my body whom I could see were very busy." It is difficult to see how random firing of cells in the visual cortex could account for experiences such as these.

Another difficulty with the anoxia hypothesis is that on occasion the early stages of the NDE, complete with a tunnel experience, are reported in cases in which the individual only perceives being about to die. In these cases, there is no question of anoxia being involved.

Here is such a case involving a woman who described herself to researchers as "Christian but not churchgoing." She said she finds organized religion "difficult to take" and is quite skeptical about spiritualism. In other words, she is not the sort of person one would expect to report an experience such as this:

> I was in a serious car accident in June 1986. I was driving in the central lane of a motorway, it was raining and although only just past midday, very dark. I realized a car in front of me had slowed down sharply, and I didn't want to brake for fear of skidding, so I steered right to the fast lane, and my car aquaplaned and went into a spin. I was struggling to control it, when suddenly I was not in the car any more.
>
> I was in a black tunnel, or funnel, shooting through it incredibly fast. I was spinning too, yet it was a different movement from that of the car. I felt I was shooting through this tunnel, head first, spinning round the edges—like water going down a plug, or like a coil. There was a loud roaring—it was very noisy, like the moment of birth. I had no time to feel afraid. I was very interested in what was happening, but I felt completely safe.
>
> When I was shooting through this tunnel, which was completely black to begin with but seemed to be getting less dark and less clearly defined further on, I was aware of a terrific debate. This part is very difficult to describe because all the words I can think of to use seem limited and therefore inadequate. . . .
>
> Around me, as the tunnel began to lighten, there were presences. They were not people, and I didn't see anything but I was aware of their minds. They were debating whether I should go back.[11]

Then suddenly, she found herself back in her car, about to be struck by an approaching car and knocked unconscious, only to awake later in a hospital. It is difficult to see how this tunnel-and-light experience could be explained as a result of lack of oxygen, when it reportedly occurred before the woman was actually in any medical danger.*

When the brain is starved for oxygen—as for instance, when air pressure is suddenly lost inside a flight cabin—a person has only a very short time before consciousness is lost. This is why the preflight instructions on an aircraft ask you to don your own oxygen mask before attending to the dependent child beside you. Pilots in training regularly undergo acute anoxia in flight simulators to make sure they can get their masks on in time. Those who fail do not have NDEs: they experience confusion and disorientation, sometimes trying to land their simulated planes on top of clouds before losing consciousness.

Finally, we have the report of a man who has experienced both anoxia and the tunnel while near death. While he was a British Royal Air Force pilot, Allan Pring experienced anoxia at high altitude and years later he had an NDE.

I found myself "floating" along in a dark tunnel, peacefully and calmly but wide awake and aware. I know that the tunnel experience has been attributed to the brain being deprived of oxygen, but as an ex-pilot who has experienced lack of oxygen at altitude I can state that for me there was no similarity. On the contrary, the whole [NDE] experience from beginning to end was crystal clear and it has remained so for the past fifteen years.[12]

EXCESSIVE CARBON DIOXIDE

Another explanation that has been proposed to account for the NDE is excessive carbon dioxide (hypercarbia) in the brain. Carbon dioxide is formed in the brain and other organs as an end product of cell metabo-

---

*It could be argued that her strange experience actually occurred after being struck by the car and was simply interpreted as having occurred before the accident. The problem with this is that she suffered a head injury in the crash, and it is possible to gauge the severity of a head injury by the length of time memory is a blank before the accident happened. In her case, the pretraumatic amnesia, as it is called, started as she saw another car coming toward her. She assumed this car struck her, but it actually swerved, and she was struck from behind by another car.

lism. Normally, the same blood supply that carries oxygen to the brain is also responsible for transporting the carbon dioxide waste out of the brain, through the veins, to be expelled in the lungs. Cessation of blood flow to the brain, as in cardiac arrest, results in a rapid buildup of carbon dioxide in the brain.

The effects of hypercarbia are well known. In the 1950s, psychiatrist L. J. Meduna studied the effects of varying degrees of hypercarbia in the hope that it would prove effective as a treatment for certain psychiatric disorders. He administered, to 150 patients with psychiatric conditions and fifty people without psychiatric conditions serving as controls, a variable number of inhalations of a gas mixture containing 30 percent carbon dioxide and 70 percent oxygen (normally air contains less than 1 percent carbon dioxide and 21 percent oxygen).

His subjects reported a range of subjective experiences, some of which resemble those found in NDEs. These included wonderful feelings, a sense of being outside of their bodies, revival of memories, and feelings of cosmic importance. Some examples are:

> I felt as though I was looking down on myself, as though I was way out here in space. . . . I felt sort of separated. It was a wonderful feeling. It was marvelous. I felt very light and I didn't know where I was. . . . And then I thought that something was happening to me. This wasn't right. I wasn't dreaming. . . . And then I felt a wonderful feeling as if I was out in space.
>
> I felt myself being separated; my soul drawing apart from the physical being, was drawn upward seemingly to leave the earth and to go upward where it reached a greater Spirit with Whom there was a communion, producing a remarkable, new relaxation and deep security.[13]

Another point in favor of the hypercarbia theory is the similarities of the accounts, which brings to mind the similarities of the NDE reports. Meduna described how the carbon dioxide treatment caused the brains of different people to produce similar or even identical phenomena, and he suggested that all the phenomena rested on some underlying physiological function of some brain structures that function independently from personality.

However, other elements of the hypercarbic experience are not associated with the NDE: these elements include perception of brightly colored geometric patterns, fantasized objects such as musical notes floating by, and seeing in duplicate or triplicate. Extreme hypercarbia also produces convulsive, sometimes violent, muscle movements that are not associated with the NDE.

Another difficulty of this explanation has been pointed out by Peter Fenwick, a neuropsychiatrist whose own study of the NDE involved over three hundred cases. As mentioned earlier, cessation of blood flow to the brain, as in cardiac arrest, rapidly results in a buildup of carbon dioxide in the brain. A heart attack can occur without cardiac arrest, but as Fenwick points out:

> No Intensive Care Unit worth its salt would tolerate a build-up of carbon dioxide in the blood of a patient who has suffered a heart-attack. It would be just as unacceptable for oxygen levels in the blood to be allowed to drop, unless there was an unavoidable catastrophic fall in blood pressure: if this happens levels of carbon dioxide in the brain would certainly rise. But we are still faced with the difficulty that catastrophic oxygen loss would accompany the carbon dioxide increase, and this would be sufficient to induce unconsciousness; brain function would then be so disturbed that it is unlikely that the brain would be able to build models or to remember them. A failing brain, by definition, produces experiences which are limited, confused and disorganized. The very opposite is true of the NDE.[14]

In other words, a cardiac arrest will certainly result in hypercarbia, but the hypercarbia will also be accompanied by hypoxia, with its attendant disorientation, confusion, and rapid descent into unconsciousness. Since the brain is even more sensitive to a lack of oxygen than to an excess of carbon dioxide, this explanation suffers from all the difficulties associated with the anoxia hypothesis.

Explanations for the NDE in terms of anoxia and hypercarbia have also been dealt a blow by a medical case discussed by Sabom of a patient whose blood gases were being monitored during the resuscitative effort. The man, a retired mechanic, had suffered a heart attack with cardiac arrest on an emergency room table and found himself outside of his body. The man later said,

> I was above myself looking down. They was working on me trying to bring me back. 'Cause I didn't realize at first that it was my body. I didn't think I was dead. It was an unusual feeling. I could see them working on me and then I realized it was me they were working on. I felt no pain whatsoever and it was a most peaceful feeling. Death is nothing to be afraid of. I didn't feel nothing. They gave me a shot in the groin.

The man went on to describe his resuscitation in great detail, as well as the amazement and disbelief of the physicians when he later told them of his ordeal. His medical record describes how his heart stopped and was started again, and mentions that "arterial blood gases were drawn during the procedure and sent to the laboratory." Sabom's own comments on the man's description of the procedure he seemed to have witnessed read, in part, "The man described 'a shot in the groin' during the resuscitation procedure. According to his medical records, arterial blood was drawn from his left femoral artery during CPR to measure the amount of oxygen in his blood. This procedure is accomplished by inserting a small needle and syringe into the groin area to obtain the blood. If observed from a distance, it could easily be mistaken as the administration of a 'shot.'"[15]

After retrieving the results of the blood test, Sabom wrote, "The results from the laboratory later indicated that his arterial oxygen level was well *above* normal (this is frequently the case when high concentrations of oxygen are administered to a patient during cardiopulmonary resuscitation) and his arterial carbon dioxide level was actually *lower* than normal (actual values were: $pO_2 = 138$, $pCO_2 = 28$, $pH = 7.46$). The fact that he had 'visually' observed this blood gas procedure indicates that the blood was obtained at the time his experience was occurring."[16]

Whether peripheral blood oxygen levels accurately reflect cerebral oxygen levels has been questioned, because the amount of oxygen delivered to the brain depends not only on the amount of oxygen in the blood but also on the rate at which oxygen is delivered to the tissues, which is determined largely by blood pressure.[17] The same reasoning holds for the amount of carbon dioxide being transported from the brain. But along with the rest of the evidence considered here, this medical case supports the position that both anoxia and hypercarbia are highly unlikely explanations for the NDE.

CAN RAPID ACCELERATION INDUCE THE NEAR-DEATH EXPERIENCE?

Rapid head-to-foot acceleration causes a problem unique to modern fighter aircraft engaged in aerial combat maneuvers: pilots sometimes pass out at the controls. The rapid and sustained acceleration causes the blood to be displaced downward in the body, away from the brain. Since the body is restrained in place in the ejection seat, the pilot is unable to assume a prone position, and under these conditions the ability of the heart to supply oxygen-rich blood to the brain is easily compromised at around 5 G (five times the normal force of gravity) in a relaxed, unprotected human.

Concerned about the loss of highly trained aircrews and multimillion-dollar aircraft, the U.S. Air Force has conducted extensive research on the effects of acceleration-induced loss of consciousness, using a ground-based human centrifuge. The goal of this research has been to develop equipment and techniques to reduce the effects of rapid acceleration in order to minimize the loss of life and expensive aircraft.

To date, data on over a thousand episodes of acceleration-induced loss of consciousness have been collected, and the effects are well documented. With the rapid onset of acceleration stress well above tolerance, consciousness is lost in about six seconds. The period of unconsciousness lasts an average of twelve seconds, and in about 70 percent of the episodes convulsions are observed during approximately the last four seconds of unconsciousness. After the subject awakens, there is a period of confusion and disorientation that lasts on average about another twelve seconds. All subjects who lose consciousness are interviewed in the centrifuge imme-diately following the episode, and all subjects are required afterward to complete a questionnaire concerning their experiences.

The most common symptom reported with rapid acceleration stress is alteration in vision. As pressure falls within the eyeballs, peripheral vision is lost. As the G forces increase, the visual field contracts further, producing what is known as tunnel vision. Finally, as blood pressure falls to the point where there is no blood flow to the retina, there is a complete loss of vision. These symptoms precede loss of consciousness, but if the increase in accel-eration is very rapid, the progression of symptoms may not be observed. In fact, the progression is usually so rapid that the last observation prior to loss of consciousness is simply some degree of tunnel vision.

Memory often returns prior to consciousness, in the form of short dreams reported by 35 to 40 percent of subjects. These dreams seem to occur during the period in which convulsions are seen to occur, as they frequently incorporate convulsive jerking movements. James Whinnery, a Navy physician who has conducted several studies on acceleration-induced loss of consciousness with the U.S. Naval Air Development Center, describes some of these short dreams: "Dreamlets in which individu-als stated they were riding on 'bumper cars' at an amusement park were reported when they rhythmically jerked their heads against the headrest of the seat. Rhythmic jerks of the arms were reported as one individual experienced a dream about fishing and pulling back on his fishing rod sev-eral times to set the hook. Floundering around in the water while being about to drown was reported in association with the rhythmic extremity jerking of the myoclonic convulsions."[18]

Another symptom commonly reported is a sense of floating; although frequently associated with a feeling of paralysis, it is nevertheless often experienced as pleasurable. Overall, most subjects find acceleration-induced loss of consciousness not only pleasurable but also euphoric.

Feelings of detachment and dissociation may persist for several hours following the experience, with individuals only feeling normal after a period of sleep. Whinnery mentions one particularly interesting side effect of the experience: "Although not a common occurrence, out-of-body experiences

(OBEs) are reported in association with G-LOC [G-force induced loss of consciousness] episodes. . . . One associated OBE, for example, occurred following multiple G-LOC episodes. The individual walking down a hallway immediately after a centrifuge exposure became aware not only that he was walking down the hallway, but also that he was above and behind himself, watching his own body walking. This duality persisted for approximately three minutes before the experience ended with what was described as a reintegration process with his body."[19]

So far, we have seen that these experiences seem to share some common ground with NDEs, including feelings of euphoria, tunnel vision, and the occasional OBE, but the most memorable aspect of the experience for the subject is usually the dream experience, when it is remembered. Whinnery elaborates on the nature of these short dreams:

> We have chosen to refer to these as dreamlets since the individuals describe them as indistinguishable from the dreams they experience during regular sleep, the only difference being the short duration of [the] dreamlets in comparison to sleep-associated dreams. . . . In any case, our dreamlets meet the characteristic features of dreams, including emotional intensity, detailed sensory imagery, illogical content and organization, uncritical acceptance, and difficulty in remembering once it is over.
>
> The dreamlets are vivid and frequently include family members and close friends. They commonly have beautiful settings and their content includes prior memories and thoughts of significance to the individual . . . they have a significant impact on individuals who experience them, and remain crystal clear for years after they occur.[20]

Here are some examples of dreamlets that Whinnery considers similar to NDEs, as dictated by three subjects. The first subject considered his experience very pleasant.

[First G-LOC episode] I was home . . . saw my mom and my brother. . . . I could not see myself. . . . I can't remember what we were doing, but when I came back [return of consciousness] I thought I shouldn't be here [in the centrifuge]. We were outdoors; it was wild. . . ! I got to go home [by dreaming] without taking [military] leave!

[Second G-LOC episode] There was a sunset. I cannot remember where. The sun was orange-red; an October sunset. . . . Maybe it was in Michigan.

The second subject also considered his experience pleasant.

I was floating in a blue ocean on my back . . . kind of asleep but not asleep. I knew the sun was up . . . like someone was trying to wake me up. Finally, I woke up and I was on the centrifuge! I did not want to wake up. . . . I could see myself on the water and also look at the sun; the sky was very blue, the sun very yellow.

The third subject did not enjoy his experience because of a sense of paralysis, as Whinnery points out:

G-LOC *subject* #3. This sense of paralysis and associated frustration is extremely common in G-LOC episodes. A typical example from a centrifuge subject is as follows:

I was in the grocery store going down one of the aisles. I was . . . being propelled by something like a magic carpet, although I could not make movements. I wanted to reach out and get a carton of ice cream but could not move my arm or even my eyes to look for it. It was intensely frustrating. . . .

It would seem as though these subjects are experiencing the effects of both anoxia and hypercarbia. Anoxia would be responsible for the loss of consciousness and hypercarbia for the dreams, feeling of floating, and the convulsive motions noted near the end of the unconscious period in most of the subjects. The experiences reported are very similar to those reported by Meduna's subjects.

The greatest similarity between acceleration-induced loss of consciousness and the NDE would seem to be the feeling of euphoria commonly reported after the experience, which is similar to the feelings of peace and joy reported as part of many NDEs. While OBEs are occasionally reported as being associated with acceleration-induced loss of consciousness, it is unclear from the literature if any of these have ever occurred during the experience.

However, the differences clearly outweigh the similarities. First of all, an experience of tunnel vision is not the same as that of perceiving a tunnel. Tunnel vision involves the absence of peripheral vision—not a region of darkness and certainly not a structured tunnel. Second, the convulsions frequently observed in the centrifuge have not been observed in cases of the NDE, although they are typical of subjects experiencing hypercarbia. Third, no panoramic life review has been reported as a result of acceleration-induced loss of consciousness. Fourth, the dreamlets do not involve deceased relatives or a being of light; unlike the visions reported as part of NDEs, the subjects describe them as "indistinguishable from the dreams they experience during regular sleep."* Fifth, the experience never ends with a decision to return. Finally, we have no evidence of lasting changes in personality and values, as is typically the case after an NDE.

In short, there is some overlap between NDE features and the symptoms of acceleration-induced anoxia and hypercarbia. It would be surprising if there were not, since most near-death experiencers do become anoxic and hypercarbic as they approach death. However, since most of the physical and mental symptoms of acceleration-induced anoxia and hypercarbia are not found in NDEs, and most of the features of NDEs are not found in acceleration-induced anoxia and hypercarbia, it makes little sense to assume they are the same phenomena.

TEMPORAL LOBE SEIZURES

Seizures are caused by abnormal electrical discharges in the brain, and seizures in the temporal lobes of the brain may cause auditory and visual

---

*In one study, 94.7 percent of respondents stated that their NDE was not like a dream, but was very *real* (Ring 1980, 82–83).

hallucinations, memory flashbacks, feelings of déjà vu, and more rarely, feelings of being out of the body. These seizures are thought by some researchers to be a primary cause of the NDE. The release of endorphins and hypoxia have both been proposed as triggers for temporal lobe seizures in the dying brain.

As we have seen, it is indeed plausible that the stress of dying may cause the release of endorphins, but whether endorphins cause seizures is, however, unclear. Endorphins appear to have both proconvulsant and anticonvulsant properties, and the authors of one medical study even suggest that endorphins may be effective in treating, not causing, temporal lobe seizures.[21]*

On the other hand, hypoxia has been shown to increase the susceptibility of the brain to seizures, including seizures of the temporal lobes.

Regardless of the triggering mechanism proposed, all of the proponents of this theory are impressed by the similarity between NDE reports and the symptoms of temporal lobe seizures. So how much similarity is there?

Pediatrician Melvin Morse, a man who has done much valuable research on NDEs in children, proposed a model of the NDE based on temporal lobe seizures, along with fellow physicians David Venecia and Jerrold Milstein. The authors write, "Support for this model begins with the work of Wilder Penfield, who identified areas of the temporal lobe associated with psychical hallucinations, memories, heavenly music, and religious visions through direct electrical cortical stimulation during neurosurgical procedures."[22]

In a book published one year later, Morse and science writer Paul Perry describe how their theories on the NDE became inspired by the research of Penfield:

Our team of researchers began to examine Penfield's work. Buried in a forty-year old textbook, we found clear reference to areas of

---

*The authors, K. Ramabadran and M. Bansinath, considered evidence that the stress of a seizure triggers the release of endorphins, which then help end the seizure. They write, "Morphine and endogenous opioid peptides have been shown to have anticonvulsant properties. . . . Therefore, it appears that endogenous opioid systems are triggered only after a stressful stimuli. . . . These studies indicate that endogenous opioid systems might play a critical role in the physiological mechanisms promoting seizure arrest and refractoriness" (Ramabadran and Bansinath 1990, 48).

the brain that, when electrically stimulated, produced out-of-body experiences. . . .

The area he was "mapping" was the Sylvian fissure, an area in the right temporal lobe located just above the right ear. When he electrically stimulated the surrounding areas of the fissure, *patients frequently had the experience of "seeing God," hearing beautiful music, seeing dead friends and relatives, and even having a panoramic life review.* (emphasis added)

This was an exciting find. . . . We had confirmed the specific area of the brain *where* NDE's occur.[23]

The only reference to Penfield's work Morse and Perry provide is a 1955 article in the *Journal of Mental Science,* and the only example in this article to anything remotely like what Morse and Perry describe is that of a 33-year-old man who suffered from seizures. When the right temporal lobe was stimulated, he "seemed confused" and shortly afterward exclaimed, "Oh God! I am leaving my body," and reportedly looked terrified. After, when asked if the experience was like his habitual seizures, he replied, "A bit, Sir," then after a pause, added, "I had the fear feeling."[24]

What Morse and Perry called "a forty-year old textbook" is presumably *The Cerebral Cortex of Man,* published in 1950, exactly forty years before their book. The only references in this book to anything remotely like what they describe are in chapter 9, titled "Psychical Seizure of Temporal Region." Like the article mentioned above, this chapter discusses experiments involving electrical stimulation of the temporal lobe in people who have seizures.

On page 172, a woman describes hearing "a lullaby her mother had been in the habit of singing to her." Penfield writes, "It was obvious that the hallucinations produced by the stimulating electrode were made up from memories, some of them quite recent."

On page 177, Penfield writes, "This man had minor seizures in which he felt very strange, as though he were 'out of this world.' The same sensation was produced by stimulation on the lower portion of the second temporal convolution."

On page 181, Penfield sums up, "Finally, the conclusion is unavoidable that when complex hallucinations are induced by stimulation of the temporal cortex the music a patient hears and the appearance before him of his mother or friend are like memories. . . . The patient is conscious of, and thinks over, these hallucinations as he would a memory which he had himself summoned." Based on his experiments, Penfield concludes that "the temporal cortex is essential to the process of remembering or interpreting things seen and heard."

We also have the conclusions Penfield published eight years later, in a book called *The Excitable Cortex in Conscious Man.*

On page 21, Penfield describes the electrical stimulation of the temporal lobe of a young woman, who said, "I hear music now, a funny little piece." Penfield adds, "The electrode was kept in place and she became more talkative, saying that the music she was hearing was something she had heard on the radio."

On page 27, Penfield describes the case of another young woman who suffered from epileptic seizures: "In summary, the localized epileptic discharges in the right temporal lobe of this young woman were causing her to experience, from time to time: (1) a sense of false familiarity (déjà vu), (2) a feeling of fear, (3) reproductions of previous experience. The first was an illusion, the second an emotion, the third a hallucination. These are all to be considered psychical phenomena, any one of which the operator might hope to reproduce by stimulation."

So Penfield duly carried out an experiment in which he electrically stimulated her right temporal lobe and concluded, "The psychical hallucinations, thus produced, were made up of experiences from this patient's past, not particularly important ones."[25]

Do any of these examples sound anything remotely like *"the experience of 'seeing God,' hearing beautiful music, seeing dead friends and relatives, and even having a panoramic life review"*?*

Similar research by other neurologists supports the conclusion that electrical stimulation of the temporal lobes results in rather mundane

---

*I asked Morse this question in a personal correspondence and received no reply.

phenomena that bear little if any resemblance to those found in the NDE. In 1978, Eric Halgren, Richard Walter, Diana Cherlow, and Paul Crandal at the Reed Neurological Research Center at the University of California, Los Angeles, School of Medicine, carried out thousands of such experiments. Regarding their conclusions, they write, "Of 3495 stimulations of the medial temporal lobe of 36 psychomotor epileptics, 267 were accompanied by reports of mental phenomena, including hallucinations of complete scenes, *déjà vu,* anxiety, visceral sensations, amnesia, and unformed sensory experiences. . . . Our findings suggest that the mental phenomena evoked by medial temporal lobe stimulation are idiosyncratic and variable, and are related to the personality of the patient stimulated."[26]*

More recently, Michael Persinger, a psychologist at Laurentian University in Canada, has mimicked temporal lobe seizure phenomena by electromagnetic stimulation. He has his subjects sit in the dark (wearing goggles) in a special chamber. Using a special helmet, weak magnetic fields are then applied across the temporal plane, and during a twenty- to thirty-minute exposure, the subjects report their experiences, which are recorded. Before leaving the chamber, each subject completes a questionnaire that rates the frequency of various experiences. Persinger reports that he has tested hundreds of volunteers in this manner.

In an article in a 1989 edition of *Journal of Near-Death Studies,* Persinger writes, "Kate Makarec and I have found that all of the major components of the NDE, including out-of-body experiences, floating, being pulled toward a light, hearing strange music, and profound meaningful experiences can occur in experimental settings during minimal

---

*The following are descriptions reported by Halgren and colleagues of the hallucinations induced by electrical stimulation of the temporal lobes of a female patient who had suffered seizures since she was twelve years old:

"Three of her hallucinations seemed to her like television shows—a 'soap opera' and programmes regarding implants or astronauts. The astronaut program seemed 'like a dream, a weird dream' . . . The remainder of her hallucinations she reported to be specific memories: a trip to Yosemite or to Reading; a scene in her home; lying on a couch watching football; a particular telephone conversation; a chocolate coke she drank once in a small town" (Halgren et al. 1978, 92).

electrical current induction within the temporal region due to exogenous spike-and-wave magnetic field sources."[27]

However, Persinger adds that "these induced experiences are fragmented and variable, whereas in NDEs these sensations are integrated and focused within a brief period." Even with this qualification, Persinger's findings may not be as impressive as the above paragraph would suggest. Five years later, he published an article that included a table summarizing the results of 153 subjects. Here is the table, with the items rearranged in order of descending frequency.

PERCENTAGE OF SUBJECTS REPORTING EXPERIENCES WITHIN EXPERIMENTAL SIMULATION OF NDE-LIKE SETTINGS

Item	Percentage Yes
Dizzy or Odd	75 %
Tingling Sensations	73 %
As If Somewhere Else	55 %
Vibrations in Body	54 %
Vivid Visual Images	52 %
Left Body/Detached	39 %
Thoughts from Childhood	35 %
Fear or Terror	32 %
Sense of Presence	30 %
Images from a Dream	29 %
Experiences Not from Own Mind	13 %
Odd Tastes	13 %
Odd Smells	6 %
Inner Voice Call Name	3 %

Source: Persinger 1994, 284–85.

The most common experiences are dizziness and tingling, which are not characteristic of NDEs. As we have seen, "vibrations," "fear or terror," "odd tastes," and "odd smells" are also rarely (if ever) reported as part of the NDE. Furthermore, the subjects in Persinger's experiments are able to converse with the experimenter and report their experiences as they occur; in other words, they remain very much "in this world" and do not experience a sense of shifting to another reality. In view of the table above, Persinger's earlier boast that "all of the major components of the NDE, including out-of-body experiences, floating, being pulled toward a light, hearing strange music, and profound meaningful experiences can occur in experimental settings" seems, in retrospect, to have been hyperbole. Does Persinger really consider "tingling sensations" and "vibrations" to be "profound meaningful experiences"?*

In 2004, Persinger's research was dealt a serious blow when a Swedish team attempted to replicate his findings, using equipment borrowed from his lab. A team at Uppsala University in Sweden, headed by Pehr Granqvist, tested eighty-nine undergraduate students, some who were exposed to the magnetic field and some who were not. A double-blind protocol was used: that is, neither the people running the experiment nor the subjects being tested knew (1) what the experiment was testing and (2) whether any particular subject was part of the test group or the control group. The Swedish team also consulted Persinger's collaborator Stanley Koren to ensure that conditions for replication were optimal.

Granqvist's team found no effect from the magnetic fields whatsoever.[28†] The only characteristic that predicted what the subjects reported was personality: subjects who were rated "highly suggestible" on the basis of a questionnaire reported strange experiences when they were wearing the helmet, *whether the current was on or off.* For instance, two of the

---

*Persinger has never agreed to any of my requests for access to his subjects for interviews, and he refused my offer to undergo his experimental procedures.

†Granqvist wrote: "In spite of high power for detecting differences between groups at a small effect size level, there were no significant differences between experimental and control group participation on any of the dependent variables. . . . Sensed presence and mystical experiences are predicted by suggestibility, not by the application of transcranial weak complex magnetic fields." (Granqvist et al. 2004)

three subjects who reported strong spiritual experiences were members of the control group, and eleven of the twenty-two who reported subtle experiences were members of the control group. Granqvist and his team concluded that the well-established psychology of suggestion was the best explanation for Persinger's results.[29]

Persinger disputed the Swedish team's findings, arguing that Granqvist's team did not generate a "biologically effective signal" because they did not use the equipment for a sufficient length of time. Granqvist dismissed his objections: "Persinger knew ahead of the experiments there would be two times of 15-minute exposures. He agreed to that time. His explanation now comes as a disappointment."[30]*

CONCLUSIONS REGARDING TEMPORAL LOBE SEIZURES AND NEAR-DEATH EXPERIENCES

We have seen that electrical stimulation of the temporal lobes produce subjective phenomena that, at most, bear little if any resemblance to the phenomena found in the NDE. How closely do *actual* seizures resemble the NDE? Ernst Rodin, medical director of the Epilepsy Center of Michigan and professor of neurology at Wayne State University, clarifies the issue. He writes:

> The hallmarks and nuclear components of NDEs are a sensation of peace or even bliss, the knowledge of having died, and, as a result, being no longer limited to the physical body. In spite of having seen hundreds of patients with temporal lobe seizures during three decades of professional life, I have never come across that symptomatology as part of a seizure.[31]

---

*Persinger's research was reported widely and favorably in the popular science press, but his fellow scientists were not so easily impressed. For instance, Mario Beauregard and Denyse O'Leary devote an entire chapter of their book *The Spiritual Brain* to a scathing review of Persinger's research. (See Beauregard and O'Leary 2007, chapter 4.)

In contrast with the peace and joy found in most NDEs, seizures are accompanied by feelings of fear, loneliness, and sadness.* Auditory hallucinations are more common than visual hallucinations, and the sensations of smell and taste so often found in seizures are absent from virtually all NDEs. The perception of the immediate environment is frequently distorted during the seizure, in contrast to the clear perception reported during many NDEs. The memory invoked during a seizure, or by electrical stimulation, is of a random, single event of no particular significance, unlike the panoramic life review found in Western NDEs. Finally, seizures and electrical stimulation of the cortex do not evoke images of communicating with deceased relatives in another world.

---

*Concerning the feelings typically experienced during a seizure, Penfield wrote, "The patients have described these feelings with the words: loneliness, sadness, scared feeling, terror" (Penfield 1955 458).

TWELVE

EXPERIENCING DEATH THROUGH DRUGS?

Some have suggested that NDEs might be nothing more than hallucinations, due to unusual biochemical changes in the brain. Pharmacologist Ronald Siegel, an expert on both drugs and hallucinations, was one of the first to extensively elaborate this position in a 1980 article in *American Psychologist*. Siegel pointed out in his paper that most hallucinations, regardless of what causes them, tend to include certain types of imagery, which he has referred to elsewhere as "form constants."[1] These form constants include lattices, honeycombs, cobwebs, spirals, funnels, and tunnels. Siegel argued specifically that tunnels, bright lights, and geometric forms that could be interpreted as cities have all been reported as part of drug hallucinations and provided the following four examples.

Tunnels in Drug Hallucinations:
   "I'm moving through some kind of train tunnel. There are all sorts of lights and colors."
   "I am traveling into a tunnel and out into space."
   Cities and Lights in Drug Hallucinations:
   "There are tall structures all around me . . . it could be buildings, it could be anything . . . and in all colors."
   "And it seems like I'm getting closer and closer to the sun, it's

very white . . . and there's like a geometric network or lattice in the distance."[2]

Siegel's position was that the core elements of the NDE are nothing more than a peculiar constellation of features that have been found in hallucinations. He argued that the nature and features of the NDE are due to the setting in which the experience occurs and to the subject's expectations. These psychological factors combine with biochemical changes in the brain that cause hallucinations, and the result is an NDE. Siegel writes, "The specific content of complex hallucinatory imagery is determined largely by set (expectations and attitudes) and setting (physical and psychological environments). For many dying and near-death experiences, the sets (fear of approaching death, changes in body and mental functioning, etc.) and settings (hospital wards, accident scenes, etc.) can influence specific eschatological thoughts and images."[3]

Most researchers simply ignored Siegel's paper when it was published. It was already known that drug-induced hallucinations and the NDE share some suspiciously common ground, so Siegel was really not saying anything new. It was even known that OBEs are sometimes reported as having occurred during drug trips, and shamans in traditional cultures sometimes ingest hallucinogenic substances to induce out-of-body travels.

The most Siegel had shown was that several elements of the NDE, taken piecemeal, tend to appear randomly in some psychedelic trips. He never demonstrated that the orderly and predictable sequence of components of the NDE—its core elements—show up consistently during psychedelic trips. One of the most striking features of the NDE is the consistency of its core elements, despite diversity across subjects (by age, sex, race, religious history, education, and so on) and situations (such as illness, accidents, suicide). By contrast, hallucinations are highly idiosyncratic and varied, with the specific content, as Siegel notes, "determined largely by set (expectations and attitudes) and setting (physical and psychological environments)."

Another problem with Siegel's model is that it doesn't specify why some features of hallucinations, such as tunnels and lights, show up in

NDEs, but not others. Cobwebs, honeycombs, and lattices are found in hallucinations, but are conspicuously absent from NDE accounts.

However, a few years later another model based on drug hallucinations was developed, a model based on a drug many recreational users believe can help an individual experience death while remaining very much alive.

THE KETAMINE MODEL

Ketamine was first synthesized in 1962 by Calvin Stevens at the Parke-Davis laboratories in Ann Arbor, Michigan. Related to the notorious drug phencyclidine (PCP), ketamine is most often used as a general anesthetic during surgery. It is classified as a dissociative anesthetic because patients or recreational users tell of being perceptually detached from their bodies or environments while under its influence.

Hallucinogenic episodes, or "emergence reactions" to the drug, were reported by Parke-Davis as occurring in approximately 12 percent of patients receiving the drug.[4] To prevent these emergence reactions, anesthetists today usually coadminister a sedative as an attempt to induce genuine unconsciousness rather than dissociation.

When taken in lower doses, ketamine induces a short psychedelic trip, sometimes so intense that users believe their experiences on the drug were not mere hallucinations, but genuine. These experiences have a tendency to involve a sense of disconnection from the surroundings and can include feelings of floating, being a disembodied mind, and going to another world.

There is little doubt that some ketamine trips resemble the NDE, as can be seen in the following two particularly vivid accounts.

My mind left my body and apparently went to what some describe as the "second state." I felt I was in a huge, well-lit room, in front of a massive throne draped in lush red velvet. I saw nothing else but felt the presence of higher intelligence tapping my mind of every experience and impression I had gathered. I begged to be released, to return

to my body. It was terrifying. Finally, I blacked out and slowly came
to in the recovery room. That is my ketamine experience.[5]

The next account was reported by a musician who had taken ketamine recreationally, while listening to music.

My perceptions were getting disoriented and when I closed my
eyes a lot of information started to happen. Colors, patterns, cross-
connections in sensory perceptions. Sounds and inner visions got
confused.

I got deeper and deeper into this state, until at one point the
world disappeared. I was no longer in my body. I didn't have a
body. . . .

Then I reached a point at which I felt ready to die. It wasn't a
question of choice, it was just a wave that carried me higher and
higher, at the same time that I was having what in my normal state
I would call a horror of death. It became obvious to me that it was
not at all what I had anticipated death to be. Except, it was death,
that something was dying.

I reached a point at which I gave it all away, I just yielded, and
then I entered a space in which there aren't any words. The words
that have been used have been used a thousand times—starting
with Buddha. I mean, at-one-with-the-universe, recognizing your
Godhead—all those words I later used to explore what I have
experienced.

The feeling was that I was "home" . . . It was a bliss state of a kind
I never experienced before.[6]

After reading accounts such as this, it may not seem surprising that
Timothy Leary described his experiences with ketamine as "experiments
in voluntary death."[7] But other ketamine trips bear only the most superficial resemblance to the NDE.

As part of a respiratory study in the early 1970s, physician Robert
Johnstone was administered ketamine and related his experiences in a

letter to the medical journal *Anesthesiology*. The major portions of his account read as follows:

> I was lying supine on a contour-flexed operating table, a pillow beneath my head. The research laboratory was dimly lit; light classical music played in the background. The investigators were friends, and all-in-all I was comfortable.
>
> I had no warning. I heard a dull buzzing and then, within seconds, I was unconscious. For about two hours I have no memory of hearing, seeing, feeling, thinking, or dreaming. . . . My first memory is of colors. I saw red everywhere, then a yellow square on the left grew and crowded out the red. My vision faded, to be replaced by a black-and-white checkerboard which zoomed to and from me. More patterns appeared and faded, always in focus, with distinct edges and bright colors.
>
> Gradually I realized my mind existed and I could think. I wondered, "What am I?" and "Where am I?" I had no consciousness of existing in a body; I was a mind suspended in space. At times I was at the center of the earth, in Ohio (my former home), on a spaceship, or in a small brightly-colored room without doors or windows. I had no control over where my mind floated. Periods of thinking alternated with pure color hallucination.
>
> Then I remembered the drug study and reasoned something had gone wrong. I remembered a story about a man who was awake during resuscitation and lived to describe his experience. "Am I dying or already dead?" I was not afraid, I was more curious. "This is death. I am a soul, and I am going to wherever souls go." During this period I was observed to sit up, stare, and then lie down.
>
> . . . Thus began my cycling into and out of awareness—a frightening experience. I perceived the laboratory as the intensive care unit; this meant something had gone wrong. I wanted to know how bad things were. I now realized I wasn't thinking properly. I recognized voices, then I recognized people. I saw some people who weren't really there. I heard people talking, but could not understand them. The

only sentence I remember is "Are you all right?" Observers reported a panicked look and defensive thrashing of my arms. I screamed "They're after me!" and "They're going to get me!" I don't recall this or remember the reassurances given me.

I then became aware of my body. My right arm seem withered and my left very long. I could not focus my eyes. I recognized the ceiling, but thought that it was covered with worms. I desperately wanted to know what was reality and to be a part of it. I couldn't speak or communicate, but once, recognizing a friend next to me, I hugged him until I faded back to abstractness.

Since he was obviously showing great distress, his friends then gave him a strong sedative, and he fell asleep. When he awoke five hours later, he "promptly vomited," fell asleep again, and after several hours was finally rational and emotionally stable. Reflecting on his bad trip, Johnstone concluded:

I have given ketamine anesthesia and observed untoward psychic reactions, but was not concerned about this possibility when the study began. After my experience, I dropped out of the study, which called for two more exposures of ketamine. In the several weeks since my ketamine trip, I have experienced no flashbacks or bad dreams. Still I am afraid of ketamine. I doubt I will ever take it again because I fear permanent psychologic damage. Nor will I give ketamine to a patient as his sole anesthetic.[8]

Anesthetist Barbara Collier conducted one of the largest studies ever undertaken on the effects of ketamine: 131 patients undergoing minor surgery were administered varying dosages of ketamine as an anesthetic, and the effects were compared with 80 patients who were given other agents. Interestingly, only 37 percent of those given ketamine would have either liked to repeat the experience or were indifferent, compared with 85 percent of the control group. Perhaps because of the hospital setting, most of those given ketamine did not find the experience worth repeating. Collier explains that "it was the strange, vivid dreaming, depersonalization and other sensory disturbances which caused most distress. Some patients considered that the vivid and frequently beautiful dreaming had been interesting and instructive, but they had no desire to repeat the experience. Several patients thought they 'had died' and others that they 'had gone mad.'"[9]

Describing the nature of the hallucinations, Collier writes:

Coloured patterns are common, but isolated objects both of a "real" and "unreal" nature are noted (*e.g.,* "Two nurses talking at the foot of the bed" "midget Chinamen" "a large tankard of beer" and a "grotesque monster"). Severe psychomotor disturbances are almost invariably associated with hallucinations. . . .

The recurrence of certain themes was notable in the ketamine groups: 67% consisted of coloured or luminous patterns with a kaleidoscopic effect; watching or being part of multiple objects and floating in outer space or down corridors. A sense of depersonalization was a common cause of profound fear and was frequently interpreted as death.[10]

Ketamine seems to produce its effects by suppressing those sections of the brain responsible for processing sensory information, while at the same time stimulating the central nervous system. The similarity of ketamine's effects with those produced by sensory deprivation was pointed out by Collier.

The phenomena seen closely resemble those described in experiments with sensory deprivation . . .—feelings of depersonalization, sensation of strangeness, even splitting of the body image may arise. Some subjects "floated" around the room. They could "look down" and see themselves sprawled on the bed. Patterned images are often seen. One subject saw a file of prehistoric monsters walking; another experienced a pastoral landscape and a third watched a series of animated cartoons; yet another subject declared that he had just awakened from a vivid dream but that "the dream was still going on."[11]

The similarity of ketamine's effects with those found in the classic NDE seems limited, at least in Collier's clinical study, to the feeling of floating outside of the body reported by some patients. In fact, in a subset of her study, in which eleven patients were given between forty and sixty milligrams of ketamine, "10 experienced a sensation of floating in space," "9 felt the 'spirit' or mind rise from the body," and "3 were able to 'look down' on their bodies lying on the trolley and note the exact time the 'spirit' re-entered it."[12]*

Perhaps the most dramatic single experience was reported by a male patient in the subset of fifty patients who were given dosages ranging from 150 to 640 milligrams. The reader will have to decide how closely this "dream of remarkable intensity" matches the classic NDE. Collier writes, "The patient ascended to Heaven, saw God, and was re-incarnated in Italy. Luminosity, green color, tranquility and marked euphoria pre-dominated. This theme occurred for over 2 hours into the awake phase during which he thought that he was speaking Italian."[13]

These accounts illustrate the similarities between some NDEs and some ketamine trips. But ketamine produces a considerably wider range of phenomena than those found in the NDE, such as color distortion, kaleidoscopic patterns, images of monsters, and so on. The NDE-like experiences reported by some people—mainly sensations of being out of the body, sometimes accompanied by feelings of bliss—seem to be subsets of a much wider variety of hallucinatory experiences.

RELEVANCE OF KETAMINE FOR THE NEAR-DEATH EXPERIENCE

Physician Lester Grinspoon and psychiatrist James Bakalar have suggested that the brain may synthesize a chemical similar to ketamine that is released when a person is severely stressed, causing the individual to experience sensations of leaving the body. This suggestion has been elabo-

---

*Other experiences for this group were not so dramatic. One patient reported "the room turned green" and "1 subject 'became' one pile of boxes" (Collier 1972, 126).

rated by psychiatrist Karl Jansen, who argues that a ketamine-like substance may be released to protect the brain from damage due to oxygen starvation or epileptic seizure.

Jansen's argument concerns the effect of the neurotransmitter glutamate, which is one of the chemical messengers used by brain cells to pass messages across the synaptic gap that separates neurons from each other. When glutamate is present in excess, neurons begin to die. Jansen cites studies providing evidence that oxygen starvation and epileptic seizures lead to an excessive release of glutamate, which appears to be the chemical mechanism causing the resulting death of brain cells.

The hallucinogenic properties of ketamine and PCP are thought to be due to the blockading of certain receptors on the synapses of the neurons, known as N-methyl-D-aspartate (NMDA) receptors. Blockading the PCP receptors is thought to prevent cell death due to an excessive release of glutamate. So according to Jansen, "This suggests that the brain may have a protective mechanism against the detected glutamate flood: a counter-flood of a substance that binds to the PCP receptor, preventing cell death. The brain is a well-protected organ with many known defenses; it is reasonable to propose that is has protective mechanisms against excitotoxicity. This hypothetical defensive flood of substances to block the PCP receptors is the only speculation in the process outlined above; the other statements are strongly supported by experimental evidence."[14]

Jansen's model therefore proposes that a ketamine-like substance is released to protect the brain from toxic damage and as a side effect produces the subjective phenomena found in the typical NDE. Jansen sums up his theory of endogenous ketamine as follows:

> The major function of such an agent in the glutamate hypothesis of the NDE is that it will protect the brain from excitotoxic cell damage, while generating a mental state that has valuable psychological aspects, such as holding overwhelming anxiety at bay—the usual function of less severe dissociative phenomena in psychology. The psychological advantage may be even greater where the forces of the unconscious are harnessed to give the person a strong message

to go back in terms of mythological drama, and that it is "not their time"—the final expression of the deep drive in the psyche to survive, presented by those parts of the brain still able to produce such a phenomenon. . . . As those who have NDEs do not in fact die, the evolutionary advantage is tremendous.[15]

The ketamine model is the most sophisticated attempt so far to provide an explanation for the NDE in terms of brain chemistry. But the model rests on two crucial assumptions: first, that the brain produces a chemical similar to ketamine when under the stress of oxygen starvation or seizure, and second, that ketamine hallucinations, or some subclass of them, strongly resemble the NDE. Both of these assumptions are crucial and so should be kept in mind during any discussion of the model.

What are we to think of this model? Are ketamine trips, as Leary suggested, literally "experiments in voluntary death," or do they tend to demonstrate, as Siegel argues, that the NDE is a type of hallucination caused by certain unusual chemical states of the brain? There seem to be three possible theories suggested by the resemblance of some ketamine hallucinations with the classic NDE.

The first theory holds that a ketamine-like substance is responsible for NDEs occurring in catastrophic circumstances. This theory is essentially that proposed by Jansen and roughly corresponds to Siegel's explanatory model. However, this model cannot account for the predictable pattern of phenomena found in the NDE and the inconsistency of ketamine trips. The NDE type of hallucinations do not invariably occur as a result of using ketamine, but are only a subtype within a wide range of hallucinatory reactions to the drug. The effects of ketamine depend greatly on set and setting, but NDEs are surprisingly similar, regardless of their cause or the circumstances under which they occur. As Peter Fenwick and Elizabeth Fenwick point out:

It seems that the mental state in the NDE bears no resemblance at all to the person's mental state before the experience. Someone who attempts suicide might be expected to be in some emotional turmoil at the time of their experience. In real life people who are depressed tend to select only depressive images and memories. And yet if we look at the experiences described . . . we can see that the depressive feelings vanish when they enter the experience; there is an awareness of peace, of something beautiful; there seems to be a healing of the "broken spirit."[16]

Another problem, perhaps even more severe, is that this model applies only to NDEs occurring in catastrophic circumstances. Some NDEs occur to individuals who are neither near death nor likely experiencing any event likely to upset the functioning of their brains. Jansen's model—postulating a release of a ketamine-like substance to protect the brain from damage—thus applies only to those NDEs occurring after a severe insult to the brain, in the form of anoxia or epilepsy. But this raises a profound problem, as Peter Fenwick points out:

Any physician dealing with head injury, epilepsy, or altered cerebral physiology knows that as cerebral function becomes compromised it becomes disorganized. Even in such simple circumstances as ordinary fainting, recovery from the faint is recovery from a confusional process. Acute cerebral catastrophes result in confusion and not clarity. This important fact is overlooked by those attributing simple chemical explanations to the NDE. Although ketamine may produce experiences that are similar to the NDE, and Jansen has argued cogently that it does, he does not explain how these same experiences can arise in a dysfunctional brain.[17]

The only way around this dilemma is to argue that the experience arises as consciousness is being lost or recovered. But memory is very sensitive to any sort of insult or injury to the brain, and events immediately preceding and following a period of unconsciousness are rarely remembered. In fact, it is well known that the length of the period of amnesia before and after unconsciousness is a way of determining the severity of the injury. Recovery after unconsciousness is marked by confusion, and so it seems highly unlikely that any thoughts or perceptions from this period would be remembered with the crystal clarity typical of the NDE.

The second theory is that ketamine induces genuine OBEs through its unusual effects on the brain. As mentioned earlier, OBEs have occasionally been reported as having occurred after the ingestion of various hallucinogenic drugs, but feelings of being outside of one's body seem to be a remarkably frequent effect of ketamine in particular. Could ketamine sometimes act on the brain in such a way as to trigger a genuine release of the mind from the body? This is the position of John Lilly, the California-based dolphin expert who pioneered the study of sensory deprivation in the 1960s. Lilly, who has experimented with ketamine past the point of excess, believes that ketamine is literally a chemical road to the OBE.

Psychiatrist Rick Strassman has toyed with this idea. After noting that ketamine exerts its effects by blockading NMDA receptors in the synapse, he asks, "Is 'everyday reality' as 'real' and compelling as it is because of NMDA receptor function? Perhaps it is the case that the NMDA receptor is blockaded when the organism is perceiving a nonmaterial world!"[18]

Surprisingly, even Jansen has conceded that there may be something to the idea that the use of ketamine opens a gate to another reality. The entire fall 1997 edition of *Journal of Near-Death Studies* was devoted to discussing the ketamine model and contained two articles by Jansen. After arguing at several points for the conventional notion that the brain is responsible for the mind, Jansen appears to reverse his position in a postscript at the end of his second article.

> I am no longer as opposed to spiritual explanations of near-death phenomena as my article and this response to the commentaries on it would appear to suggest. Over the past two years . . . I have moved more toward the view put forward by John Lilly and Stanislav Grof: namely, that drugs and psychological disciplines such as meditation and yoga may render certain "states" more accessible. . . .
>
> After 12 years of studying ketamine, I now believe that there most definitely is a soul that is independent of experience. It exists when we begin, and may persist when we end. Ketamine is a door to

a place we cannot normally get to; it is definitely not evidence that such a place does not exist.[19]

Yet it seems like special pleading to suggest that the OBE- and NDE-like aspects of ketamine trips are sometimes just what they appear to be, while the other effects of ketamine, such as seeing cartoon figures, geometric patterns, prehistoric monsters, and so on, are mere hallucinations. We would have to argue that these other, idiosyncratic features merely occur as side effects en route to the threshold of a genuine OBE or NDE, but an experience occurring with a brain that is still functioning, albeit in an intoxicated manner. There have been numerous anecdotal reports of accurate perception occurring during the out-of-body component of the NDE. What are needed to support the idea that ketamine can induce a genuine separation of mind and body are similar reports indicating veridical perception during a drug-induced OBE. So far, these have been lacking.

The third theory holds that ketamine hallucinations are nothing more than pseudo-NDEs. Scott Rogo, an author who has reviewed the effects of ketamine, writes:

It may be that ketamine, in and by itself, doesn't really produce NDE hallucinations at all. While researching [the effects of ketamine], I found relatively few cases of classic NDEs reported by people taking the drug in recreational settings. They seem to be almost exclusively reported by patients recovering in the hospital from surgery. Now this pattern could be a by-product of the high dosages needed to produce general anesthesia. But perhaps the NDE-like hallucinations result from the hospital setting in which the drug is usually administered. We know that ketamine often induces in the patient some sense of disembodied existence. Now a patient coming out of surgery might naturally be concerned with death and surviving the ordeal. The patient might then misinterpret these dissociative sensations and build up an elaborate fantasy based on them. Such a fantasy would be concerned with themes such as leaving the body, going to a heavenly realm, and other hallucinations typical of ketamine use. But it could be the patient's mind that is producing the imagery and not the drug. Experts on ketamine have often remarked that the specific nature of the ketamine "trip" can be influenced by the setting under which the drug is taken.[20]

Strassman, a psychiatrist who has directly participated in extensive clinical research on the effects of various hallucinogenic drugs, is not impressed with comparisons between the effects of ketamine and the NDE. He writes:

Regarding differences, I have been struck by the fearful experiences many anesthetized patients describe as they are awakening from ketamine anesthesia, when blood levels compare to those attained with nonmedical or "recreational" use. These so-called "emergence phenomena," while partaking of some of the particular perceptual and cognitive properties of the NDE, often are not pleasant nor desired to be repeated, and lack the equanimity and reinforcing effects that recreational ketamine users describe. Nor are they felt to be beneficial over the long run, that is, lessening fear of death and enhancing appreciation of life.[21]

Interestingly, Kenneth Ring, one of the most prominent NDE researchers, has taken the drug experimentally several times. In a personal communication with me from January 16, 2003, he writes:

As to my experiences with Ketamine, in my day I took the drug a total of 9 times. My trips were extremely variable and while often transcendent, nothing I experienced, either in content or texture, had any particular overlap with the classic NDE. For me personally, therefore, I had no cause to conclude that Ketamine provides an analogous experience to the classic, beatific NDE. And since I've known quite a few people who have also taken Ketamine, I daresay most if not all of them would agree with me. However, it may certainly be that for some people there may be features of the Ketamine experience that mimic the NDE—that's an empirical matter. I don't personally know any NDErs who have taken Ketamine, but I would be very interested in their judgments about the similarity.

As with other hallucinogenic drugs, the nature of the ketamine trip seems to depend on set and setting. But some NDEs occur when the patient did not expect to die, as when sudden cardiac arrest causes the patient to lose consciousness before realizing what is happening. If a ketamine-like substance floods the brain, then why don't these patients frequently report the features of ketamine hallucinations that are not found in the classic NDE?

The ketamine model postulates that a ketamine-like substance will be released during anoxia to protect the brain from neurotoxic cell damage "while generating a mental state that has valuable psychological aspects, such as holding overwhelming anxiety at bay," as Jansen states. In assessing the validity of the ketamine model, we must remember that ketamine experiences that contain at least some NDE-like features are usually reported in hospitals, where the setting may cause the hallucinations to be interpreted as stages of dying. But many of the emergence reactions that occur in a hospital setting do not induce calmness, but rather feelings of fear and anxiety. What survival value could such fearful experiences possibly have? The feeling of bliss sometimes reported seems to result almost exclusively from ketamine use in recreational settings, where the user is less likely to interpret the experience as "death."

CONCLUDING REMARKS

What is needed in order to rigorously evaluate the ketamine model is a detailed statistical comparison between the frequencies of occurrence for the various features found in ketamine trips and the NDE. So far, this has been lacking. In addition, the ranking of ketamine trips on the standardized scales of the NDE that have been developed by Greyson and Ring would be useful. These scales are commonly used in NDE studies to rank NDEs in terms of depth, and so would enable a more rigorous assessment of how closely some ketamine experiences resemble the classic

NDE. Finally, the administration of ketamine to volunteers who have had NDEs may provide some useful subjective comparisons.

As it is, the ketamine model is both speculative and vague. It hinges on the speculation that the brain produces its own endogenous ketamine-like substance in response to anoxia, for which, at this point, we have no evidence. It also hinges on the assertion that ketamine hallucinations resemble those experiences people frequently report while near death. However, it has not been demonstrated that they bear anything more than an occasional superficial resemblance.

With regard to hallucinations as an explanation of the NDE—whether caused by anoxia, temporal lobe seizures, or drugs—psychiatrist Bruce Greyson, editor of *Journal of Near-Death Studies,* notes, "Without exception, every report of a large study of NDEs published in a mainstream medical journal has concluded that these phenomena cannot be explained as hallucinations. Such unanimity among scientific researchers is unusual and should tell us something. Why is it that scientists who have done the most near-death research believe the mind is not exclusively housed in the brain, whereas those who regard NDEs as hallucinations by and large have not conducted any studies of the phenomena at all?"[22]

In response to one critic's assertion these scientists are biased and that near-death research has been influenced by the researchers' beliefs, Greyson retorted that "he has it backwards: the researchers' beliefs have been influenced by their consistent research findings. Most near-death researchers did not go into their investigations with a belief in mind-body separation, but came to that hypothesis based on what their research found."[23]

In fact, one researcher, Michael Sabom, entered the field of NDE research specifically to debunk reports of the NDE. He writes, "When I began my study of the NDE, I was convinced that the NDE would readily be accounted for using some traditional scientific explanation. I have searched for such an explanation over the past five years and have not yet found one that is adequate. In recent years I have begun to consider another approach toward explaining the NDE, an approach which holds open the possibility that the perception of an 'out-of-body' experience at the point of death may be accurate, i.e., that is somehow *does* occur 'out-of-body.'"[24]

THIRTEEN

THE "DYING BRAIN" THEORY OF SUSAN BLACKMORE

British psychologist Susan Blackmore has outlined a "dying brain" theory of the NDE that combines aspects of several physiological and psychological theories. As described in her book *Dying to Live,* in essence it contains the following elements:

- Feelings of peace and bliss caused by endorphins
- Tunnel and light caused by anoxia
- Life review caused by temporal lobe seizures, triggered by endorphins
- Experience of being "out-of-body" due to a breakdown of body image and model of reality
- Accurate perceptions of immediate environment during the NDE due to "prior knowledge, fantasy and lucky guesses and the remaining operating senses of hearing and touch"[1]

There is little that is new in Blackmore's attack on the transcendental interpretation of the NDE. It is essentially a combination of various physiological and psychological theories, strung together in an attempt to provide a materialist explanation for several aspects of the experience. We have already examined the physiological theories in great detail and have seen how they are refuted by the evidence. What we have not yet dealt with is Blackmore's only original contribution to the controversy—her attempt to provide a psychological explanation for the out-of-body component of the NDE.

Before she attempts to explain the OBE, Blackmore leaves us with no doubt about her materialist leanings. She writes, "I want to be quite clear. It is my contention that there is no soul, spirit, astral body or anything at all that leaves the body during NDEs and survives after death. These, like the very idea of a persisting self, are all illusions and the NDE can be accounted for without recourse to any of them."[2]

Seeking to provide a purely materialistic explanation for the OBE, Blackmore proposes that the OBE "is the brain's way of dealing with a breakdown in the body image and model of reality"[3] when near death. The various reasons for this breakdown "may be a lack of input, confusion through pain, injury and actual physical distortion; it may be that the brain is no longer capable of building a good body image even if it had the information because it is ceasing to function properly."[4]

So when the normal model of reality can no longer be sustained, what, according to Blackmore, can the dying brain do?

I suggest that one possibility is to try to get back to normal by using whatever information is available to build a body image and a world. If the sensory input is cut off or confused this information will have to come from memory and imagination. Memory can supply all the information about your body, what it looks like, how it feels and so on. It can also supply a good picture of the world. "Where was I? Oh, yes, I was lying in the road after that car hit me."

However, there is one crucial thing we know about memory images. They are often built in a bird's-eye view. Siegel uses a good example. Recall the last time you were walking along the seashore. Do you see the beach as though from where your eyes would be? Or are you looking from above? Many people recall such scenes in a kind of bird's-eye view. It seems likely, therefore, that in the event of nearly dying, or any other circumstance in which the normal model of reality has broken down, such a bird's-eye memory model may take over as "real."

At last we have a simple theory of the OBE. The normal model of reality breaks down and the system tries to get back to normal by building a new model from memory and imagination. If this model is in a bird's eye view, then an OBE takes place.[5]

To have the dying brain hypothesis explain the OBE in terms of memory and imagination, Blackmore must be able to account for the aerial perspective commonly reported during the NDE. She does this by claiming that memories are "often built in a bird's-eye view" and provides Siegel's example in support. The example comes from Siegel's 1977 article titled "Hallucinations," which focuses on his work giving an unspecified number of subjects various drugs of unspecified doses and recording the subsequent hallucinations. As Blackmore noted, Siegel did at one point mention memories from an aerial perspective:

Common complex images included childhood memories and scenes associated with strong emotional experiences that the subjects had undergone. These hallucinatory images were more than pictorial replicas; many of them were elaborated and embellished into fantastic scenes. This constructive aspect of imagery can be illustrated by a simple exercise. Recall the last time you went swimming in the ocean. Now ask yourself if this memory includes a picture of yourself running along the beach or moving about in the water. Such a picture is obviously fictitious, since you could not have been looking at yourself, but images in the memory often include fleeting pictures of this kind. Our subjects often reported equally improbable images, such as aerial perspectives and underwater views. . . . During the peak hallucinatory periods . . . [the] subjects frequently reported feeling dissociated from their bodies.[6]

Blackmore also cited an article by Georgia Nigro and Ulric Neisser to support her contention of a bird's-eye view. So the aerial perspective for Blackmore's dying brain hypothesis rests on the works of Nigro and Neisser, and of Siegel.

Nigro and Neisser reported finding two types of memory, which they called observer memory and field memory. In observer memory, "one seems to have the position of an onlooker or observer, looking at the situation from an external vantage point and seeing oneself 'from the outside.'" In field memory, "the scene appears from one's own position; one seems to have roughly the field of view that was available in the original situation and one does not 'see oneself.'"[7]

The researchers recruited a sample of undergraduates and high school students to participate in their study. They also cautioned against making too much of their study, writing, "Our investigation is only a preliminary one. So far, we have studied only a few situations, a few recall instructions, an unrepresentative sample of subjects, and an uncontrolled range of recencies."[8]

Nevertheless, Nigro and Neisser found that field memories tended to be more clear and vivid, and were more likely to include the recall of emotions and feelings associated with the event. Observer memories, in contrast, were not as vivid, but did occur almost half the time when subjects were asked to recall the "concrete, objective circumstances" of an occasion. Overall, however, the investigators found that "as in earlier studies, there were more field than observer memories." They concluded:

> A deliberate attempt to remember the "objective circumstances" of an event leads to relatively more observer memories; a focus on feelings leads to more field memories. People who are given no special recall set generally focus on their own feelings in remembering an event. This tendency may help to explain the overall preponderance of F [field] memories in our data. Another reason for that preponderance may be simply that recent memories tend to be in the field mode, and our open-ended instructions tended to elicit recall of recent events. It is also possible, of course, that there are simply more F [field] memories altogether.[9]

Nigro and Neisser wondered what could account for the fact that some memories are from an observer perspective, and they considered

Freud's theory that observer memories are a product of imaginative reconstruction. However, they write:

> Another hypothesis also merits consideration. Freud's assumption that original impressions are necessarily F [field] may not be justified: it is also possible to have observer experiences. Both of us (the authors) can attest to the possibility of experiencing events from a "detached" perspective as they occur. In such instances we are conscious of how the entire scene would appear (or does appear in fact) to an onlooker who sees *us* as well as our surroundings. . . . It is not clear how these experiences are best interpreted . . . but it is clear that they exist.[10]

Later in the article, they comment further on the possible reasons why some memories are in the observer rather than the field mode.

> Observer memories do occur. We are inclined to agree with Freud that they are often produced by a process of reconstruction in memory. We do not think that all of them originate in this way, however, because there may well be O [observer] *experiences* as well as O [observer] memories. In particular, events involving high degrees of emotional self-awareness may be experienced from an observer perspective. Our finding that such events produce a relatively high proportion of O [observer] memories is consistent with that hypothesis.[11]

In short, Nigro and Neisser wrote that observer memories may be the results of events that were *experienced* from an observer perspective. These observer experiences described by Nigro and Neisser seem to strongly resemble the separation of the mind from the body, in other words, an OBE.

So Blackmore's dying brain hypothesis needs the bird's-eye view to explain OBEs, and the evidence for memories in a bird's-eye view depends on Nigro and Neisser's article, which they described as a preliminary study based on an unrepresentative sample, and in which observer experiences may account for many observer memories. It is hard to imagine a more tenuous connection between Blackmore's bird's-eye view explanation of the OBE and Nigro and Neisser's article.

However, Blackmore's OBE explanation also rests on Siegel's 1977 article on hallucinations, in which one paragraph mentioned the bird's-eye perspective. Siegel gave us his opinion on the aerial perspective, but did not cite any data or studies on memory reconstruction, such as the study Nigro and Neisser conducted. Siegel's article was not even on memory, but on drug hallucinations, and so this foundation of Blackmore's bird's-eye view explanation of the OBE is even more flimsy than her citation for Nigro and Neisser's article.

Blackmore's case—that the OBE is due to a breakdown of body image with a subsequent reconstruction of what happened when the person was unconscious—is somewhat stronger when she attempts to explain accurate perceptions by the remaining senses of touch and hearing. She notes that during unconsciousness the senses are not all lost at once. Sometimes the senses of hearing and touch are still available to the seemingly unconscious person. So the possibility exists that people hear conversations, feel medical procedures being performed, and use this data to reconstruct a plausible account of what happened during the time they were apparently unconscious.

In this regard, Blackmore quoted from the case described earlier by Sabom, in which a man claimed to have witnessed "a shot" being administered near his groin while out of his body ("I was above myself looking down"). As mentioned earlier, the patient did not receive an injection but in fact had blood withdrawn from his femoral artery. Sabom felt that the patient's mistake was understandable only on the hypothesis that the perception of the scene was visual, not auditory. If the patient's description was based on remarks overheard, then he would not have confused the withdrawal of blood with an injection. Blackmore suggested that the man never left his body but felt the pain of the needle while semiconscious and later built this up into a visual picture of what was happening during his resuscitation.[12]

But health psychologist William Serdahely, who has written an excellent critique of the dying brain hypothesis, points out that this raises an interesting question. He asks,

If reconstruction of stimuli from other senses is indeed the case, then why do we not find out-of-body perceptions from a supine or prone or even a sitting position, at least occasionally? Using Blackmore's explanations and given the preliminary nature of Nigro and Neisser's study, which in any event found that field memories— that is, memories from the original perspective—occur more frequently than observer memories, one would expect NDErs to say that during an OBE they looked up to see living relatives and/or medical providers.[13]

Given the extremely tenuous support provided by the work of Nigro and Neisser and of Siegel for her theory, on which it is based, and given the prediction that a mental reconstruction of memories in which field memories predominate should yield at least some, if not many, sightings from a prone perspective, Serdahely seems correct in concluding that Blackmore's theory of the OBE "just does not seem to hold up."

NEURAL DISINHIBITION AND THE OUT-OF-BODY EXPERIENCE

At several points in *Dying to Live,* a case is made that the disinhibition of brain cells may be an important factor in leading the dying brain to produce NDEs. As described earlier, neurons interact with each other by sending chemical messages across the synaptic gaps that separate them. These messages have two main effects, either to excite the next cell or to inhibit it. Blackmore cites a study of the effects of anoxia on rat brain cells in support of the idea that anoxia abolishes inhibitory potentials before excitatory ones. Based on this, she postulates that with anoxia affecting large areas of the brain, we should expect global disinhibition and therefore random excitation of whole brain areas.

Blackmore writes that there are other substances or conditions known to cause cortical disinhibition, such as psychedelic drugs, surgical anesthetics, temporal lobe seizures, brain chemicals such as endorphins, fever, and exhaustion. Several of these substances or conditions have been associated with OBEs, NDEs, or both. She concludes, "The key is not in anoxia itself but in the disinhibition and consequent excitation it can produce. It may well be that this kind of disorganized activation is the common thread running through *all* the experiences we are considering."[14]

Blackmore asks, "Why . . . should disinhibition and random excitation produce NDEs"?[15] and answers that question with a materialist response. Serdahely, not being committed to a materialist position, examined the same data and points out another possible interpretation:

> However, it is possible that the disinhibition she described in the visual cortex and especially in the temporal lobes with its concomitant neural excitation may be the physiological condition that 'opens the gate,' so to speak, to release the soul from the physical body. After all, if there is a soul, then it has to interface with the physical body somehow.[16]

This is an intriguing suggestion, one that proposes that at least some OBEs experienced during non-life-threatening circumstances involve a genuine separation, with neural disinhibition being the mechanism that separates mind from body.

PERCEPTION OF DEAD RELATIVES

Serdahely is mentioned twice in *Dying to Live,* in connection with two cases he has researched. The first concerns a seven-year-old boy, Pat, who was fishing with a friend from a bridge when he fell off. He dropped about ten feet and hit his head on a rock in the pond below, where he spent five to ten minutes underwater before a police officer rescued him. Pat's heart had stopped beating, and he was not breathing. An ambulance took him to a local hospital, where he was resuscitated, and then he was flown by helicopter to a larger hospital for more specialized care. He was in a coma all that day and the next, but eight days later he was discharged from the hospital.

Later, in a series of interviews with Serdahely, the boy described how he had seen himself in the water, the police officer coming to rescue him, the ambulance ride, and the trip in a blue, orange, and white helicopter with three other people on board. He also described entering a black tunnel, where he met his dog and cat, both of which had died when he was three years old. Blackmore remarks, "This fitted with Serdahely's finding that when children have NDEs and all their loved ones are alive, they tend to have animals or other alternative beings to meet them." She then comments on the case.

Pat was in a coma when transported to the hospital and therefore if he had the details of the helicopter colours and the people on board correct it would be most interesting. Serdahely has been trying to contact the boy's mother for confirmation of these details but has received no replies. This is just one of many cases that may or may not be potential evidence, but frustratingly, we cannot find out.

Blackmore continues:

Serdahely has, however, had more success with another case, that of Ben Bray, a little boy of six.
"I Went to Heaven and Talked to God" says the headline in the tabloid paper, the *Globe;* "Boy, 6, snaps out of coma and bares startling proof." Ben Bray had to have a heart transplant for an inherited heart defect, from which his older brother had already died. Ben was able to describe his journey to a beautiful, light and happy place with angels in white robes and a "big, bright, yellow light far ahead, down a long, long, white room." During his experience he met his [deceased] brother Matthew and his two dead grandfathers, one with black hair and the other with brown. Ben's mother explained that he had only seen his grandfathers—whether in real life or in pictures—with grey hair, so it was surprising that he had these details right. Or, as she puts it in the paper, "It just absolutely stunned us that he got the color of their hair right and that he pinpointed which was which."

Dr. Serdahely wrote to Ben's mother and she replied that the article had exaggerated the story in most parts but confirmed that Ben recalled the colour of his grandfathers' hair. Of course, brown and black are both descriptions that could cover a variety of hair colours and the probability of getting them right by chance is quite high. The case is hardly the "startling proof" of the popular headline.[17]

We may agree that neither of these cases constitutes "startling proof," but they do raise another interesting question that Blackmore simply has not dealt with. Serdahely writes:

> As mentioned, Blackmore attributed the tunnel, light, and noises to disinhibition. With that as my premise, my question is how the dying brain hypothesis accounts for seeing deceased relatives during an NDE. If relatives are encountered in the course of an NDE, almost always they are said to be deceased. So how does the disinhibited brain know to call up these memories only, and not memories or images of living loved ones? It would seem that if the brain alone is responsible for an NDE, then it is more likely that the brain would recall images of *living* loved ones to provide the comfort and assurance that NDErs report from encountered deceased beings . . . if there is a random firing of disinhibited neurons, then why do these neurons almost always produce images of deceased loved ones?[18]

THE PHYSIOLOGY OF THE DYING BRAIN

A major difficulty with all dying brain theories of the NDE is that they assume that clear memories can be formed at a time when cerebral function is severely compromised. We have touched on this issue earlier, in our discussion of anoxia, hypercarbia, and the chemical explanations, but it seems desirable at this point to outline in greater detail what we know about the physiology of the dying brain.

Several of the most scientifically rigorous studies of the NDE have involved interviewing all survivors of cardiac arrest during a set time period, shortly after their resuscitation in a hospital. Such prospective studies have several obvious advantages: the resulting sample is not self-selected, there is a nearly identical control group (the survivors who do not report an NDE), detailed medical records are readily available, and both subjects and witnesses are interviewed shortly after the event. But another excellent advantage of these studies, as physicians Sam Parnia, D. G. Walker, R. Yeates, and Peter Fenwick point out, is that

> the mental state of cardiac arrest survivors is the closest model to that of a dying brain. This is due to the fact that cardiac arrest patients by definition exhibit two out of three criteria required to pronounce an individual dead (no cardiac output, no spontaneous respiratory effort) and usually in the clinical setting of an arrest they develop all three (fixed dilated pupils) due to the loss of brainstem activity.[19]

This British team has undertaken just such a prospective study. In addition, a Dutch team led by cardiologist Pim van Lommel has completed a much larger study using an almost-identical methodology, and the results of these studies have been published in the medical journals *Resuscitation* and *The Lancet,* respectively.[20] Both sets of authors have carefully considered the physiology of the dying brain in relation to their findings on the NDE. As can be gathered from these articles, there is extensive medical literature available on the physiology of cardiac arrest, obtained from studies of both humans and animals. This is what we know.

THE EFFECTS OF CARDIAC ARREST

Weighing approximately three pounds, the human brain is only about 2 percent of the body's mass, yet under normal circumstances it receives 15 percent of the oxygenated blood pumped out by the heart. With its enormous oxygen requirement, the brain is an organ especially dependent on a constant supply of oxygen-rich blood.

After the onset of cardiac arrest, anoxia of the total brain occurs within seconds. As soon as the heart stops, blood flow to the brain ceases, and consciousness is lost within seconds. Breathing soon stops due to anoxia of the lower portion of the brain stem, which controls autonomic functions. As the anoxia continues, other brain stem reflexes are lost, such as the gag reflex and the pupil reflex, leading after a few minutes to fixed, dilated pupils. This loss of function can be reversed by timely and adequate cardiopulmonary resuscitation (CPR), but if the cessation of blood flow to the brain continues for more than five to ten minutes, irreparable damage occurs to the cells of the brain and irreversible brain death is then said to have occurred.

In clinical practice, an electroencephalogram (EEG) monitor is often used to assess the amount of oxygen being received by the brain during cardiac surgery and neurosurgery. Patients have suffered cardiac arrest while connected to an EEG, and the effects of cardiac arrest on brain activity have been well documented. The initial slowing of the EEG waves occurs within an average of 6.5 seconds after circulation stops. Within ten to twenty seconds of cardiac arrest, the monitor shows a flat line.[21]

Strictly speaking, a flat line on the EEG monitor only indicates no electrical activity in the cerebral cortex, the outermost section of the brain. It is currently believed that activity in the cerebral cortex is associated with the higher cognitive functions and that other parts of the brain handle the instinctive drives, motor movements, and autonomic functions such as respiration and digestion. However, it can be argued that even with a flat EEG, some residual consciousness is still possible, sustained by some of the more primitive structures of the brain. Concerning this claim, cardiologist Pim van Lommel has commented:

The frequently cited counter-argument that the loss of blood flow and a flat EEG do not exclude some activity somewhere in the brain, because an EEG is primarily a registration of the electrical activity of the cerebral cortex, misses the point in my view. The issue is not whether there is any immeasurable brain activity of any kind whatsoever, but whether there is any brain activity of the specific form regarded by contemporary neuroscience as essential for the experience of consciousness. And there is no sign whatsoever of those specific forms of cerebral activity in the EEGs of cardiac arrest patients.[22]

Modern neuroscience provides no reason to suppose that some residual consciousness can be sustained during a flat EEG, because no neuroscientific model has ever been proposed that implicates deep brain structures in the kind of higher-level mental activity required to produce or sustain consciousness. Also, during cardiac arrest, blood flow to the brain ceases completely, so it is highly implausible that *any* parts of the brain could remain active in the absence of oxygen and glucose. Finally, studies using animals with electrodes implanted deep in their brains have demonstrated that an absence of cortical activity as measured by the EEG is associated with an absence or reduction in activity of the deep brain structures as well.[23] Shortly after electrical activity in the cerebral cortex disappears, electrical activity in the deeper structures also disappears completely.[24]

In cases of prolonged cardiac arrest, EEG activity may not return to normal for several minutes or even several hours, depending on the duration of cardiac arrest. The duration of arrest also can vary substantially, depending on the location in which the arrest occurs. In a cardiac care unit, it is usually 60 to 120 seconds; on a cardiac ward, two to five minutes; and an out-of-hospital cardiac arrest usually lasts five to ten minutes.[25]

Parnia and Fenwick, both physicians, point out the problems these data cause for any dying brain hypothesis.

The occurrence of lucid, well structured thought processes together with reasoning, attention and memory recall of specific events during a cardiac arrest (NDE) raise a number of interesting and perplexing questions regarding how such experiences could arise. These experiences appear to be occurring at a time when cerebral function can be described at best as severely impaired, and at worst absent. . . . In addition cerebral localization studies have indicated that thought processes are mediated through a number of different cortical areas, rather than single areas of the brain. Therefore a globally disordered brain would not be expected to produce lucid thought processes.

From a clinical point of view any acute alteration in cerebral physiology such as occurring in hypoxia, hypercarbia, metabolic, and drug induced disturbances and seizures leads to disorganized and compromised cerebral function. Furthermore . . . any reduction in cerebral blood flow leads to impaired attention and higher cerebral function. . . . NDEs in cardiac arrest are clearly not confusional and in fact indicate heightened awareness, attention and consciousness at a time when consciousness and memory would not be expected to occur.[26]

The only alternative is to argue that these experiences occur as consciousness is being lost or recovered. One problem with the first possibility is that with cardiac arrest the transition to unconsciousness can occur within a second and often appears immediate to the subject. Another problem is that any sort of insult to the brain typically results in a loss of memory, and the length of amnesia before and after unconsciousness is typically used to assess the severity of the injury. The major difficulty with the idea that the experiences occur during recovery is that recovery from any sort of insult to the brain is via a state of confusion. Even recovery from simple fainting is recovery via a confusional process. An acute cerebral insult results in even greater confusion. So it seems hard to imagine how experiences during a confused mental state could result in clear memories of an NDE. Peter Fenwick, in the large-scale study he conducted with his wife, Elizabeth Fenwick, found several specific accounts that illustrated this point.

We had patients who were head-injured and whose arousal was confusional and showed all the characteristics and mental states that would be expected after a severe head injury. Yet within this dense confusional state, but attributed by the individual to the time of unconsciousness, was full memory of a wonderfully clear NDE. It is worth noting that in severe head injury memory for the accident and for the confusional awakening in hospital is absent, and this was so in our cases of head injury. Except by special pleading, it is not possible with our current understanding of cerebral functioning to explain, on a simple chemical theory, how, within dense unconsciousness and with absence of memory, the brain can structure and remember a clear comprehensive experience. This is an interesting point and is a challenge to our current understanding of brain function.[27]

Finally, patients almost invariably think that their NDE occurred during the time they appeared to be unconscious, and not during recovery. This, by itself, is of course no guarantee that the experience did not in fact occur during recovery. But the reports of patients being able to see and recall detailed events that occurred during the period they seemed to be unconscious that are later corroborated by hospital staff, such as details relating to their resuscitation, cannot be explained away as imaginative reconstruction. This leads us to the strongest evidence against the dying brain hypothesis.

FOURTEEN

VERIDICAL NEAR-DEATH
EXPERIENCES

In her 1993 book *Dying to Live,* Blackmore reviewed several anecdotal reports of individuals who claimed to have had accurate perception of the immediate environment at the time they remembered being out of their bodies. She proposes several counter-explanations and concludes, "The suspicion must be, rightly or wrongly, that there may be no properly corroborated cases that cannot be accounted for by the perfectly normal processes of imagination, memory, chance and the use of the remaining senses."[1]

Her comments were perhaps justified at the time they were written. As mentioned earlier, it has been rare for investigators to provide corroborating evidence to support claims that events or objects were seen in a way that defies a normal explanation. Many of these reports were gathered years after the experience, and by this time potential witnesses were often simply unavailable. However, perhaps because Blackmore's critique served as a wake-up call, researchers have since gathered several impressive and corroborated accounts of accurate perception of events that occurred during the time subjects were considered comatose, yet they remembered being conscious observers, located outside of their bodies.

In 2007, NDE researcher Janice Holden searched for every single case of apparently veridical perception during an NDE that had been reported since 1975. She found 107 such cases, from thirty-nine different publications by thirty-seven different authors or author teams. Using the most stringent criterion—that a case would be classified as inaccurate if even one detail was found to not correspond to reality—Holden found that only 8 percent involved some inaccuracy. In contrast, 37 percent of the cases—almost five times as many—were determined to be accurate by independent objective sources, such as the investigation of researchers reporting the cases.[2]

Some NDEs do involve perceptual errors, and it would indeed be surprising if no errors were ever reported. Human beings, after all, are fallible. It would also be surprising if people never hallucinated while near death. However, as Holden remarks, these results "certainly call into question how an allegedly hallucinatory phenomenon could produce only 8 percent of cases with any apparent error whatsoever and 37 percent of cases with apparently completely accurate content that had been objectively verified."[3]

Let us now examine some of these cases in detail.

CASE OF THE MISSING DENTURES

Results from one of the largest scientific studies of the NDE ever undertaken were reported in a 2001 issue of the medical journal *The Lancet*. The methodology of the study involved interviewing 344 consecutive patients who were successfully resuscitated after cardiac arrest in ten Dutch hospitals. The researchers compared medical, psychological, and demographic data between patients who reported an NDE after resuscitation and those who did not. In addition, the two groups were reinterviewed two and eight years later to study the long-term aftereffects and to see if the stories changed as time passed.

The researchers found that sixty-two patients (18 percent) reported an NDE, which forty-one (12 percent) described a notably deep or a "core" experience. None of the patients reported a distressing or frightening NDE, and no medical or psychological factor affected the likelihood of the experience.

In an early phase of the study, a coronary-care-unit nurse reported the following experience of a resuscitated patient. It concerns a man, comatose and turning blue from lack of oxygen, who had been brought in by ambulance during a night shift.

After admission, he receives artificial respiration without intubation, while heart massage and defibrillation are also applied. When we want to intubate the patient, he turns out to have dentures in his mouth. I remove these upper dentures and put them onto the "crash car."* Meanwhile, we continue extensive CPR. After about an hour and a half the patient has sufficient heart rhythm and blood pressure, but he is still ventilated and intubated, and he is still comatose. He is transferred to the intensive care unit to continue the necessary artificial respiration. Only after more than a week do I meet again with the patient, who is by now back on the cardiac ward. I distribute his medication. The moment he sees me he says: "Oh, that nurse knows where my dentures are." I am very surprised. Then he elucidates: "Yes, you were there when I was brought into hospital and you took my dentures out of my mouth and put them onto that car, it had all these bottles on it and there was this sliding drawer underneath and there you put my teeth." I was especially amazed because I remembered this happening while the man was in deep coma and in the process of CPR. When I asked further, it appeared the man had seen himself lying in bed, that he had perceived from above how nurses and doctors had been busy with CPR. He was also able to describe correctly and in detail the small room in which he had been resuscitated as well as the appearance of those present like myself. At the time that he observed the situation he had been very much afraid that we would stop CPR and that he would die. And it is true that we had been very negative about the patient's prognosis due to his very poor medical condition when admitted. The patient tells me that he desperately and unsuccessfully tried to make it clear

---

*A crash car (or "cart") is a cabinet on wheels containing equipment needed to resuscitate someone who "crashes" (has a cardiac arrest).

to us that he was still alive and that we should continue CPR. He is deeply impressed by his experience and says he is no longer afraid of death. 4 weeks later he left hospital as a healthy man.[4]

"FLAPPING HIS ARMS AS IF TRYING TO FLY . . ."

The following case was reported to researchers in 1990. Two years earlier, fifty-six-year-old van driver Al Sullivan was taken to Hartford Hospital in Connecticut to have an irregular heartbeat diagnosed. During diagnostic testing, one of his coronary arteries became blocked and he was rushed into the operating room for bypass surgery. During the operation, he had a clear sensation of leaving his body in an upward direction. He also reported that, to his amazement, he saw himself lying on a table covered with light blue sheets, with his chest cut open. But this was not all he apparently saw.

> I was able to see my surgeon, who just moments ago had explained to me what he was going to do during my operation. He appeared to be somewhat perplexed. I thought he was flapping his arms as if trying to fly. . . . It was at this point I noticed one of the three figures I saw on my arrival . . . was that of my brother-in-law who had died almost two years before. . . . It was then that I turned my attention to the lower right-hand side of the place I was at. I saw the most brilliant yellow light coming from, what appeared to be, a very well lit tunnel. . . . The light that came from the tunnel was of a golden yellow hue and although the brightest I had ever looked into, it was of no discomfort to the eyes at all. Then, preceded by warmth, joy and peace and a feeling of being loved, a brown cloaked figure drifted out of the light toward me. As my euphoria rose still more, I, much to my delight, recognized it to be that of my mother. My mother had died at age thirty-seven when I was seven years old. I am now in my fifties and the first thought that came to my mind was how young my mother appeared. She smiled at me and appeared to be shaping words with her mouth and these was [sic] not audible

to me. Through thought transfer we were soon able to communicate. All at once my mother's expression changed to that of concern. At this point she left my side and drifted down toward my surgeon. She placed the surgeon's hand on the left side of my heart and then returned to me. I recall the surgeon making a sweeping motion as if trying to rid the area of a flying insect. My mother then extended one of her hands to me, but try as I might I could not grasp it. She then smiled and drifted back toward the lit tunnel . . .[5]

Shortly after he regained consciousness, Sullivan told his cardiologist, Anthony LaSala, what he had observed during the operation. The cardiologist's first reaction was to attribute Sullivan's experience to the anesthetics he had been given. When Sullivan then described seeing the cardiac surgeon, Hiroyoshi Takata, flapping his elbows as if to fly, LaSala's eyes widened, and he asked who had told Sullivan about that. Sullivan told the physician that he had seen it himself, from above his body in the operating room. LaSala then explained that this was a peculiar habit of Takata's: if the surgeon had not yet scrubbed in and did not want his hands touching anything, he would flatten his palms against his chest and give instructions to his assistants by pointing with his elbows.

In the fall of 1997, psychiatrist and NDE researcher Bruce Greyson spoke with both Takata and LaSala. Takata could not remember if he had flapped his elbows during Sullivan's surgery, but he did confirm that this is a regular habit of his. LaSala confirmed to Greyson that Sullivan had told him about the experience shortly after he regained consciousness. He also confirmed that Takata has this peculiar habit of flapping his elbows, and he added that he has never seen any other surgeon do this.

OPERATION "STANDSTILL"

The following case concerns one of the deepest NDEs ever reported. The experience occurred during neurosurgery at the Barrow Neurological Institute in Phoenix, Arizona, on an August morning in 1991. Thirty-five-year-old Pam Reynolds was being operated on for a giant aneurysm in the wall of her basilar artery, located at the base of her brain. A weakness in the wall of the large artery had caused it to balloon out like a bubble on the side of a faulty inner tube. Unless removed, the eventual rupture of the aneurysm would be immediately fatal.

Pam had been referred to surgeon Robert Spetzler of the Barrow Institute, as Spetzler had pioneered a daring surgical procedure known as hypothermic cardiac arrest that would allow Pam's aneurysm to be removed with a reasonable chance of success. This operation, nicknamed "standstill" by the surgeons who perform it, would require her body temperature to be lowered to sixty degrees Fahrenheit, her heartbeat and breathing stopped, the electrical activity in her brain extinguished, and the blood drained from her head. In ordinary clinical terms, Pam would be dead.

This extraordinary episode in the history of NDE research is described in great detail by Michael Sabom in chapter 3 of his book *Light and Death*. As Sabom notes, the medical documentation of the events surrounding this case "*far exceeds* any recorded before and provides us with our most complete scientific glimpse yet into the near-death experience."[6]

As described by Sabom, Pam was wheeled into the operating room at 7:15 a.m., given general anesthesia to induce unconsciousness, and then prepped for surgery. Instruments were set up to monitor her blood pressure, body temperature, and heartbeat. In addition, EEG electrodes were taped to her head to record brain activity in the cerebral cortex. The auditory nerve center located in the brain stem was tested repeatedly using 100 decibel clicks emitted from small speakers inserted into her ears, at a rate of 11.3 per second, creating a loud staccato noise in both ears. As long as Pam's brain stem was still functioning, these clicks would evoke sharp spikes on the electrogram.

By 8:40 a.m., Pam was ready for surgery, and over twenty physicians, nurses, and technicians had scrubbed in. Spetzler began the surgery by opening the scalp with a surgical blade, and folded the scalp back to expose the skull. A nurse handed Spetzler the Midas Rex pneumatically powered bone saw, and a loud buzzing noise filled the room as the thumb-sized motor hidden in the brass head of the bone saw revved up. Spetzler then began to carve out a section of Pam's skull. According to Pam, her experience began at about this time.

> The next thing I recall was the sound: It was a natural *D*. As I listened to the sound, I felt it was pulling me out of the top of my head. The further out of my body I got, the more clear the tone became. I had the impression it was like a road, a frequency that you go on. . . . I remember seeing several things in the operating room when I was looking down. It was the most aware that I think I have ever been in my entire life. . . . I was metaphorically sitting on Dr. Spetzler's shoulder. It wasn't like normal vision. It was brighter and more focused and clearer than normal vision. . . . There was so much in the operating room that I didn't recognize, and so many people.
>
> I thought the way they had my head shaved was very peculiar. I expected them to take all of the hair, but they did not. . . .
>
> The saw thing that I hated the sound of looked like an electric toothbrush and it had a dent in it, a groove at the top where the saw appeared to go into the handle, but it didn't. . . . And the saw had interchangeable blades, too, but these blades were in what looked like a socket wrench case. . . . I heard the saw crank up. I didn't see them use it on my head, but I think I heard it being used on something. It was humming at a relatively high pitch and then all of a sudden it went *Brrrrrrrrrr!* like that.[7]

Spetzler removed the section of bone from Pam's skull, exposing the outermost membrane of her brain. This was cut open with scissors, and the operating microscope was swung into position. While this was going on, a female cardiac surgeon located the femoral artery and vein in Pam's right groin. These vessels turned out to be too small to handle the large flow of blood required by the cardiopulmonary bypass machine, and so the left femoral artery and vein were prepared instead. Pam later claimed to remember this point in the surgery:

I distinctly remember a female voice saying "We have a problem. Her arteries are too small." And then a male voice: "Try the other side." It seemed to come from further down the table. I do remember wondering "what are they doing there," because this is brain surgery![8]

After cutting through the tough fibrous membrane, Spetzler probed deep into Pam's brain until he located the aneurysm on the neck of the giant basilar artery. As feared, it turned out to be, as Spetzler noted in his medical records, "extremely large and extended up into the brain." The risky procedure of hypothermic cardiac arrest (operation standstill) would unfortunately be needed.

At 10:50 a.m., the cardiac surgeon and heart-pump technicians inserted tubes into the femoral artery and vein and connected these tubes to plastic hoses leading to and from the cardiopulmonary bypass machine. Warm blood traveled from the artery into the large reservoir cylinders of the bypass machine, where it was cooled before being returned to Pam's body. Pam's body temperature began to fall.

At 11:00 a.m., Pam's core body temperature had dropped twenty-five degrees, and the cardiac monitor's warning tone indicated cardiac malfunction. Pam's heart began beating in the irregular, disorganized pattern known as ventricular fibrillation. Sabom describes what the surgical team did next.

Five minutes later, the remaining electrical spasms of Pam's dying heart were extinguished with massive intravenous doses of potassium chloride. Cardiac arrest was complete.

As Pam's heart arrested, her brain waves flattened into complete electrocerebral silence. Brain-stem function weakened as the clicks from the ear speakers produced lower and lower spikes on the monitoring electrogram.

Twenty minutes later, her core body temperature had fallen another 13 degrees to a tomblike 60 degrees Fahrenheit. The clicks from her ear speakers no longer elicited a response. Total brain shutdown.

Then, at precisely 11:25 a.m., Pam was subjected to one of the most daring and remarkable surgical maneuvers ever performed in an operating room. The head of the operating table was tilted up, the cardiopulmonary bypass machine was turned off, and the blood was drained from Pam's body like oil from a car.[9]

Pam recalled that sometime during this period she felt a sensation of being pulled quickly through a vortex that she describes as being "like a tunnel but it wasn't a tunnel."

At some point very early in the tunnel vortex I became aware of my grandmother calling me. But I didn't hear her call me with my ears. . . . It was a clearer hearing than with my ears. I trust the sense more than I trust my own ears. The feeling was that she wanted me to come to her, so I continued with no fear down the shaft. It's a dark shaft that I went through, and at the very end there was this very little tiny pinpoint of light that kept getting bigger and bigger and bigger.

Pam describes how she entered the light and there sensed presences that at first she could not see. Then she was able to discern different figures in the light, which slowly began to form shapes she could recognize.

I could see that one of them was my grandmother. I don't know if it was reality or projection, but I would know my grandmother, the sound of her, anytime, anywhere.

Everyone I saw, looking back on it, fit perfectly into my understanding of what that person looked like at their best during their lives.

I recognized a lot of people. My uncle Gene was there. So was my great-great Aunt Maggie, who was really a cousin. On Papa's side of the family, my grandfather was there. . . . They were specifically taking care of me, looking after me.

They would permit me to go no further. . . . It was communicated to me—that's the best way I know how to say it, because they didn't speak like I'm speaking—that if I went all the way into the light something would happen to me physically. They would be unable to put this me back into the body me, like I had gone too far and they couldn't reconnect. So they wouldn't let me go anywhere or do anything.

When all the blood had drained from Pam's brain, the aneurysm "collapsed like a deflated balloon." It was removed by Spetzler, the cardiopulmonary machine was turned back on, and warmed blood was pumped back into Pam's body. As her body temperature began to rise, blips on the electrogram registered the first signs of life as the brain stem began to again respond to the clicking speakers in Pam's ears. Soon after, waves on the EEG screen indicated electrical activity in her higher brain centers. Pam's body appeared to be waking up.

Then, at noon, the surgical team faced a serious problem. The initially silent heart monitor indicated Pam's heart was beating again, but with the irregular rhythm of ventricular fibrillation. If not corrected, Pam's heart would be damaged within minutes. The cardiac surgeon placed the two defibrillator paddles on Pam's chest and shocked her heart. When 50 joules of electricity produced no response, the machine was charged with 100 joules. A second jolt restored the normal heart rhythm, bringing sighs of relief from the cardiac surgical team, who were preparing to cut open her chest.

Pam described how her NDE came to a close:

My grandmother didn't take me back through the tunnel, or even send me back or ask me to go. She just looked up at me. I expected to go with her, but it was communicated to me that she just didn't think she would do that. My uncle said he would do it. He's the one who took me back through the end of the tunnel. Everything was fine. I did want to go.

But then I got to the end of it and saw the thing, my body. I didn't want to get into it. . . . It looked terrible, like a train wreck. I looked like what it was: dead. I believe it was covered. It scared me and I didn't want to look at it.

It was communicated to me that it was like jumping into a swimming pool. No problem, just jump right into the swimming pool. I didn't want to, but I guess I was late or something because he [the uncle] pushed me. I felt a definite repelling and at the same time a pulling from the body. The body was pulling and the tunnel was pushing. . . . It was like diving into a pool of ice water. . . . It hurt!

By 12:32 p.m., Pam's body was warmed to a life-sustaining but still subnormal temperature of 89.6 degrees, and the bypass machine was turned off. Her surgical wounds were closed, and the record indicates that at 2:10 p.m., she was taken to the recovery room in stable condition.

By three clinical tests—flat EEG, no brain stem activity, no blood flowing through the brain—Pam's brain was dead, with almost certainly no activity whatsoever. Yet Pam reported the deepest NDE ever investigated by Sabom.

Pam was interviewed on CBS's *48 Hours,* along with Sabom and Spetzler. As Pam's attending surgeon, Spetzler left no doubt about Pam's clinical condition during hypothermic cardiac arrest: "If you would examine that patient from a clinical perspective during that hour, that patient by all definition would be dead. At this point there is no brain activity, no blood going through the brain. Nothing, nothing, nothing."[10]

Like the Dutch patient and Al Sullivan, Pam Reynolds described seeing events, from an elevated location, that could not have been perceived or inferred by auditory means. Initially, Sabom was very skeptical when he first listened to Pam's description of a bone saw that "looked like an electric toothbrush" with "interchangeable blades." But he was shocked at the accuracy of Pam's description when he received a user manual from the Midas Rex Company in Fort Worth, Texas. Photographs from the manual show a tool that resembles an electric toothbrush, with interchangeable blades that are stored in what Pam described as a "socket wrench case."[11]

In addition, Pam reported that shortly after part of her skull was removed, she heard a female voice say "something about my veins and arteries being very small," and the medical records indicate that words to this effect were indeed spoken.[12] At the time, Pam's ears were blocked by small molded speakers inserted to monitor the auditory nerve center in her brain stem. The speakers continuously played 100 decibel clicks into her ears at a rate of 11.3 per second (100 decibels is about the level a symphony orchestra plays at full volume. Prolonged exposure to sound more intense than 85 decibels will cause hearing loss).*

Although her brain stem response was absent during removal of the aneurysm, it was not yet absent when the surgeon began cutting into her skull or at the time the cardiac surgeon made the remarks that she remembers hearing. In other words, the veridical parts of Pam's experience—that is, the parts that were later verified as genuine by others—occurred while she was not yet clinically dead, but was under heavy general anesthetic, with her eyes taped shut and molded speakers playing 100-decibel clicks into her ears.

Therefore, it does not seem at all plausible that Pam could have overheard operating room conversation in the normal fashion. Sabom writes, "These speakers occlude the ear canals and altogether eliminate the possibility of physical hearing."[13]

In 2007, in response to skeptical objections that Pam may have simply overheard the surgeon's remarks, Sabom added even more detail to this account.

Steven Cordova, Neuroscience Manager at the Barrow Neurological Institute, who was the intraoperative technologist responsible for inserting small molded speakers into Spetzler's patients in the early 1990s when Reynolds's surgery was performed, told me that after these speakers were molded into each external auditory canal, they were further affixed with "mounds of tape and gauze to seal securely the ear piece into the ear canal." This "tape and gauze" would "cover

---

*Studies estimate that up to 52 percent of orchestra musicians may suffer some degree of noise-induced hearing loss (Stephen Strauss, "Piccolo Peril," *The Globe and Mail* [Toronto], May 18, 1996).

the whole ear pinnae" making it extremely unlikely that Reynolds could have physically overheard operating room conversation one hour and twenty minutes after anesthesia had been induced.[14]

Ordinary conversation is at around 60 decibels, and the 100 decibel clicks were 10,000 times more intense than that.* In her testimony, Pam neither mentions hearing loud clicks nor struggling to hear through them.

Pam's neurosurgeon Dr. Robert Spetzler added these words:

I don't think that the observations she made were based on what she experienced as she went into the operating theater. They were just not available to her. For example, the drill and so on, those things are all covered up. They aren't visible; they were inside their packages. You really don't begin to open until the patient is completely asleep, so that you maintain a sterile environment. . . . At that stage in the operation nobody can observe, hear in that state. And I find it inconceivable that the normal senses, such as hearing, let alone the fact that she had clicking modules in each ear, that there was any way for her to hear through normal auditory pathways. I don't have an explanation for it. I don't know how it's possible for it to happen.[15]

The other parts of Pam's NDE involved a journey through a dark shaft toward a pinpoint of light that grew larger and brighter as she approached, entering the light, and meeting there with several deceased relatives before being sent back to her body, which was described by Pam as looking "like what it was: dead." Her experience clearly began before standstill was initiated, which raises the question, did her NDE continue during the period of flat EEG and no blood flow to the brain? As Sabom correctly points out,

---

*The decibel scale is a logarithmic scale based on multiples of ten, so a sound at 70 decibels is ten times more intense than a sound at 60 decibels. Perceived loudness depends on both intensity and frequency, and so loudness is partially a function of intensity, but not exactly the same.

The question is not when Reynolds's NDE *began* but when it *ended*. Reynolds described her NDE as an uninterrupted, continuous experience perceived to be as real at the beginning, during her "out-of-body" experience, as it was throughout. According to her, the NDE ended at the close of surgery around 2:00 P.M., a time frame that included the period of "standstill" and "flat EEG."

My construction of Reynolds's combined autoscopic and transcendental NDE as a continuous, unbroken encounter was based entirely on her testimony—testimony correlated at times with events in the operating room. Interestingly, Reynolds's claim of continuity within her experiences is consistent with virtually all other reports of combined NDEs that I have studied over the past 30 years.[16]

What about the time delay between the operation and the time Sabom interviewed her? Pam's operation occurred in August 1991, but Sabom did not interview her until November 11, 1994. Could Pam's memory of the event have become embellished during the three-year interval?

Not likely. Several independent statistical studies have demonstrated no significant alteration in peoples' memories of NDEs over years, or even over decades. Greyson, for instance, readministered a questionnaire to seventy-two individuals who had been given an identical questionnaire after their NDE an average of almost twenty years previous, in order to compare the responses. Detailed statistical analysis revealed, "Contrary to expectations, accounts of near-death experiences were not embellished over a period of almost two decades. These data support the reliability of near-death experience accounts."[17]

Pam's case is one of the best documented and most extraordinary NDEs ever reported. Other extraordinary cases of visual perception during an NDE have come from those who normally have little or no visual perception at all.

FIFTEEN

NEAR-DEATH EXPERIENCES OF PEOPLE WHO ARE BLIND

For decades there had been rumors of NDEs occurring to people who are blind, in which they could clearly see their surroundings while seemingly outside of their bodies. These stories remained little more than unsubstantiated anecdotes until researchers Kenneth Ring and Sharon Cooper launched an in-depth investigation of NDEs in people who are blind, and published their results in a book they titled *Mindsight*.

These researchers found twenty-one cases in which people who were blind had an NDE, which was defined as "any type of conscious experience associated with a condition that was unquestionably life-threatening, regardless of whether it conformed to the familiar classic pattern of the Moody-type NDE."[1] Out of these twenty-one cases, fifteen individuals claimed to have some sort of sight during their NDE, three were not sure whether they saw or not, and the remaining three did not appear to see at all. Ring and Cooper also collected ten cases of OBEs not associated with a medical crisis, and here the figures are even more impressive: nine out of ten people who were blind claimed to have had sight while they remembered being out of their bodies (the other person was not sure). Their total sample included fourteen individuals who were blind from birth, and from among this group, nine individuals, or 64 percent, reported sight during an NDE or OBE.

Ring and Cooper summarize what people who are blind tend to report seeing in these circumstances.

> In general, blind people report the same kinds of visual impressions as sighted persons do in describing NDEs and OBEs. For example, ten of our twenty-one NDErs said they had some kind of vision of their physical body, and seven of our ten OBErs said likewise. Occasionally, there are other this-worldly perceptions as well, such as seeing a medical team at work on one's body or seeing various features of the room or surroundings where one's physical body was. Otherworldly perceptions abound also, and seem to take the form characteristic for transcendental NDEs of sighted persons—radiant light, otherworldly landscapes, angels or religious figures, deceased relatives, and so forth.[2]

These visual perceptions also tended to be "extremely clear and detailed, especially when they found themselves in the otherworldly portions of their near-death journeys."[3]

Here is one example of apparent visual perception by a woman who was blind and who experienced cardiac arrest while at home. The case did not come from Ring and Cooper's sample, but was forwarded to them by a Swedish colleague, Ingegerd Bergstrom, a nurse and NDE researcher.

> This woman had the ability only to distinguish light and darkness. She could, for example, see daylight coming through a window in an otherwise darkened room. She could not, however, make out silhouettes nor walk in dimly lit corridors.
>
> She had suffered from this limited vision for many years when she had a cardiac arrest at home. At that moment, she was sitting in the kitchen by her kitchen table. A sink was nearby, but she later claimed that she had not seen it for the past ten years.
>
> When this woman came to be interviewed, she arrived in a

wheelchair, accompanied by her husband, and agreed to allow the interview to be tape-recorded.

At one point, in asking her a question, I expressed myself badly by saying, "Did you on any occasion see? . . ." That was very embarrassing because I knew she was blind. Her husband reacted with disappointment, which was obvious to me by the look on his face and his body language.

But the woman herself, on the contrary, was pleased at the question, and answered: "It's fine you ask about that because there is one thing that I thought a lot about. When I had my cardiac arrest, I suddenly saw the sink with the surroundings—and I hadn't seen any of that for ten years."

The husband reacted with surprise, and wondered why she didn't tell him that. He always thought she told him everything. She answered then "You never asked if I saw anything at the time my heart stopped." She then told how the sink "appeared out of the fog." And that there was unwashed china piled up in it.

That was the husband's responsibility and he looked very guilty. . . .[4]

Another case described by Ring and Cooper came from their own study and is backed up by independent witnesses and medical records. It concerns a woman named Nancy who entered a California hospital in September 1991 for what was supposed to be a routine biopsy of a large tumor in her chest. Unfortunately, in the course of the operation, the major vein that returns blood from the upper body to the heart, the superior vena cava, was accidentally cut. In the resulting panic, the vein was accidentally sewn shut, blocking the flow of blood, without anyone realizing this had been done. In the recovery room several hours later, Nancy's upper extremities began to swell and turn purple. Nancy remembers waking up and telling people, "I'm blind, I'm blind," with medical staff thinking that her inability to see was due to the swelling in her head.

At some point after waking, Nancy stopped breathing and lost consciousness. A device known as an "ambu bag" was strapped over her nose and mouth, forcing her to breath, and she was wheeled out of recovery on a gurney to have an angiogram. On the way to the x-ray room, the panicked staff slammed the gurney into the elevator door, at which point Nancy's experience began.

> I was on the gurney. I wasn't really aware of what I looked like but as the gurney hit the elevator I stepped out of myself, stood, like next to the elevator, and was watching. I then looked away from myself on the gurney and looked down the hall about fifteen or twenty feet. And there were two men standing there. One of the men was/is my son's father. I have an eight-and-a-half-year-old son. The other man was my lover at the time. And they were just standing there—just kind of looking. And I thought to myself, "Why aren't they coming up and doing something or saying something? You know, this is probably going to be the last chance they're gonna have to see me."[5]

At this point, Nancy remembers noticing a beautiful white light, clear and focused, and then moving toward the light. After entering the light, she remembers being urged to return and eventually deciding to come back.

Ring and Cooper retrieved Nancy's medical records, which essentially confirm the details of her surgical mishap. They also interviewed the two men Nancy claims to have seen standing in the hall while her body was on the gurney. Both men corroborated the essential details of Nancy's story. Leon, her lover at the time of the mishap, described seeing Nancy being wheeled out of the recovery room toward the elevator, with her face and body greatly swollen.

> I think I was still in a state of shock. I mean, it had been a long day for me. You're expecting an hour procedure and here it is, approximately ten hours later and you don't have very many answers. I believe a nurse did. I know I asked. And I think Dick [the father of Nancy's child] was there at the same time. I think he and I were talking in the hallway. . . . I believe Dick was right next to me as

well. . . . She was on the gurney. There were IVs . . . I'm not sure—I think she had some sort of a breathing apparatus. I'm not sure if it was an ambu bag or what it was.[6]

Ring and Cooper also consulted an ophthalmologist, who concurred that the obstruction of the superior vena cava could damage the optic nerve within minutes, causing complete cortical blindness. From Leon's notes and Nancy's medical records, it is clear that at least six hours, and probably more, had passed from the time her vein was accidentally sewn shut until she was wheeled out on the gurney in the presence of Leon and Dick. From the medical records and the testimony of the three individuals, the researchers concluded:

Therefore, it is certainly possible, even highly likely, that Nancy's assertion that she was blind at that moment was true and that she couldn't have seen these men through normal vision. But even if she *had* retained some residual physical vision at this time, having the ambu bag on her head, as we discovered when we examined this device ourselves, would have prevented the kind of lateral vision necessary to see them from her supine position, to say nothing of the obstructive shield provided by the attendants surrounding her gurney.[7]

SIXTEEN

THE SCIENTIFIC CHALLENGE
TO MATERIALISM

It is only in searching for refutations that science can hope to learn and to advance. It is only in considering how its various theories stand up to tests that it can distinguish between better and worse theories and so find a criterion of progress.

KARL POPPER, *CONJECTURES AND REFUTATIONS*

The cases above seem to provide strong evidence that consciousness and perception can operate independently of a properly functioning brain and sense organs. Materialism simply cannot accommodate corroborated reports of enhanced mental processes and accurate perception of the environment at a time when brain processes are severely impaired or entirely absent.

As we have seen, a variety of alternative psychological and physiological explanations have been proposed, and so the interpretation of the NDE as a genuine separation of mind and body is still strongly resisted by many scientists and philosophers. Many more simply ignore the evidence that appears to prove materialism false, including the other lines of evidence, such as the evidence for reincarnation, apparitions, and messages from the dead, that will be discussed in the next book of this series. When such scientists and philosophers are confronted with the evidence, their reaction is often anything but rational. Philosopher Neal Grossman describes how he discovered this for himself.

> I was devouring everything on the near-death experience I could get my hands on, and eager to share what I was discovering with colleagues. It was unbelievable to me how dismissive they were of the evidence. "Drug-induced hallucinations," "last gasp of a dying brain," and "people see what they want to see" were some of the commonly used phrases. One conversation in particular caused me to see more clearly the fundamental irrationality of academics with respect to the evidence against materialism.
>
> I asked, "What about people who accurately report the details of their operation?"
>
> "Oh," came the reply, "they probably just subconsciously heard the conversation in the operating room, and their brain subconsciously transposed the audio information into a visual format."
>
> "Well," I responded, "what about cases where people report veridical perception of events remote from their body?"
>
> "Oh, that's just a coincidence or a lucky guess."
>
> Exasperated, I asked, "What will it take, short of having a near-death experience yourself, to convince you that it's real?"
>
> Very nonchalantly, without batting an eye, the response was: "Even if I were to have a near-death experience myself, I would conclude that I was hallucinating, rather than believe that my mind can exist independently of my brain."[1]*

In other words, Grossman's colleague simply stated that nothing could possibly convince him that materialism was false. Like others before him, Grossman realized at that moment that for some people materialism is

---

*Grossman's article is well worth reading, as it is an excellent discussion of the collective irrationality of the academic world with respect to the evidence against materialism (Grossman 2002).

an ideology, a dogma. For such individuals, materialism is not a scientific hypothesis that is open to potentially being proved false; it is an article of faith that "must" be true, regardless of evidence to the contrary. As Grossman shrewdly pointed out, a complicating factor is that materialists are typically under the impression that their belief in materialism is not ideological, but empirical. That is, they talk as though their adherence to materialism is rigorously scientific, when in fact it is merely an expression of faith.

It is this confusion, this implicit equation of materialism with science, that explains the widespread practice of ignoring and dismissing the objectionable evidence as somehow "unscientific." Materialism is upheld as an incontestable dogma on which, it is thought, rests the entire edifice of science. But the difference between science and ideology is not that they are based on different dogmas; rather, it is that scientific beliefs are *not* held as dogmas, but are open to testing and hence possible rejection. Science cannot be an objective process of discovery if it is wedded to a metaphysical belief that is accepted without question and that leads to the exclusion of certain lines of evidence on the grounds that these lines of evidence contradict the metaphysical belief.

Grossman makes this point clearly:

Science is a methodological process of discovering truths about reality. Insofar as science is an objective process of discovery, it is, and must be, metaphysically neutral. Insofar as science is not metaphysically neutral, but instead weds itself to a particular metaphysical theory, such as materialism, it cannot be an objective process for discovery. There is much confusion on this point, because many people equate science with materialist metaphysics, and phenomena that fall outside the scope of such metaphysics, and hence cannot be explained in physical terms, are called "unscientific." This is a most unfortunate usage of the term. For if souls and spirits are in fact a part of reality, and science is conceived epistemologically as a system of investigation of reality, then there is no reason why science cannot devise appropriate methods to investigate souls and spirits.[2]

If science is metaphysically neutral, then lines of evidence can be admitted that not only contradict materialism as a metaphysical theory, but prove materialism false as a scientific hypothesis. But the equation of materialism with science is so deeply ingrained in the academic establishment that even some sophisticated near-death researchers fall prey to it. For instance, Peter Fenwick and Elizabeth Fenwick write:

> So far we've taken a largely scientific, and therefore a rather limited, view of the NDE. We've been looking at mechanism, and almost everything we have said has been based on the assumption that the NDE takes place in or is constructed by the brain. We've confined "mind" to the brain because, scientifically . . . we have no other option. When the brain dies, the mind dies; the scientific view does not allow for the possibility of a soul, or for any form of personal survival.
>
> It is only by looking at some non-scientific views that we might find a wider interpretation of the NDE. . . .[3]

As Grossman points out, if the term "materialistic" is substituted for "scientific," then the above passage is an accurate statement. This semantic point needs to be stressed, because the term "scientific" carries a lot of emotional weight. In our modern world, science and scientists hold a great deal of prestige, and so few people want to be thought of as unscientific. To be labeled unscientific is enough to have one's work dismissed from serious consideration by the academic establishment. If to be scientific is good and unscientific bad, and if the term "scientific" is thought to be synonymous with the term "materialistic," then any talk of disembodied minds or spirits is antimaterialist, unscientific, and therefore bad.* The long-standing confusion of materialism with science is what largely accounts for the persistent social taboo responsible for the ignorance and dismissal of the substantial amount of evidence that proves materialism false.

---

*For the materialists, the term "unscientific" seems to be the modern equivalent of the term "heretical," and is invoked for the same purpose: to exclude from consideration ideas that challenge the believers' faith.

Greyson has also elaborated on this confusion. He states, "Materialists often claim credit for the scientific advances of the past few centuries. But it is the scientific method of empirical hypothesis testing, rather than a materialistic philosophy, that has been responsible for the success of science in explaining the world. If it comes to a choice between the empirical method and a materialistic worldview, the true scientist will choose the former."[4]

It is also important to stress at this point that although the evidence appears to prove false the hypothesis that consciousness is produced by the brain, it does not follow that any particular transmission theory discussed earlier is therefore proved correct. This is a subtle point and is worth explaining.

It is important to distinguish between factual and theoretical hypotheses: gravity is considered an empirical fact, but we attempt to explain *how* gravity works with various theoretical hypotheses. The ancient hypothesis that biological evolution occurs also now appears to be a fact (after all, there is the fossil record); yet we have theories of evolution to account for how it works. Factual hypotheses may be proven correct beyond all reasonable doubt, but our scientific theories—which propose relationships between facts—can never be, and must forever remain conjectures, or speculation. Similarly, it may be proved beyond all reasonable doubt that the brain works as a receiver-transmitter, but the details of precisely *how* the mind and brain work together is the task of the various quantum mechanical theories of mind/brain interaction described earlier.

As discussed at length in chapter 15 of my previous book, *Parapsychology and the Skeptics,* our scientific theoretical hypotheses are never proved correct; they may be *disproved* by observations that contradict their predictions, but no amount of observation can logically prove that our universal theories are correct. Rather, they are *corroborated* by unsuccessful attempts to refute them and by successful attempts to refute rival hypotheses.

Only in the nonempirical fields of mathematics and pure logic are general statements proved correct not only beyond all reasonable doubt, but beyond all conceivable doubt. That is because in these fields, we are either deducing conclusions from premises that are accepted as axioms, or we are simply expressing the same idea in different ways. In the field of empirical science, there is no mathematical or logical certainty that what seems to be correct is indeed correct. We can never know in advance in what ways our beliefs will eventually have to be modified.

Despite having said that, the hypothesis that the brain works as a receiver-transmitter of consciousness has two decisive advantages over its rival: (1) the production hypothesis has been proved false by the data, and (2) the transmission hypothesis can accommodate the facts that refute the production theory. In terms of the production hypothesis, the cases of veridical out-of-body perception during times of severely compromised if not entirely absent brain function are completely inexplicable, except in terms of fraud. This desperate last resort is always available, of course, but we should wonder why the defenders of materialism are left with no other realistic option.

In practice, the defenders of materialism largely ignore the evidence, rather than deal with it. This is one available tactic; another is to continually insist that more and more evidence be presented, thereby delaying any day of reckoning to some continually receding point in the future. Another is to insist that alternatives to materialism be proved logically correct beyond all possible doubt; yet another is to treat materialism as an ideology rather than a scientific theory. Popper does not refer to challenges to any specific theory when he writes,

> We can always immunize a theory against refutation. There are many such immunizing tactics; and if nothing better occurs to us, we can always deny the objectivity—or even the existence—of the refuting observation. Those intellectuals who are more interested in being right than in learning something interesting but unexpected are by no means rare exceptions.[5]

One such intellectual would almost certainly be Michael Shermer: historian, author, director of the Skeptic Society, and publisher of *Skeptic* magazine, who also has a regular column, "Skeptic," in *Scientific American* magazine. After flirting in his youth with various New Age practices such as pyramid power, Shermer is currently on a crusade to expose ESP, OBEs, and alien abductions for what he now thinks they are: complete nonsense.

In his book *The Borderlands of Science,* Shermer provides his readers with a series of criteria for distinguishing between real science and "baloney." He particularly warns us against people who have ideologies to pursue, whose pattern of thinking "consistently ignores or distorts data not for creative purposes but for ideological agendas."[6] But Shermer clearly seems to have an ideological agenda of his own. His column in the March 2003 issue of *Scientific American* is devoted to the brain and contains the subheading: "If the brain mediates all experience, then paranormal phenomena are nothing more than neuronal events."

Fair enough. In his article, Shermer concentrates on the OBE, writing, "Nowadays people are reporting out-of-body experiences, floating above their beds. What is going on here? Are these elusive creatures and mysterious phenomena in our world or in our minds? New evidence adds weight to the notion that they are, in fact, products of the brain."

Shermer then quotes a variety of studies in an attempt to show that OBEs "are nothing more than neuronal events." He claims that Persinger, whom we met earlier in our discussion of temporal lobe seizures, "can induce all these perceptions in subjects by subjecting their temporal lobes to patterns of magnetic fields. (I tried it myself and had a mild OBE.)"[7]*

He then quotes a Swiss study reported in the September 19, 2002, issue of *Nature* that describes how a female patient experienced an OBE of sorts after electrical stimulation of an area of the brain near the temporal lobe. The woman saw herself lying in bed, from above, but said that "I only see my legs and lower trunk." When asked to watch her real legs during electrical stimulation, she reported seeing her legs "becoming shorter" and then "she reported that her legs appeared to be moving quickly toward

---

*The reader may recall that Persinger's claims do not stand up to close critical scrutiny, and that a Swedish team failed to replicate Persinger's results.

her face, and took evasive action."[8] Of course, this experiment does not prove that all OBEs are illusions, and at any rate, the Swiss researchers did not say whether they attempted to test if the woman could accurately perceive anything during the time she reported seeing herself.

Shermer then mentions a study that scanned the brains of meditating monks and speculates on what the findings may imply for alien abductions. The last study Shermer mentions seems to have the most relevance for his suggestion that OBEs are "products of the brain."

> Sometimes trauma can become a trigger. The December 15, 2001, issue of the *Lancet* published a Dutch study in which 12 percent of 344 cardiac patients resuscitated from clinical death reported near-death experiences, some having a sensation of being out of body, others seeing a light at the end of a tunnel. Some even described speaking to dead relatives. Because the everyday occurrence is of stimuli coming from the outside, when a part of the brain abnormally generates these illusions, another part of the brain interprets them as external events. Hence, the abnormal is thought to be the paranormal. *These studies are only the latest to deliver blows against the belief that mind and spirit are separate from brain and body. In reality, all experience is mediated by the brain.* (emphasis added)[9]

Shermer must have hoped that his readers would not consult the original article in *The Lancet,* for if they do they are in for a surprise. This study was the source of the NDE reported above in the section headed "Case of the Missing Dentures." In it, the authors acknowledge that experiences similar to the classic NDE can be induced in several ways, such as electrical stimulation of the brain, excessive carbon dioxide, and with certain drugs. But they then point out that "induced experiences are not identical to NDE."

Instead of concluding that their research indicates that all experience is mediated by the brain, these medical researchers came to the opposite conclusion! This is what cardiologist van Lommel and his coauthors write:

With lack of evidence for any other theories for NDE, the thus far assumed, but never proven, concept that consciousness and memories are localised in the brain should be discussed. How could a clear consciousness outside one's body be experienced at the moment that the brain no longer functions during a period of clinical death with flat EEG? Also, in cardiac arrest the EEG usually becomes flat in most cases within about 10 s [seconds] from onset of syncope [fainting]. Furthermore, blind people have described veridical perception during out-of-body experiences at the time of this experience. NDE pushes at the limits of medical ideas about the range of human consciousness and the mind-brain relation.[10]

Science writer and TV host Jay Ingram, normally a fan of Shermer's writing, was startled when he read Shermer's column because he had interviewed van Lommel earlier and knew the study well. He expressed his disappointment with Shermer in his newspaper column, stressing how he can't stand it "when influential figures misrepresent the research of others to make a point." He wondered, "Is this now considered justifiable if you have some sort of scientific axe to grind?"[11]

SUMMARY

The reports of enhanced mental processes and out-of-body perception of the environment at a time when we would expect brain processes to be severely impaired or entirely absent quite clearly seem to prove the production hypothesis false in favor of the rival view that the brain acts as a two-way receiver-transmitter, one that also restricts and filters out certain forms of consciousness and perception.

According to the materialists, these reports must be hallucinations somehow produced by a malfunctioning brain. Apart from the fact that we have found no plausible mechanism that can account for such hallucinations, the reports of accurate perception are simply inexplicable by this model. Greyson compares the two models:

The major advantage of the hallucination model is its compatibility with the materialistic worldview favored by a majority of neuroscientists (though not by a majority of physicists). The major *disadvantage* of the hallucination model is that it fails to account for the phenomenon [accurate perceptions], and is plausible only if we discredit or discount much of our data. As astronomer and spectroscopy pioneer Paul Merrill quipped, "If you eliminate the data that do not agree, the remaining data agree very well." But disregarding disagreeable data is the hallmark of pseudoscience, not science.[12]

If we accept any of the veridical reports above as genuine, then it seems only one conclusion follows: although the operations of mind and brain are undeniably closely linked during biological life, at times the mind can operate in an unimpaired manner independently of a properly functioning brain. In other words, materialism has been proven false.

Does this imply that consciousness survives the death of the body?

SEVENTEEN

THE NEAR-DEATH EXPERIENCE AS EVIDENCE FOR SURVIVAL

There is no question that the NDE leaves most of those who experience it with little doubt, as the following three quotes indicate.

> As a result of that [experience], I have very little apprehension about dying my natural death . . . because if death is anything at all like what I experienced, it's gotta be the most wonderful thing to look forward to, absolutely the most wonderful thing.
>
> I have a message to others living an ordinary life . . . "There is more." Our identity will continue to be—in a greater way. Friends will not be lost to you. You will know beauty and peace and love.
>
> It gave me an answer to what I think everyone must really wonder about at one time or another in this life. Yes, there is an afterlife! More beautiful than anything we can begin to imagine. Once you know it, there is nothing that can equal it! You just know![1]

The question is whether the NDE provides evidence for survival for those of us who have not had such an experience.

BUT ARE THEY REALLY DEAD?

One objection that has been raised over and over again to the idea that the NDE offers evidence for survival is presented vigorously by philosopher Gerd Hovelmann when he writes that "one of the most obvious and utterly devastating objections to the survival interpretation of near-death experiences lies in the fact that those who were still capable of telling the tale and having their experiences recorded, by definition, cannot have been dead and therefore cannot have had any experience of death."[2]

Hovelmann refers to talk of a resuscitated person being dead as "linguistic slovenliness" because "by definition, 'being resuscitated' and 'being dead' are mutually exclusive; that is, a person (or animal) who has been resuscitated may not, at the same time, be said to have been dead before. So, if someone claims . . . that a person has been 'resuscitated' after he 'really was dead,' the claimant may be said to be ignorant of how the words 'resuscitated' and 'dead' are to be used."[3]

But definitions are always somewhat arbitrary, and we are free to question Hovelmann's assertion that those who report NDEs "by definition, cannot have been dead and therefore cannot have had any experience of death." Becker refers to this as "specious question-begging because it assumes as a fact the premise that no one ever revives once truly dead, which is precisely the issue in question."[4]

The definition Hovelmann is using implies that death is an irreversible event, but the meanings of words are determined by how people use those words in conversation and in writing, regardless of how those words may be defined in any dictionary. Dictionary definitions may be obsolete or unrepresentative of how some words are in fact used, as shown by the fact that the meaning of many words has changed over time.

The issue is whether the word "death" is used in such a manner as to imply irreversibility, or whether the very concept of death implies irreversibility. This is by no means clear; rather, it seems that whether the concept of death is considered reversible depends on the beliefs of the person using the word and on the context in which the word is used.

One of the earliest recorded "returns" from death is Plato's story of Er, told in Book X of his *Republic,* written circa 360 BCE. Er was killed in battle, and when the bodies of the slain were collected ten days later, his was found intact, although the others were by now in a state of decay. Two days later, "as he was lying on the funeral pile, he returned to life and told them what he had seen in the other world." He told a story about how, along with his fallen comrades, he had traveled to a mysterious place, from where he saw souls departing and others arriving. But he was not allowed to go further and was told he was to be a messenger, and "they bade him hear and see all that was to be heard and seen in that place." He saw, among other things, souls choosing their next lives and then drinking from a river of forgetfulness to obliterate former memories. Er was not allowed to drink, but after falling asleep suddenly awakened and found himself lying on the funeral pyre.

Other ancient accounts from the Western tradition include the Old Testament report of Elisha resuscitating the widow's dead son,[5] and in the New Testament, John says that the raising of Lazarus after four days was one of the direct causes of the priest's plan to do away with Jesus. In addition, we have seen that similar stories of people returning from the dead have been told in hunter-gatherer and pastoral societies. Someone may object that many of these stories may only be myths, but that is completely beside the point. The point is that the concept of death has historically often been used as a reversible concept.

However, death as a reversible concept is completely inadequate in the medical environment. There it has been necessary to determine—with as much accuracy as possible—the point at which the process of death is irreversible so that life-support measures may be stopped. In the effort to determine a clinical definition of irreversible death, a variety of criteria have been proposed.

As one physician has noted, "The scientific definition of death is a medical quagmire."[6] Traditionally, people were declared dead when they were found unconscious without pulse or respiration. The absence of breathing was checked by holding a mirror underneath the person's nose. The invention of the stethoscope in the mid-nineteenth century enabled physicians to diagnose death based on the absence of heart sounds, and so somewhat reduced the fear of being buried alive.

However, the advent of CPR allowed patients who would have previously been pronounced dead to be resuscitated. By the 1960s, improvements in medical technology enabled the artificial maintenance of respiration—and consequently heartbeat—in patients who had sustained brain damage so severe that they could no longer breathe on their own. An inevitable consequence of these developments was the requirement for a new set of criteria to define clinical death.

The result was a new definition of death: the loss of brain function. But what part of the brain? As already described, the brain stem controls involuntary functions of respiration and certain reflexes, the cerebellum controls balance and coordination, and it is believed that conscious thought is mediated through the cerebral cortex. But with CPR and artificial respiration, it was found that the cortex is more vulnerable to a temporary loss of blood and oxygen than the brain stem. If a person has lost all higher brain functions yet retains a fully functional brain stem—and therefore can breathe on his own despite remaining unconscious—the person is said to be in a "persistent vegetative state." Should such individuals be declared "clinically dead"? Debate still rages.

The legal definition of brain death varies between jurisdictions. In the United States, a special presidential commission in 1981 led to the Uniform Determination of Death Act, which states that "an individual with irreversible cessation of all functions of the entire brain, including the brain stem, is dead."[7] However, the report qualified this definition, indicating that "functions of the entire brain" referred only to those functions that could be clinically assessed.

In contrast to the "whole-brain" definition of clinical death, the British definition of brain death is based exclusively on loss of function of the brain stem.[8] In practice, the difference is that in the United States, it is much more common to combine a diagnosis of an inactive brain stem with a record of a flat EEG, indicating no activity in either the brain stem or the cerebral cortex. It has been suggested that the somewhat stricter American criteria are considered necessary to protect physicians against "the malevolent ravages of opportunistic lawyers."[9]

In Canada, the definition is different from those of both the United

States and the United Kingdom, requiring "irreversible global brain dysfunction." Not only are the definitions of clinical death different but even the measurements required to determine that the brain stem is inactive differ between these three countries. Clearly, it is possible to be dead in one country but alive in another.

In practice, three criteria are commonly used to diagnose brain death. The first is lack of brain stem activity. This can be determined in various ways, including checking for the absence of pupil dilatation or auditory evoked potentials, similar to those elicited by the ear speakers in Pam Reynolds' surgery. The second is a flat EEG reading, indicating nonfunction of the cerebral cortex. The third is documentation of no blood flow to the brain.

Even by these exhaustive criteria, there can be little doubt that some people, such as Pam Reynolds, have not only survived clinical death but have also reported fully conscious experiences during the time they were clinically dead. So either we must say that our clinical definition of death is inaccurate and that—except in cases of extreme trauma or until decay of the corpse occurs—we can never really be sure if someone is alive or dead; or we must say that some people have in fact returned from death.

But this is simplistic. Since different parts of the body cease functioning in stages, it should be clear that biological death is a process and not a single definable event. Of course, it is clear that none of the near-death experiencers crossed an irreversible threshold. But rather than argue pointlessly over whether they were "really dead," the most reasonable position, given our present understanding, would seem to be that the subjects experienced the early stages of death and returned to tell of their experience.

Regardless of how we settle this issue, it is of course true that people reporting NDEs were not *irreversibly* brain dead. This may seem like a purely semantic issue, but as we will see, it is a very relevant point.

FEATURES OF THE NEAR-DEATH EXPERIENCE SUGGESTING SURVIVAL

The specific features of the NDE that would seem to suggest survival are:

1. Normal or enhanced mental processes at a time when brain processes are severely impaired or entirely absent
2. Out-of-body view of one's own body and of the surrounding environment
3. Perception of deceased acquaintances
4. Corroborated perception of events not accessible to one's biological sense organs, apparently while out of the body

The first feature suggests that mental clarity is not entirely dependent on a properly functioning brain, the second that consciousness can function apart from the physical body, the third that those who have died before us continue to exist, and the fourth that these experiences are not entirely subjective.

The most common of these features is the first: in one study it was found that, among 130 patients who had been close to death, 120 (92 percent) reported that their sensory and cognitive functioning had been either normal or enhanced, despite their seriously impaired physiological condition. We have also seen that the OBE is fairly commonly reported, by about 57 percent of Western subjects. Perception of deceased acquaintances is somewhat less frequent. The rarest cases—and the most important—are those in which the observations of the seemingly unconscious person are corroborated by independent testimony.

We have reviewed many cases that contain several of these features, but two in particular—those of Al Sullivan and Pam Reynolds—contain all four features. Perhaps most important in terms of evidence, both Sullivan and Reynolds described visual events from an elevated perspective that they could not have inferred by auditory means, and in both cases, their reports were corroborated shortly afterward by witnesses. It could perhaps be suggested that such perception was in fact clairvoyant, but clairvoyant descriptions associated with remote viewing are not typically from an elevated perspective and are certainly not from an elevated position directly above the viewer's own body. An even stronger objection to the clairvoyance hypothesis is that these perceptions were reported when we have every reason to believe that the subjects' cerebral processes were either impaired or entirely absent.

The NDE proves false the notion that the mind depends on a functioning brain, and so allows us to conclude that consciousness can continue to function, at least temporarily, after brain activity ceases. The NDE suggests the existence of a continuing afterlife, and of those people who have had this experience, the overwhelming majority are convinced that life continues long after the body has died. But, strictly speaking, because those who returned did not suffer irreversible brain death, the NDE alone does not provide more than suggestive evidence in favor of conscious life after the point of irreversible brain death.

Near-death experiences may suggest an afterlife, but other lines of evidence more directly prove false the arguments against survival. These lines include the evidence for reincarnation, for apparitions, and for genuine communication from the deceased. Many have argued that together, along with the NDE, these lines of evidence converge to make a very strong case for survival. Before we consider these other remarkable lines of evidence in the third book of this series, let us first examine the near-death experiences of those who most certainly did cross the threshold of death.

PART III

Deathbed Visions

It's beautiful over there.

THOMAS EDISON,
OCTOBER 18, 1931,
SHORTLY BEFORE HE DIED

EIGHTEEN

REPORTS FROM ENGLAND
TO INDIA

Extraordinary visions experienced shortly before death have been reported throughout history, but the first systematic attempt to study the phenomenon was made by a physics professor at the Royal College of Science in Dublin, Sir William Barrett.

On the night of January 12, 1924, Sir Barrett's wife, a physician, rushed home to tell her husband of a remarkable event she had witnessed. She had been called in to deliver the child of a woman named Doris, and although the baby was delivered safely, Doris herself was dying. Lady Barrett describes what happened:

> Suddenly, she looked eagerly toward one part of the room, a radiant smile illuminating her whole countenance. "Oh, lovely, lovely," she said. I asked, "What is lovely?" "What I *see*," she replied in low intense tones. "What do you see?" "Lovely brightness—wonderful beings." It is difficult to describe the sense of reality conveyed by her intense absorption in the vision. Then—seeming to focus her attention more intently on one place for a moment—she exclaimed, almost with a kind of joyous cry, "Why, it's Father! Oh, he's so glad I'm coming; he *is* so glad. It would be perfect if only W. (her husband) would come too."

Her baby was brought for her to see. She looked at it with interest, and then said, "Do you think I ought to stay for baby's sake?" Then turning toward the vision again, she said, "I can't—I can't stay; if you could see what I do, you would know I can't stay."

Apparently the young woman "saw" something she found so appealing that she was willing to give up her life and her own baby! Sir Barrett considered the possibility that the vision was some sort of wish-fulfilling hallucination, but rejected it because among the apparitions of the dead was someone Doris had not expected to see. Her sister Vida had died three weeks earlier, but Doris had not been informed because of her precarious health. This explains the surprise Doris expresses when the following occurred:

She spoke to her father, saying, "I am coming," turning at the same time to look at me, saying, "Oh, he is so near." On looking at the same place again, she said with a rather puzzled expression, "He has Vida with him," turning again to me saying, "Vida is with him." Then she said, "You do want me, Dad; I am coming."[1]

Doris died shortly afterward.

Barrett was so impressed with his wife's report that he collected this and other cases he could find into a small book titled *Death Bed Visions,* published in 1926. Barrett found that deathbed visions tend to be of apparitions of the dead, who seem to dying people to appear with the purpose of taking them away. He also found that when such visions occur, the dying person is usually rational and clear-minded and that the dying person often reacts with emotions of joy or serenity.

Thirty years later, Barrett's book inspired respected parapsychologist Karlis Osis to undertake a systematic survey of deathbed experiences, using modern survey methods and techniques of statistical analysis not available in Barrett's time. In 1959 and 1960, Osis asked thousands of physicians and nurses in the United States about their experiences with the dying and received 640 responses covering over thirty-five thousand dying patients. This pilot study was followed up with a larger American study from 1961 to 1964, in which 1,004 responses were received, representing approximately fifty thousand deathbed observations. The results from the second survey were consistent with results from the first, and both sets of data were generally in agreement with Barrett's earlier findings.

As might be expected, some of the "visions" reported appeared to be no more than just pathological hallucinations, ramblings about this-world concerns, or the reliving of old memories. But most were visions of otherworldly visitors—usually deceased relatives—who were said to appear with the expressed purpose of taking the dying away to another mode of existence. The majority (two-thirds) of apparitions perceived by the dying portrayed deceased rather than living people; just the opposite was found to be true of hallucinations of people in normal health.

An interesting relationship was found between the expressed purpose of the apparitions and the time elapsed between the vision and death: in the pilot study, of those who died almost instantly (within ten minutes) after seeing the apparition, 76 percent said the apparition had come to take them away; of those who died after a period of one hour or longer, the percentages varied from 25 to 44 percent. In the total American sample of deathbed visions, 87 percent of those who died within sixty minutes reported apparitions with a take-away purpose, as compared with 46 percent of those who died after longer intervals.[2] Similar to what Barrett had found, dying patients tended to experience mood elevation, accompanied by emotions of joy or serenity, in response to their visions.

Osis began to statistically analyze the medical and psychological variables surrounding deathbed visions, but he and others wondered what influence, if any, cultural factors might have on the frequency and content of the visions. American culture has a background of biblical religion, and so it was suggested that the visions might be a playback of biblical stories heard at some point in the past. It became clear to Osis and his colleagues that American deathbed visions had to be compared with similar experiences reported from a culture in which the Bible is not part of the population's religious upbringing. Japan and India were suggested, and after considering all the factors, India became the choice.

REPORTS FROM INDIA

India's predominant Hindu religion differs in several respects from Christianity, with its emphasis on karma instead of Judgment Day and reincarnation instead of heaven and hell.

The Indian survey was conducted in 1972 and 1973 by Osis along with parapsychologist Erlendur Haraldsson and resulted in 255 cases of death-bed visions and 120 cases of NDEs. When combined with the results from the second American survey, Osis and Haraldsson now had 877 cases with which to test the competing hypotheses of survival and destruction that they had formed on the basis of results from the pilot study.

The results from the Indian survey were in agreement with results from the earlier surveys on almost all points. All three studies found that the hallucinations of people in deathbed visions mainly portray otherworldly visitors—usually apparitions of deceased relatives, but sometimes of beings interpreted as religious figures. The percentages were remarkably similar on both sides of the globe: 78 percent for the United States and 77 percent for India.[3] By contrast, only a small minority of hallucinations in the general population are concerned with otherworldly apparitions. Osis and Haraldsson emphasize this point, writing, "In both the United States and India, the visions of the dying and of near-death patients were overwhelmingly dominated by apparitions of the dead and religious figures. This finding is loud and clear: *When the dying see apparitions, they are nearly always experienced as messengers from a postmortem mode of existence.*"[4]

Second, all three studies were in agreement about the main purpose of the apparitions portrayed in the visions: it was to take the dying patient away to another mode of existence. This purpose was expressed in 69 percent of the American cases and in 79 percent of the cases in India.[5]

As mentioned earlier, Osis and Haraldsson sometimes found reports in which the dying person hallucinated figures of living people. Of course, such hallucinations are not at all related to the afterlife hypothesis and are more likely the result of brain malfunction. Osis and Haraldsson write, "Naturally, in our surveys, we came across a few such experiences, and their frequency was quite similar in the United States and in India.

However, *we found not one case in which the take-away purpose was attributed to an apparition of the living.* In both countries, the apparitions of the dead mostly expressed take-away purpose (United Sates, 82 percent, India, 71 percent)." (emphasis added)[6]

The two researchers also encountered cases in which the purpose of the apparition was at odds with the expectations of the patient, the will of the patient, and even the medical prognosis.

> Several medical observers expressed amazement and surprise when confronted with cases in which patients died—after seeing apparitions calling them—despite good medical prognoses. For example, a Hindu patient in his sixties was hospitalized because of a bronchial asthmatic condition. His doctor's prognosis predicted a definite recovery. The patient himself expected to live and wished to live. Suddenly, he exclaimed, "Somebody is calling me." Afterward he reassured his relatives, saying, "Don't worry, I will be all right," but the "call" seemed to have been more potent than he himself thought. The patient died within ten minutes.[7]

Another such case concerned a college-educated Indian man in his twenties who was recovering from mastoiditis. He was doing very well, and both patient and doctor expected a definite recovery. Osis and Haraldsson write, "He was going to be discharged that day. Suddenly at 5:00 a.m. he shouted, 'someone is standing here dressed in white clothes. I will not go with you!' He was dead in ten minutes."[8]

Osis and Haraldsson concluded that these findings contradict predictions implied by the destruction hypothesis and so serve to corroborate the alternative hypothesis of survival.

DIFFERENCES BETWEEN THE AMERICAN AND INDIAN SURVEYS

If the hypothesis of destruction is true, then deathbed visions should vary greatly between different cultures. On the other hand, if there is an afterlife, then we should expect the influence of culture to be only moderate. Osis and Haraldsson carefully set out the assumptions and predictions of each hypothesis and compared deathbed visions in the United States and India on fourteen points: on almost all points, visions in the two cultures agreed, leading the authors to conclude, "In our judgment, the similarities between the core phenomena found in the deathbed visions of both countries are clear enough to be considered as supportive of the postmortem survival hypothesis."[9]

However, while Osis and Haraldsson found that nationality and culture did not determine the frequency of afterlife-related apparitions, they did find some influence on the type of vision experienced. There were essentially two differences.

First, although the overwhelming majority of deathbed visions in both countries involved otherworldly apparitions, there was cultural variation in the type of apparition seen. In the United States, the vast majority of otherworldly apparitions were identified as deceased people known to the dying patient. In India, more apparitions were identified as religious figures or were of unknown people. In the United States, apparitions not identified as deceased relatives were often identified as angels; in India, as messengers of Yamaraj, the Hindu god of death. But as Osis and Haraldsson remind us, "Let us be aware that such apparitions do not wear name tags or speak their names. It is the patient who announces the apparition's name and title."[10] Only occasionally would a dying patient refrain from interpreting an unknown apparition as a figure from their religious background.*

Second, although the majority of patients in both countries wished to go, there were far more cases of nonconsent in India. While only one

---

*Here is an example of a case of an engineer in his fifties, struck by coronary thrombosis. His physician reported: "He saw a 'bearded man' standing at the opening to a long golden corridor. He was shaking his head and motioning him to go back, said: 'Not now, later.' This made the patient very happy. He said I [the doctor] need not give him medicine anymore: 'I am not wanted up there.' It was right after this experience that he started getting better" (Osis and Haraldsson 1977, 150). Obviously, a more emotional patient would have jumped to the conclusion that the bearded man was somebody from the patient's religious teachings.

American patient did not wish to go when called, one out of every three Indians who experienced a take-away apparition refused to consent.

Several physicians in India suggested that the reason so many Indian patients experienced take-away apparitions against their will is because the Indian patients tended to die at a younger age. However, when Osis and Haraldsson analyzed the data, they found only the slightest relationship between the age of the patient and the perceived purpose of the apparition.

It appears that Indian mythology about Yamaraj and his messengers may partly explain why some Indians are unwilling to accept the call of the take-away apparitions. Yamadoots are supposed to appear at the bedside of the dying to take the person away to the land of the dead. The appearance of the yamadoot is supposed to depend on the karma of the patient; if the patient has led a good life, a pleasant yamadoot is said to appear.

Osis and Haraldsson found that in the nonconsent cases, the apparition is nearly always that of a stranger, sometimes interpreted as a yamadoot, as in the following case, which includes a perceived visitor with a neutral appearance. It concerns a Hindu clerical worker hospitalized with septicemia. His temperature was 103 degrees Fahrenheit, and he was mildly affected by drugs, but his consciousness seemed clear to his nurse when he suddenly exclaimed, "Somebody is standing there! He has a cart with him so he must be a yamadoot! He must be taking someone with him. He is teasing me that he is going to take *me*! But Mamie, I am not going; I want to be with you!" Then he said someone was pulling him out of bed. He pleaded, "Please hold me; I am not going." His pain increased and he died.[11]

NINETEEN

ALTERNATIVE EXPLANATIONS

According to the hypothesis that the destruction of the brain entails the destruction of the mind, deathbed visions are nothing more than products of drugged, diseased, and dying brains. This hypothesis would predict that the presence of hallucinogenic drugs and brain disease would increase the frequency of such visions and that religious beliefs and expectations would influence the content. Osis and Haraldsson tested the destruction hypothesis by considering each of these factors in turn.

Of the 425 patients on whom the researchers had information regarding medication, 61 percent had received no medication at all. An additional 19 percent had received such small doses that the reporting physicians did not consider them to have been psychologically affected at all. All in all, 80 percent of the patients who were considered to be "terminal" and who had apparitional experiences did not seem to have been affected by drugs.

Morphine, Demerol, and other potent hallucinogenic drugs are frequently given to the dying to ease their pain, but the researchers found, "Only a small minority of the patients who had deathbed visions had received such drugs. Those who had received medication had not greater frequency of afterlife visions than the other patients."[1]

Hallucinations sometimes occur in the aftermath of brain diseases and other diseases that affect the brain. But only about 12 percent of the patients with apparitional experiences were suffering from afflictions that could have been of a hallucinogenic nature, such as stroke, brain injury, or uremic diseases. The researchers investigated the relationship between the type of illness and the frequency of visions. They write, "We discovered that in both countries apparitional hallucinations and total hallucinations were not affected by the type of illness. This was true with only one exception: Patients with brain diseases or nephritis saw significantly fewer apparitional figures than did patients who had other diseases. We may, therefore, state that hallucinogenic types of diseases tend to reduce rather than generate the possibility of seeing an apparitional hallucination."[2]

Neither sex nor age seemed to be related to the frequency of reported visions. However, in both the American and Indian samples, the percentage of patients with a college education was several times higher than that of the general population of the same average age. Of course, within each sample there was wide variation in educational attainment.

Yet the researchers found no marked difference between patients who had attended only grade school and those who had gone to college. The phenomenon seems independent of sex, age, and education.

Osis and Haraldsson carefully considered the effect of religious belief on the experiences reported. In fact, the very reason for the Indian study was to see if religious differences resulted in marked differences in the frequency or type of deathbed vision. Therefore, the researchers carefully evaluated the kind of religion patients belonged to and the degree of their religious involvement.

The religious affiliations of the combined sample fell into two broad groups: 48 percent Hindu and 43 percent Christian. Within the American sample, the distribution between Protestant, Catholic, Jewish, unaffiliated, and other religions was in reasonable agreement with the religious distribution of the entire U.S. population. The Indian sample was 85 percent Hindu, 10 percent Christian, and 5 percent Muslim, roughly matching the distribution of these religious groups in the province in the north of India where the survey was conducted. Accordingly, Osis and Haraldsson concluded that "it appears that the kind of religious affiliation was not a determining factor in the occurrence of this phenomenon."[3]

Data concerning the degree of religious involvement were much harder to solicit. Respondents remembered and knew the patients' involvement in only 58 percent of the cases, and as might be expected, of these the largest group (47 percent) was deeply involved. Patients with a low degree of involvement might not bother mentioning their experience. At any rate, the researchers were not aware of any figures from the two countries regarding the degree of religious involvement of the populations.

Within each sample, the patient's personal involvement in religion did not affect the subject matter at all, but it did affect the patient's reaction. Those patients who were more deeply involved more frequently had a positive emotional response to their vision.

However, the authors found no significant relationship between religious involvement and seeing any type of apparition. Benign otherworldly apparitions also appeared to patients who had no religious concerns or interest.

Critics who refuse to accept NDEs and deathbed visions as evidence for survival sometimes point to the fact that different people often report different afterlife environments populated by different kinds of beings. This is especially true for people from different cultural backgrounds, as a comparison of Western and Indian NDEs and deathbed visions has made clear. These differences, the critics assert, are evidence that these experiences are idiosyncratic or culturally determined hallucinations.

This objection carries no weight whatever. If there is indeed an afterworld, then it does not follow that this world must be one homogeneous environment. Consider the reports from three people who claim to have visited a place called Africa: one reports seeing large, cosmopolitan cities populated with both white and black people; another describes vast deserts in which live people of Arabic appearance; and the third tells of dense jungles inhabited by small hunter-gatherers called pygmies. Are we to conclude from the differences in these reports that the existence of Africa is a myth?

Also, differences in culture influence our perceptions and our descriptions, as Greyson emphasizes.

Individual differences in cultural expectations influence our perceptions of the *physical* world; why should we expect them not to influence our perceptions of a transcendental dimension, if one exits—particularly when the NDErs report, as many do, that what they experienced was ineffable?

As an analogy, imagine that three of your acquaintances describe to you their alleged visit to a place they call "France." One, a hedonistic gourmand, details the sumptuous meals she enjoyed, but does not mention architecture or people. The second, a religious artist, describes in detail the magnificent cathedrals with their paintings and stained glass windows, but does not mention food or people. The third, a high-powered businessman, rails about the rude taxi drivers and street merchants, but does not mention food or architecture. Their descriptions of their purported visits to a place called "France" largely conform to their expectations and their interests. Do you assume therefore that their visits to "France" took place only in their imaginations, and that no such realm actually exists?[4]

As mentioned, there was some difference in content between the American and Indian visions, with some seemingly due to a different interpretation of the perceived visitors. But patients often saw the unexpected, something contrary to their beliefs. In further support of the postmortem survival hypothesis, Osis and Haraldsson write, "We reached the impression that cultural conditioning by Christian and Hindu teaching is, in part, contradicted in the visionary experiences of the dying. It seems to us that besides symbolizations based on inculcated beliefs, terminal patients do 'see' something that is unexpected, untaught, and a complete surprise to them."[5]

Expectations and desires can be possible causes of hallucinations. For instance, someone dying of thirst in the desert might be expected to "see" a mirage of water. Similarly, patients who expect to die might be expected to indulge in otherworldly fantasies. But both samples showed that the purpose of reported apparitions was not significantly related to the expectations of the patient.

On the contrary, the reports seem to indicate that apparitions show a purpose of their own, often contradicting the intentions of the patients.

Osis and Haraldsson write, "Especially dramatic were those cases in which apparitions called a patient for transition to the other world, and the patient, not willing to go, cried out for help or tried to hide. Fifty-four of these 'no-consent' cases were observed, nearly all in India. Such cases can hardly be interpreted as projected wish-fulfillment imagery, and they are even more impressive when the apparition's prediction of death was not only correct but contradictory to the medical prognosis of recovery."[6]

The skeptic may at this point argue that, consciously or subconsciously, the patients knew they were dying and that the "no-consent" visions were really just unpleasant hallucinations created by their dying brains, similar to nightmares. Perhaps patients who are especially apprehensive of dying have unpleasant hallucinations, whereas other patients have pleasant hallucinations of being visited by relatives that they know are deceased.

One problem with this view is the clarity of the minds of these people. In contrast with the delirium typical of most hallucinating patients, these dying patients are frequently able to carry on lucid conversations with others in the room at the same time they claim to see deceased friends and relatives. We have also noted the absence of a correlation between these visions and drugs, disease, and religious belief. An even more serious problem concerns cases such as that of Doris, who when dying saw her dead sister Vida, who she did not know had died. And this is not the only case of this type on record.

The following case was reported by Minot Savage, a physician. It involves two American girls, eight years of age—Jennie and Edith—who were close friends. In June 1889, both caught diphtheria, and Jennie died at noon on a Wednesday. Edith's parents decided not to tell her that Jennie had died, and shortly before Edith died, she asked her parents to give Jennie two photographs and to say good-bye to Jennie for her. According to witnesses:

> She appeared to see . . . friends she knew were dead. . . . But now suddenly, and with every appearance of surprise, she turned to her father and exclaimed, "Why Papa, I am going to take Jennie with me! . . . Why Papa! You did not tell me that Jennie was here!" And

immediately she reached out her arms as if in welcome, and said, "Oh, Jennie, I'm so glad you are here!"[7]

A more modern case involving a person from a non-Western culture was reported by two nurses who have spent decades working with the dying.

A dignified Chinese woman, Su was getting devoted care from her daughter, Lily. Both were Buddhists, and very accepting of the mother's terminal status.

"I've had a good life for ninety-three years," she said. "And I've been on this earth long enough!" She dreamed often of her husband, who had died some years before.

"I will join him soon," she said.

But one day Su seemed very puzzled.

"Why is my sister with my husband?" she asked. "They are both calling me to come."

"Is your sister dead?" I asked.

"No, she still lives in China," she said. "I have not seen her for many years."

When I related this conversation to the daughter, she was astonished and tearful.

"My aunt died two days ago in China," Lily said. "We decided not to tell Mother—her sister had the same kind of cancer. It was a very painful death; she lived in a remote village where good medical care wasn't available. We didn't want to upset or frighten Mother, since she is so sick herself."[8]

When the mother was told of her sister's illness and death, she smiled and said "Now I understand." She died three weeks later, at peace.

Another modern case was described by Natalie Kalmus, a pioneer developer of the Technicolor process. Natalie's sister Eleanor was dying, with Natalie beside her at the last moments of her life.

I sat on her bed and took her hand. It was on fire. Then Eleanor seemed to rise up in bed, almost to a sitting position.

"Natalie," she said, "there are so many of them. There's Fred and Ruth—what's she doing here?"

An electric shock went through me. She had said Ruth! Ruth was her cousin, who had died suddenly the week before. But I knew that Eleanor had not been told of the sudden death. . . . I felt on the verge of some wonderful, almost frightening knowledge. . . .

Her voice was surprisingly clear. "It's so confusing. There are so many of them!" Suddenly her arms stretched out happily. "I am going up," she murmured.[9]

Shortly after, Eleanor died.

The skeptic must say that the dying person telepathically or clairvoyantly gains true information about a recently deceased friend or relative, but about nothing else, and that the rest of the content of the vision is pure hallucination. It should be clear that this is a purely ad hoc theory, created to explain these cases and nothing else. If this theory is to be more than merely dogma, it must be independently testable, and for this theory to be testable, from it certain predictions must follow. But there is not a shred of independent evidence that the dying become more clairvoyant or telepathic in the final moments of life, and not a shred of independent evidence that ESP "dresses up" knowledge of unpleasant occurrences into pleasant hallucinations. The predictions of the theory in its testable form are not borne out, and if the theory is still maintained, then it is just another example of what Popper called an "immunizing tactic."

TWENTY

COMPARISON WITH THE NEAR-DEATH EXPERIENCE

Osis and Haraldsson noted that they had collected 120 cases in which patients had come back from near-death states and had reported seeing apparitions, with the number of cases split almost evenly between the United States and India. They had expected to find more apparitions of the living in the comeback cases, but the data proved them wrong. Apparitions related to the afterlife were as common in the comeback cases (80 percent) as in the cases of those who died (81 percent). The emotional reactions to these apparitions was also similar—mostly feelings of serenity and peace.

In one respect the comeback cases were different from the terminal cases. In the comeback cases in which unambiguous information was available concerning the purpose of the apparition, 78 percent were said to have a take-away purpose. But one-third of these take-away apparitions were said to have sent the patient back to life in no uncertain terms. In the remaining cases, no explicit postponement was expressed. Osis and Haraldsson suspected that the explicit postponement was higher than one-third, but that it got lost in the process of communication with the health professionals. Unfortunately, some of the accounts only mentioned that the patient reported seeing an apparition and then recovered.

The experiences of the Indian patients were similar to those of the American patients. About 80 percent saw otherworldly apparitions, and about one-third of those who reported take-away apparitions also reported being explicitly sent back by the apparitions. However, whereas the American patients were usually told something to the effect that it was not their time or that they had unfinished work to do, the manners of the Indian apparitions seemed more bureaucratic. As mentioned earlier, messengers would sometimes bring the patient to a clerk, who would then consult some records and announce that a mistake had been made. As in the Indian terminal cases, about one-third of the Indian patients did not want to go with the visitor.

Deathbed visions are broadly similar to NDEs, and the effect of culture on each appears to be about the same. In one important respect, the causes of the experiences differ. This difference was revealed when Osis and Haraldsson began to wonder why the distribution of causes of death in their sample was so different from that of the general population. For instance, the share of patients suffering heart disease in their American sample (29 percent) was much lower than that of the general U.S. population (38 percent). With regard to cancer, the discrepancy was even greater: 37 percent in their sample, compared with 18 percent in the general population. As Osis and Haraldsson conclude, "Apparently, slow death is more conducive to these experiences."[1]

This is in direct contrast with most reported NDEs, which are usually the result of accidents, heart attacks, drowning, or suicide attempts. Throughout this book, we have seen that there is not a single good reason to doubt that these experiences are in fact what they appear to be. If that is so, then the NDE is a sudden thrust into another world, while the deathbed vision is a gradual transition.

NEXT

The gate is straight, deep and wide
Break on through to the other side

JIM MORRISON

In the experiences people have at the borderland near death, we find a finger obstinately pointing toward consciousness beyond death. Yet in this book, we have gone no further than death's door. We have stopped at the gate, perhaps at the gate of eternity.

My next book will investigate reports of children who claim to remember previous lives, reports of apparitions, and most impressive of all, accounts from several individuals who appear to have broken through to the other side and found a way to keep the lines of communication open.

Finally, we will arrive at a solution to this deep and ancient mystery.

NOTES

FOREWORD

1. Planck, *Scientific Autobiography*, 33–34.
2. Kelly, Kelly, Crabtree, et al. *Irreducible Mind*, 421.
3. James, *The Works of William James: Essays in Psychical Research*, 184.
4. Grossman, "Four Errors Commonly Made by Professional Debunkers," 227–35.
5. Carter, *Parapsychology and the Skeptics: A Scientific Argument for the Existence of ESP;* also, of course, the book that is now in your hands.

INTRODUCTION

1. Schoolcraft, *Travels in the Central Portion of the Mississippi Valley*, 397.
2. Frazer, *The Belief in Immortality*, vol. 1, London, Macmillan, 1913. Quoted in Lorimer, *Survival? Body, Mind and Death in the Light of Psychic Experience*, 20.
3. Greely, *The Sociology of the Paranormal: A Reconnaissance.*
4. Haraldsson and Hontkooper, "Psychic Experiences in the Multinational Human Values Study: Who Reports Them?" 145–65.

CHAPTER 1. ANCIENT AND MODERN THEORIES

1. As quoted in Lorimer, *Survival? Body, Mind and Death in the Light of Psychic Experience*, 112.
2. Russell, *Portraits from Memory*, 152.
3. Ibid., 145–46.
4. Herbert, *Quantum Reality: Beyond the New Physics*, 46.
5. Russell, *Portraits from Memory*, 149.
6. Eccles, *Facing Reality: Philosophical Adventures of a Brain Scientist*, 83.
7. Russell, *Why I Am Not a Christian, and Other Essays*, 88–93.
8. Ryle, *The Concept of Mind*, 13.
9. Lamont, *The Illusion of Immortality*, 86–108.
10. Ibid., 89–113.
11. Schiller, *Riddles of the Sphinx*, 295.
12. James, *The Will to Believe*, 15.

13. Ibid., 22.
14. Burt, *ESP and Psychology,* 60.

CHAPTER 2. OBJECTIONS OF SKEPTICS

1. Edwards, *Reincarnation: A Critical Examination,* 297.
2. Ibid., 280–81.
3. Ibid., 286.
4. Ducasse, *A Critical Examination of the Belief in a Life after Death,* chap. VI.
5. Ibid.
6. Edwards, *Reincarnation: A Critical Examination,* 287.

CHAPTER 3. OPINIONS FROM NEUROSCIENCE

1. Penfield, *The Mystery of the Mind,* 55.
2. Ibid., 77–78.
3. Edwards, *Reincarnation: A Critical Examination,* 291.
4. Penfield, *The Mystery of the Mind,* 88.
5. Ibid., 79.
6. Ibid., 79–80.
7. Ibid., 113–14.
8. Eccles, *Facing Reality: Philosophical Adventures of a Brain Scientist,* 126–27. See also Eccles, *The Neurophysiological Basis of Mind,* 285.
9. Eccles, *Facing Reality: Philosophical Adventures of a Brain Scientist,* 58.
10. Ibid., 84.

CHAPTER 4. PHYSICS AND CONSCIOUSNESS

1. Koestler, *The Sleepwalkers: A History of Man's Changing Vision of the Universe,* 427–28.
2. Isaac Newton, from *Optics,* 1704; quoted in Stapp, *Mindful Universe,* 6.
3. Rosenblum and Kuttner, "Consciousness and Quantum Mechanics: The Connection and Analogies."
4. Ibid.
5. Herbert, *Elemental Mind: Human Consciousness and the New Physics,* 145–46.
6. Wigner, "Remarks on the Mind-Body Problem."
7. Squires, *The Mystery of the Quantum World,* 68, 81.
8. Kaku, *Hyperspace,* 317.
9. Polkinghorne, *The Quantum World,* 68.
10. Radin and Nelson, "Evidence for Consciousness-Related Anomalies in Random Physical Systems," 1510–11.
11. Schmidt, Morris, and Rudolph, "Channeling Evidence for a PK Effect to Independent Observers," 3.
12. Ibid.
13. Squires, *The Mystery of the Quantum World,* 65.
14. Ibid., 68.

15. Ibid.
16. Herbert, *Quantum Reality: Beyond the New Physics*, 226–27; Squires, *The Mystery of the Quantum World*, 98–102.
17. Quoted in Herbert, *Quantum Reality: Beyond the New Physics*, 29.
18. Quoted in Koestler, *The Roots of Coincidence*, 51.
19. Stapp, *Mindful Universe*, 136.
20. Jeans, *The Mysterious Universe*, 137.
21. William James, 1892; quoted in Stapp, *Mindful Universe*, 38.
22. Stapp, *Mindful Universe*, 38.
23. Herbert, *Elemental Mind: Human Consciousness and the New Physics*, 251.
24. Stapp, "Quantum Interactive Dualism: An Alternative to Materialism," 50.
25. Ibid., 51.
26. Stapp, *Mindful Universe*, 43.
27. Herbert, *Elemental Mind: Human Consciousness and the New Physics*, 260.
28. Walker, "A Review of Criticisms of the Quantum Mechanical Theory of Psi Phenomena," 279.
29. Stapp, *Mindful Universe*, 49.
30. Ibid., 49.
31. Beauregard and O'Leary, *The Spiritual Brain*, 141.
32. Ibid., 130.
33. Quoted in Beauregard and O'Leary, *The Spiritual Brain*, 126.
34. Carter, *Parapsychology and the Skeptics: A Scientific Argument for the Existence of ESP*, 57–60.
35. Beauregard and O'Leary, *The Spiritual Brain*, xii.
36. Quoted in Beauregard and O'Leary, *The Spiritual Brain*, 115.
37. Beauregard and O'Leary, *The Spiritual Brain*, 122.
38. Broad, *The Mind and its Place in Nature*, 623.
39. Quoted in Koestler, *The Roots of Coincidence*, 77.
40. Pauli, *The Influence of Archetypal Ideas on the Scientific Theories of Kepler: The Interpretation of Nature and the Psyche*, 208.
41. Popper, "Natural Selection and the Emergence of Mind."
42. Morowitz, "Rediscovering the Mind," 12.
43. Beauregard and O'Leary, *The Spiritual Brain*, 123.
44. Searle, *The Rediscovery of the Mind*, 3–4.
45. Lycan, "Giving Dualism Its Due."
46. Rao, "Consciousness."
47. Beloff, "The Mind-Brain Problem."
48. Popper and Eccles, *The Self and Its Brain*, 182.
49. Dennett, *Consciousness Explained*, 33.
50. Ibid., 35.
51. Ibid., 37.
52. Stapp, *Mindful Universe*, 81.
53. Rosenblum and Kuttner, "Consciousness and Quantum Mechanics: The Connection and Analogies," 248.

54. Broad, *The Mind and its Place in Nature,* 103.
55. Wallace, *The Taboo of Subjectivity: Toward a New Science of Consciousness,* 136.
56. Jeans, *The Mysterious Universe,* 137.
57. Stapp, *Mindful Universe,* 167–68.

CHAPTER 5. ARE MEMORIES STORED IN THE BRAIN?

1. Edwards, *Reincarnation: A Critical Examination,* 297.
2. Ibid., 284–85.
3. Ibid., 297.
4. Popper and Eccles, *The Self and Its Brain,* 542.
5. Boycott, "Learning in the Octopus," 44.
6. Sheldrake, *The Presence of the Past,* 165.
7. As quoted in Sheldrake, "Can Our Memories Survive the Death of Our Brains?" in *What Survives?* ed. by Gary Doore, 115.
8. Sheldrake, *The Presence of the Past,* 164.

CHAPTER 6. THEORIES OF LIFE

1. Firsoff, "Life and Quantum Physics," 115.
2. Sheldrake, *The Rebirth of Nature,* 111.
3. Sheldrake, *A New Science of Life,* 185–91.
4. Ertel, "Testing Sheldrake's Claims of Morphogenetic Fields."
5. Sheldrake, *The Rebirth of Nature,* 116–17.
6. Sheldrake, *The Presence of the Past,* 217.
7. Ibid., 218–19.
8. Teuber, "Recovery of Function after Brain Injury in Man," 160.
9. Sheldrake, "Can Our Memories Survive the Death of Our Brains?" 119.
10. Penfield, *The Mystery of the Mind,* 31.
11. Sheldrake, "Can Our Memories Survive the Death of Our Brains?" 120.
12. Huxley, *The Doors of Perception,* 19–20.
13. Ibid., 22.
14. Osis and Haraldsson, *At the Hour of Death,* 31.

CHAPTER 7. REPORTS FROM THE BRINK

1. Valarino, *On the Other Side of Life,* 86.
2. Sabom, *Recollections of Death,* 56–57.
3. Parnia et al., "A Qualitative and Quantitative Study of the Incidence, Features and Aetiology of Near Death Experiences in Cardiac Arrest Survivors."
4. van Lommel et al., "Near-Death Experience in Survivors of Cardiac Arrest: A Prospective Study in the Netherlands."
5. Lorimer, *Survival? Body, Mind and Death in the Light of Psychic Experience,* 248; Rogo, *The Return from Silence,* 58–61.
6. Irwin, *An Introduction to Parapsychology,* 199–200.

7. Moody, *Life after Life,* 21.

8. Valarino, *On the Other Side of Life,* 104.

9. Ibid., 45; originally found in Moody, *Life after Life.*

10. Ring and Valarino, *Lessons from the Light,* 15.

11. Ring, *Heading Toward Omega,* 42.

12. Ibid., 43.

13. Ring, *Life at Death,* 53.

14. Ibid., 54.

15. Sabom, *Recollections of Death,* 42.

16. Ibid.

17. Ibid.

18. Ring, *Life at Death,* 56.

19. Fenwick and Fenwick, *The Truth in the Light,* 75.

20. Sabom, *Recollections of Death,* 41.

21. Fenwick and Fenwick, *The Truth in the Light,* 77–78.

22. Ibid., 88.

23. Ibid., 116.

24. Morse and Perry, *Closer to the Light: Learning from Children's Near-Death Experiences,* 114–15.

25. Fenwick and Fenwick, *The Truth in the Light,* 114.

26. Ring, *Life at Death,* 139–40.

27. van Lommel et al., "Near-Death Experience in Survivors of Cardiac Arrest: A Prospective Study in the Netherlands," 2042–43.

28. Groth-Marnat and Summers, "Altered Beliefs, Attitudes and Behaviors following Near-Death Experiences," 118–20.

29. Ibid., 111.

30. Greyson, "Near-Death Experiences and Attempted Suicide"; Ring and Franklin, "Do Suicide Survivors Report Near-Death Experiences?" 191–208.

31. Ring and Franklin, "Do Suicide Survivors Report Near-Death Experiences?" 206.

32. Fenwick and Fenwick, *The Truth in the Light,* 200.

33. Ibid., 133–34.

34. Ibid., 134.

35. Morse and Perry, *Closer to the Light: Learning from Children's Near-Death Experiences.*

36. Ring, *Life at Death;* Sabom, *Recollections of Death.*

37. Ring, *Heading Toward Omega,* 44–45.

38. Ring, *Life at Death,* 136; Sabom, *Recollections of Death,* 57.

39. Owens, Cook, and Stevenson, "Features of 'Near-Death Experience' in Relation to Whether or Not Patients Were Near Death."

CHAPTER 8. INTO THE ABYSS: HORRIFIC NEAR-DEATH EXPERIENCES

1. As quoted in Rogo, *The Return from Silence,* 133.

2. Sabom, as quoted in Rogo, *The Return from Silence,* 136.

3. Rogo, *The Return from Silence*, 137–38.

4. Ring, "Solving the Riddle of Frightening Near-Death Experiences: Some Testable Hypotheses and a Perspective Based on *A Course in Miracles*," 8.

5. Ibid.

6. Ibid., 9.

7. Greyson and Bush, "Distressing Near-Death Experiences," 102.

8. Kircher, *Love Is the Link*, 116.

9. Greyson and Bush, "Distressing Near-Death Experiences," 104.

10. Ring, "A Note on Anesthetically-Induced Frightening Near-Death Experiences," 19.

11. Fenwick and Fenwick, *The Truth in the Light*, 188.

12. Ibid., 189.

13. Ibid., 190.

14. Grey, *Return from Death*, 63.

15. Ibid., 63–64.

16. Ibid., 68–69.

17. Ibid., 72.

18. Bush, "Afterward: Making Meaning after a Frightening Near-Death Experience," 104.

19. Ibid., 105.

20. Ibid., 108.

21. Ibid., 124.

22. Ibid., 124.

CHAPTER 9. NEAR-DEATH EXPERIENCES ACROSS CULTURES

1. Zhi-ying and Jian-xun, "Near-death Experience among Survivors of the 1976 Tangshan Earthquake," 39. Eleven years later, Feng Zhi-ying and Liu Jian-xun interviewed eighty-one survivors and found that 40 percent reported NDEs.

2. Osis and Haraldsson, *At the Hour of Death*.

3. Pasricha, "A Systematic Survey of Near-Death Experiences in South India," 166.

4. Ibid., 167.

5. Schoolcraft, *Travels in the Central Portion of the Mississippi Valley*, 407.

6. Neidhardt, *Black Elk Speaks*, 241–43.

7. Barrett, *Geronimo: His Own Story*, 167–68.

8. Green, "Near-Death Experiences in a Chammorro Culture," 6.

9. Ibid., 7.

10. Ibid.

11. King, *Being Pakeha: An Encounter with New Zealand and the Maori Renaissance*, 87–88.

11. Kellehear, "Culture, Biology, and the Near-Death Experience," 154.

12. Ibid., 155.

CHAPTER 10. PROPOSED PSYCHOLOGICAL EXPLANATIONS

1. Abramovitch, "An Israeli Account of a Near-Death Experience."
2. Wilson and Barber, "The Fantasy-prone Personality: Implications for Understanding Imagery, Hypnosis, and Parapsychological Phenomena."
3. Greyson, "Commentary on 'Psychophysiological and Cultural Correlates Undermining a Survivalist Interpretation of Near-Death Experiences,'" 130.
4. Noyes, "Depersonalization in the Face of Life-Threatening Danger: A Description," 20–21.
5. Noyes, "The Experience of Dying," 181.
6. Sabom, *Recollections of Death,* 162–63.
7. Noyes, "Near-Death Experiences: Their Interpretation and Significance," 85–86.
8. Gabbard and Twemlow, *With the Eyes of the Mind.*
9. Irwin, "The Near-Death Experience as a Dissociative Phenomenon: An Empirical Assessment."
10. Sabom, *Recollections of Death,* 165.
11. Ibid., 170.
12. Fenwick and Fenwick, *The Truth in the Light,* 37.
13. Sabom, *Recollections of Death,* chap. 7.
14. Ibid., 153.
15. Ibid., 155.
16. Ibid.
17. Ibid., 156.
18. Sagan, *Broca's Brain: Reflections on the Romance of Science,* 304.
19. Blackmore, "Birth and the OBE: An Unhelpful Analogy."
20. Becker, "Why Birth Models Cannot Explain Near-Death Phenomena," 159.
21. Ibid., 157–58.
22. Ibid., 160.

CHAPTER 11. PROPOSED PHYSIOLOGICAL EXPLANATIONS

1. Quoted in Sabom, *Recollections of Death,* 171.
2. Sabom, *Recollections of Death,* 172.
3. Lindley, Bryan, and Conley, "Near-Death Experiences in a Pacific Northwest American Population: The Evergreen Study," 120.
4. As mentioned in Sabom, *Recollections of Death,* 176.
5. Fenwick and Fenwick, *The Truth in the Light,* 309–10.
6. Parnia et al., "A Qualitative and Quantitative Study of the Incidence, Features and Aetiology of Near Death Experiences in Cardiac Arrest Survivors," 154.
7. Ibid., 153.
8. Blackmore and Troscianko, "The Physiology of the Tunnel."
9. Blackmore, "Near Death Experiences in India: They Have Tunnels Too," 111.
10. Kellehear et al., "The Absence of Tunnel Sensations in Near-Death Experiences from India," 112.
11. Fenwick and Fenwick, *The Truth in the Light,* 69–72.

12. Ibid., 309.

13. Sabom, *Recollections of Death,* 177.

14. Fenwick and Fenwick, *The Truth in the Light,* 313.

15. Sabom, *Recollections of Death,* 109.

16. Ibid., 178.

17. Fenwick and Fenwick, *The Truth in the Light,* 308; Gliksman and Kellehear, "Near-Death Experiences and the Measurement of Blood Gases."

18. Whinnery, "Psychophysiologic Correlates of Unconsciousness and Near-Death Experiences," 240.

19. Ibid., 243.

20. Ibid., 244–45.

21. Ramabadran and Bansinath, "Endogenous Opioid Peptides and Epilepsy."

22. Morse, Venecia, and Milstein, "Near-death Experiences: A Neurophysiologic Explanatory Model," 47.

23. Morse and Perry, *Closer to the Light: Learning from Children's Near-Death Experiences,* 104.

24. Penfield, "The Role of the Temporal Cortex in Certain Psychical Phenomena," 458.

25. Penfield, *The Excitable Cortex in Conscious Man,* 31.

26. Halgren et al., "Mental Phenomena Evoked by Electrical Stimulation of the Human Hippocampal Formation and Amygdala," 110.

27. Persinger, "Modern Neuroscience and Near-Death Experiences: Expectancies and Implications. Comment on 'A Neurobiological Model for Near-Death Experiences,'" 234.

28. Granqvist et al., "Sensed Presence and Mystical Experiences Are Predicted by Suggestibility, Not by the Application of Transcranial Weak Complex Magnetic Fields."

29. Ibid., 2.

30. Quoted in Beauregard and O'Leary, *The Spiritual Brain,* 97.

31. Rodin, "Comments on 'A Neurobiological Model for Near-Death Experiences,'" 256.

CHAPTER 12. EXPERIENCING DEATH THROUGH DRUGS?

1. Siegel, "Hallucinations," 132.

2. Ibid., 253.

3. Siegel, "The Psychology of Life after Death," 926.

4. As reported in Rogo, *The Return from Silence,* 121.

5. Siegel, "The Psychology of Life after Death," 924.

6. Rogo, *The Return from Silence,* 123.

7. Leary, *Flashbacks,* 375.

8. Johnstone, "A Ketamine Trip."

9. Collier, "Ketamine and the Conscious Mind," 126.

10. Ibid., 129.

11. Ibid., 133.

12. Ibid., 130.

13. Ibid., 125.

14. Jansen, "The Ketamine Model of the Near-Death Experience: A Central Role for the N-Methyl-D-Aspartate Receptor," 12–13.

15. Jansen, "Response to Commentaries on 'The Ketamine Model of the Near-Death Experience: A Central Role for the N-Methyl-D-Aspartate Receptor,'" 86.

16. Fenwick and Fenwick, *The Truth in the Light,* 194.

17. Fenwick, "Is the Near-Death Experience Only N-Methyl-D-Aspartate Blocking?" 45.

18. Strassman, "Endogenous Ketamine-Like Compounds and the NDE: If So, So What?" 39.

19. Jansen, "Response to Commentaries on 'The Ketamine Model of the Near-Death Experience: A Central Role for the N-Methyl-D-Aspartate Receptor,'" 94–95.

20. Rogo, *The Return from Silence,* 128.

21. Strassman, "Endogenous Ketamine-Like Compounds and the NDE: If So, So What?" 29.

22. Greyson, "Commentary on 'Psychophysiological and Cultural Correlates Undermining a Survivalist Interpretation of Near-Death Experiences,'" 140.

23. Ibid., 141.

24. As quoted in Greyson, "Commentary on 'Psychophysiological and Cultural Correlates Undermining a Survivalist Interpretation of Near-Death Experiences,'" 141.

CHAPTER 13. THE "DYING BRAIN" THEORY OF SUSAN BLACKMORE

1. Blackmore, *Dying to Live: Near Death Experiences,* 115.

2. Ibid., 114.

3. Ibid., 261.

4. Ibid., 176.

5. Ibid., 177.

6. Siegel, "Hallucinations," 136.

7. Nigro and Neisser, "Point of View in Personal Memories," 467–68.

8. Ibid., 481.

9. Ibid.

10. Ibid., 468–69.

11. Ibid., 481.

12. Blackmore, "Near Death Experiences in India: They Have Tunnels Too," 124–25.

13. Serdahely, "Questions for the 'Dying Brain Hypothesis," 45.

14. Blackmore, *Dying to Live: Near Death Experiences,* 65.

15. Ibid., 66.

16. Serdahely, "Questions for the 'Dying Brain Hypothesis," 51.

17. Blackmore, *Dying to Live: Near Death Experiences,* 126.

18. Serdahely, "Questions for the 'Dying Brain Hypothesis,'" 52.

19. Parnia et al., "A Qualitative and Quantitative Study of the Incidence, Features and Aetiology of Near Death Experiences in Cardiac Arrest Survivors," 150.

20. van Lommel et al., "Near-Death Experience in Survivors of Cardiac Arrest: A Prospective Study in the Netherlands."

21. Parnia and Fenwick, "Near Death Experiences in Cardiac Arrest: Visions of a Dying Brain or Visions of a New Science of Consciousness"; Clute and Levy, "Electroencephalographic Changes during Brief Cardiac Arrest in Humans."

22. van Lommel, *Endless Consciousness: A Scientific Approach to the Near-Death Experience,* chapter 8.

23. Parnia and Fenwick, "Near Death Experiences in Cardiac Arrest: Visions of a Dying Brain or Visions of a New Science of Consciousness," 8.

24. Lavy and Stern, "Electroencephalographic Changes Following Sudden Cessation of Articial Pacing in Patients with Heart Block"; Mayer and Marx, "The Pathogenesis of EEG Changes During Cerebral Anoxia," 5–11.

25. Sam Parnia, "What is the Effect of Anoxia to the Function of the Brain?" (unpublished paper).

26. Parnia and Fenwick, "Near Death Experiences in Cardiac Arrest: Visions of a Dying Brain or Visions of a New Science of Consciousness," 8.

27. Fenwick, "Is the Near-Death Experience Only *N*-Methyl-D-Aspartate Blocking?" 46.

CHAPTER 14. VERIDICAL NEAR-DEATH EXPERIENCES

1. Blackmore, *Dying to Live: Near Death Experiences,* 128.

2. Holden, "More Things in Heaven and Earth: A Response to 'Near-Death Experiences with Hallucinatory Features.'"

3. Ibid., 41.

4. van Lommel et al., "Near-Death Experience in Survivors of Cardiac Arrest: A Prospective Study in the Netherlands," 2041.

5. Cook, Greyson, and Stevenson, "Do Any Near-Death Experiences Provide Evidence for the Survival of Human Personality after Death? Relevant Features and Illustrative Case Reports," 399.

6. Sabom, *Light and Death,* 38.

7. Ibid., 41.

8. From the BBC documentary *The Day I Died.* Also see Sabom, *Light and Death,* 42.

9. Sabom, *Light and Death,* 43.

10. Ibid., 50.

11. Ibid., 187–89.

12. Ibid., 185.

13. Ibid., 184.

14. Sabom, "Commentary on 'Does Paranormal Perception Occur in Near-Death Experiences?'" 259.

15. From the BBC documentary *The Day I Died.*

16. Sabom, "Commentary on 'Does Paranormal Perception Occur in Near-Death Experiences?'" 258.

17. Greyson, "Commentary on 'Psychophysiological and Cultural Correlates Undermining a Survivalist Interpretation of Near-Death Experiences,'" 407. See also van Lommel et al., "Near-Death Experience in Survivors of Cardiac Arrest: A Prospective Study in the Netherlands."

CHAPTER 15. NEAR-DEATH EXPERIENCES OF PEOPLE WHO ARE BLIND

1. Ring and Cooper, *Mindsight,* 16.
2. Ibid., 75.
3. Ibid., 76.
4. Ibid., 109.
5. Ibid., 112.
6. Ibid., 116.
7. Ibid., 120.

CHAPTER 16. THE SCIENTIFIC CHALLENGE TO MATERIALISM

1. Grossman, "Who's Afraid of Life After Death?" 8.
2. Ibid., 10–11.
3. Fenwick and Fenwick, *The Truth in the Light,* 249.
4. Greyson, "Commentary on 'Psychophysiological and Cultural Correlates Undermining a Survivalist Interpretation of Near-Death Experiences,'" 142.
5. Popper, *The Philosophy of Karl Popper,* 983.
6. Shermer, *The Borderlands of Science,* 19.
7. Shermer, "Demon Haunted Brain."
8. Blanke et al., "Stimulating Illusory Own-Body Perceptions," 269.
9. Shermer, "Demon Haunted Brain."
10. van Lommel et al., "Near-Death Experience in Survivors of Cardiac Arrest: A Prospective Study in the Netherlands," 2044.
11. Ingram, "Why I'm Skeptical—Even of the Skeptic."
12. Greyson, "Commentary on 'Psychophysiological and Cultural Correlates Undermining a Survivalist Interpretation of Near-Death Experiences,'" 141–42.

CHAPTER 17. THE NEAR-DEATH EXPERIENCE AS EVIDENCE FOR SURVIVAL

1. Ring and Valarino, *Lessons from the Light,* 275–76.
2. Hovelmann, "Evidence for Survival from Near-Death Experiences? A Critical Appraisal," 660–61.
3. Ibid., 662.
4. Becker, *Paranormal Experience and Survival of Death,* 93.
5. 2 Kings 4:32.
6. Sabom, *Light and Death,* 48.
7. McCullagh, *Brain Dead, Brain Absent, Brain Donors,* 11.

8. Ibid., 11.
9. Ibid., 43.

CHAPTER 18. REPORTS FROM ENGLAND TO INDIA

1. Barrett, *Death Bed Visions,* 14.
2. Osis and Haraldsson, *At the Hour of Death,* 87.
3. Ibid., 91.
4. Ibid., 184.
5. Ibid., 88.
6. Ibid., 91.
7. Ibid., 87.
8. Ibid., 44.
9. Ibid., 190.
10. Ibid., 152.
11. Ibid., 90.

CHAPTER 19. ALTERNATIVE EXPLANATIONS

1. Osis and Haraldsson, *At the Hour of Death,* 187.
2. Ibid., 104–5.
3. Ibid., 75.
4. Greyson, "Commentary on 'Psychophysiological and Cultural Correlates Undermining a Survivalist Interpretation of Near-Death Experiences,'" 138–39.
5. Osis and Haraldsson, *At the Hour of Death,* 191.
6. Ibid., 87–88.
7. Dr. Minot Savage, *Psychic Facts and Theories.* Cited in Currie, *You Cannot Die!* 160.
8. Callanan and Kelley, *Final Gifts,* 93–94.
9. R. DeWitt Miller, *You DO Take It With You.* Cited in Currie, *You Cannot Die!* 161.

CHAPTER 20. COMPARISON WITH THE NEAR-DEATH EXPERIENCE

1. Osis and Haraldsson, *At the Hour of Death,* 72.

BIBLIOGRAPHY

Abramovitch, Henry. "An Israeli Account of a Near-Death Experience." *Journal of Near-Death Studies* 6, no. 3 (1988): 175–84.

Alexander, John A. "Enhancing Human Performance: A Challenge to the Report." *New Realities* 9, no. 4 (1989): 10–15, 52–53.

Almeder, Robert. *Death and Personal Survival.* Lanham, Md.: Rowman and Littlefield, 1992.

Barrett, S. M. *Geronimo: His Own Story.* New York: E. P. Dutton, 1970.

Barrett, William. *Death Bed Visions.* London: Methuen, 1926.

Bartley, W. W. "The Philosophy of Karl Popper Part II: Consciousness and Physics." *Philisophia* 7, no. 3–4 (July 1978): 675–716.

Bauer, Henry. "Arguments over Anomalies: II. Polemics." *Journal of Scientific Exploration* 3, no. 1 (1989): 1–14.

Beauregard, Mario, and Denyse O'Leary. *The Spiritual Brain.* New York: HarperOne, 2007.

Becker, Carl. *Paranormal Experience and Survival of Death.* Albany: State University of New York Press, 1993.

———. "Why Birth Models Cannot Explain Near-Death Phenomena." In *The Near-Death Experience,* edited by Bruce Greyson and Charles Flynn, 154–62. Springfield, Ill.: Charles Thomas, 1984.

Beloff, John. "Mind-Body Interactionism in Light of the Parapsychological Evidence." *Theoria to Theory* 10 (1976): 125–37.

———. "The Mind-Brain Problem." *The Journal of Scientific Exploration* 8, no. 4 (1994): 509–22.

———. *The Relentless Question.* Jefferson, N.C.: McFarland and Company, 1990.

———. *Parapsychology: A Concise History.* London: The Athlone Press. 1993.

———. "Parapsychology and Physics: Can They Be Reconciled?" *Theoretical Parapsychology* 6 (1988): 23–29.

Bem, D., and C. Honorton. "Does Psi Exist?" *Psychological Bulletin* 115, no. 1 (1994): 4–18.

Berger, Rick. "Discussion: A Critical Examination of the Blackmore Psi Experiments."

Journal of the American Society for Psychical Research 83 (April 1989): 123–44.

———. "Reply to Blackmore's 'A Critical Response to Rick Berger.'" *Journal of the American Society for Psychical Research* 83 (April 1989): 155–57.

Bergson, Henri. *The Creative Mind.* New York: Citadel Press, 1946.

Blackmore, Susan. *The Adventures of a Parapsychologist.* Buffalo, N.Y.: Prometheus Books, 1986.

———. "Birth and the OBE: An Unhelpful Analogy." *Journal of the American Society for Psychical Research* 77 (July 1983): 229–38.

———. "A Critical Response to Rick Berger." *Journal of the American Society for Psychical Research* 83 (April 1989): 145–54.

———. *Dying to Live: Near Death Experiences.* Buffalo, N.Y.: Prometheus Books, 1993.

———. "If the Truth Is Out There, We've Not Found It Yet." *The Times,* August 27, 1999, higher education supplement, 18.

———. *In Search of the Light: The Adventures of a Parapsychologist.* Amherst, N.Y.: Prometheus Books, 1996.

———. "Into the Unknown." *New Scientist,* no. 2263 (November 4, 2000): 55.

———. "Near Death Experiences in India: They Have Tunnels Too." *Journal of Near-Death Studies* 11, no. 4 (Summer 1993): 205–17.

———. "Out-of-Body Experiences." In *The Encyclopedia of the Paranormal,* edited by G. Stein. Amherst, N.Y.: Prometheus Books, 1996.

Blackmore, S., and T. S. Troscianko. "The Physiology of the Tunnel." *Journal of Near-Death Studies* 8 (1989): 15–28.

Blanke, O., S. Ortigue, T. Landis, and Margitta Seeck. "Stimulating Illusory Own-Body Perceptions." *Nature* 419 (September 2002): 269.

Boycott, B. B. "Learning in the Octopus." *Scientific American* 212 (1965): 42–50.

Braude, Stephen. *The Limits of Influence.* New York and London: Routledge and Kegan Paul, 1986.

Broad, C. D. *Lectures on Psychical Research.* New York: Humanities Press, 1962.

———. *The Mind and its Place in Nature.* New York: Harcourt, Brace and Co., 1929.

———. "The Relevance of Psychical Research to Philosophy." *The Journal of the Royal Institute of Philosophy* XXIV, no. 91 (October 1949): 291–309.

Broughton, Richard. *Parapsychology: The Controversial Science.* New York: Ballantine Books, 1991.

Brown, Rosemary. *Immortals By My Side.* London: Bachman and Turner, 1974.

Burt, Cyril. *ESP and Psychology.* London: Weidenfeld and Nicolson, 1975.

Bush, N. E. "Afterward: Making Meaning after a Frightening Near-Death Experience." *Journal of Near-Death Studies* 21 (2002): 99–133.

Callanan, Maggie, and Patricia Kelley. *Final Gifts.* New York: Poseidon Press, 1992.

Carter, Chris. *Parapsychology and the Skeptics: A Scientific Argument for the Existence of ESP.* Pittsburgh, Pa.: Sterlinghouse, 2007.

Cerf, Christopher, and Victor Navasky. *The Experts Speak: The Definitive Compendium of Authoritative Misinformation.* New York: Pantheon Books, 1984.

Clark, Jerome. "Skeptics and the New Age." In *New Age Encyclopedia,* edited by J.

Gordon Melton, Jerome Clark, and Aidan Kelly, 417–27. Detroit, Mich.: Gale Research, 1990.

Clute, H. L., and W. J. Levy. "Electroencephalographic Changes during Brief Cardiac Arrest in Humans." *Anesthesiology* 73 (1990): 821–25.

Collier, Barbara. "Ketamine and the Conscious Mind." *Anaesthesia* 27 (1972): 120–34.

Collins, H. H. *Changing Order: Replication and Induction in Scientific Practice.* Beverly Hills, Calif.: Sage, 1985.

Cook, E., B. Greyson, and Ian Stevenson. "Do Any Near-Death Experiences Provide Evidence for the Survival of Human Personality after Death? Relevant Features and Illustrative Case Reports." *Journal of Scientific Exploration* 12, no. 3 (1998): 377–406.

Costa de Beauregard, Olivier. "The Expanding Paradigm of the Einstein Theory." In *The Iceland Papers,* edited by A. Puharich, 161–91. Amherst, Wis.: Essentia Research Associates, 1979.

———. "Quantum Paradoxes and Aristotle's Twofold Information Concept." In *Quantum Physics and Parapsychology,* edited by Laura Oteri, 91–102. New York: Parapsychology Foundation, 1975.

Crace, John. "Richard Wiseman: Fortune Teller." *The Guardian,* Tuesday, March 2, 2004.

Currie, Ian. *You Cannot Die!* Toronto: Somerville House, 1978.

Dennett, D. C. *Consciousness Explained.* New York: Little Brown, 1991.

Druckman, Daniel, and John A. Swets, eds. *Enhancing Human Performance: Issues, Theories, and Techniques.* Washington, D.C.: National Academy Press, 1988.

Ducasse, Curt. *A Critical Examination of the Belief in a Life after Death.* Springfield, Ill.: Charles C. Thomas. 1961.

———. "What Would Constitute Conclusive Evidence of Survival after Death?" *Journal of the Society for Psychical Research* 41, no. 714 (December 1962): 401–6.

Dunne, B., and R. Jahn. "Experiments in Remote Human/Machine Interaction." *Journal of Scientific Exploration* 6 (1992): 311–32.

Eccles, John. *Facing Reality: Philosophical Adventures of a Brain Scientist.* New York, Heidelberg, Berlin: Springer-Verlag, 1970.

———. *The Neurophysiological Basis of Mind.* Oxford: Oxford University Press, 1953.

Edwards, Paul. *Reincarnation: A Critical Examination.* New York: Prometheus Books, 1996.

Elitzur, Avshalom, Beverly Sackler, and Raymond Sackler. "Consciousness Can No More Be Ignored." *Journal of Consciousness Studies* 2, no. 1 (1995): 353–57.

Ertel, Suitbert. "Testing Sheldrake's Claims of Morphogenetic Fields." In *Research in Parapsychology 1991,* edited by Emily Cook and Deborah Delanoy, 169–92. London: The Scarecrow Press, 1994.

Evans, Christopher. "Parapsychology—What the Questionnaire Revealed." *New Scientist* 25 (January 1973): 209.

Eysenck, H., and Carl Sargent. *Explaining the Unexplained: Mysteries of the Paranormal.* London: Book Club Associates, 1982.

Fenwick, Peter, and Elizabeth Fenwick. *The Truth in the Light*. London: Headline Book Publishing, 1995.

Fenwick, Peter. "Is the Near-Death Experience Only *N*-Methyl-D-Aspartate Blocking?" *Journal of Near-Death Studies* 16, no. 1 (Fall 1997): 43–53.

———. "Science and Spirituality: A Challenge for the 21st Century." *Journal of Near-Death Studies* 23, no. 3 (Spring 2005): 131–57.

Ferris, Timothy. *Coming of Age in the Milky Way*. New York: Doubleday, 1988.

Feuer, L. *Einstein and the Generations of Science*. New York: Basic Books, 1974.

Firsoff, V. A. "Life and Quantum Physics." In *Quantum Physics and Parapsychology*, edited by L. Oteri, 109–20. New York: Parapsychology Foundation, 1975.

Frazier, Kendrick, ed. *Paranormal Borderlands of Science*. Buffalo, N.Y.: Prometheus Books, 1981.

Gabbard, G., and S. Twemlow. *With the Eyes of the Mind*. New York: Praeger, 1984.

Gardner, Howard. *The Mind's New Science: A History of the Cognitive Revolution*. New York: Basic Books, 1985.

Gliksman, M., and A. Kellehear. "Near-Death Experiences and the Measurement of Blood Gases." *Journal of Near-Death Studies* 9, no. 1 (Fall 1990): 41–43.

Granqvist, Pehr, Mats Fredrikson, Dan Larhammar, Marcus Larsson, and Sven Valind. "Sensed Presence and Mystical Experiences Are Predicted by Suggestibility, Not by the Application of Transcranial Weak Complex Magnetic Fields." *Neuroscience Letters* (2004): doi:10.1016/j.nuelet.2004.10.057.

Greely, A. "Mysticism Goes Mainstream." *American Health* 7 (1987): 47–49.

———. *The Sociology of the Paranormal: A Reconnaissance*. Sage Research Papers in the Social Sciences. Beverly Hills, Calif., and London: Sage Publications, 1975.

Green, J. Timothy. "Near-Death Experiences in a Chammorro Culture." *Vital Signs* 4 (1984): 6–7.

———. "Near-Death Experiences in a Southern California Population." *Anabiosis: Journal for Near-Death Experiences* 3 (June 1983): 77–95.

Greene, John. "The Kuhnian Paradigm and the Darwinian Revolution in Natural History." In *Paradigms and Revolutions*, edited by Gary Gutting. Notre Dame, Ind.: University of Notre Dame Press, 1980.

Grey, Margot. *Return from Death*. Boston: Arkana, 1985.

Greyson, Bruce. "Commentary on 'Psychophysiological and Cultural Correlates Undermining a Survivalist Interpretation of Near-Death Experiences.'" *Journal of Near-Death Studies* 26, no. 2 (Winter 2007): 127–45.

———. "Consistency of Near-Death Experience Accounts over Two Decades: Are Reports Embellished over Time?" *Resuscitation* 73 (2007): 407–11.

———. "Near-Death Experiences and Attempted Suicide." *Suicide and Life Threatening Behavior* 11 (1981): 10–16.

Greyson, Bruce, and Nancy Evens Bush. "Distressing Near-Death Experiences." *Psychiatry* 55 (1992): 95–109.

Grossman, Neal. "Four Errors Commonly Made by Professional Debunkers." *Journal of Near-Death Studies* 26, no. 3 (2008): 227–35.

———. "Who's Afraid of Life After Death?" *Journal of Near-Death Studies* 21, no. 1 (Fall 2002): 5–24.

Groth-Marnat, G., and R. Summers. "Altered Beliefs, Attitudes and Behaviors following Near-Death Experiences." *Journal of Humanistic Psychology* 38 (1998): 110–25.

Haku, Michio. *Hyperspace.* New York: Doubleday, 1994.

Halgren, E., R. Walter, D. Cherlow, and Paul Crandall. "Mental Phenomena Evoked by Electrical Stimulation of the Human Hippocampal Formation and Amygdala." *Brain* 101 (1978): 83–117.

Hansen, George. "CSICOP and the Skeptics: An Overview." *Journal of the American Society for Psychical Research* 86 (January 1992): 19–63.

———. "Magicians and the Paranormal." *Journal of the American Society for Psychical Research* 86 (April 1992): 151–85.

———. "Magicians Who Endorsed Psychic Phenomena." *Linking Ring* 70, no. 8 (1990): 52–54.

———. "Magicians Who Endorsed Psychic Phenomena." *Linking Ring* 70, no. 9 (1990): 63–65, 109.

Haraldsson, E. "Survey of Claimed Encounters with the Dead." *Omega* 19, no. 2 (1988–1989): 103–13.

Haraldsson, Erlendur, and Joop M. Houtkooper. "Psychic Experiences in the Multinational Human Values Study: Who Reports Them?" *Journal of the American Society for Psychical Research,* 85, no. 2 (1991): 145–65.

Harman, W. *Global Mind Change.* Indianapolis, Ind.: Knowledge Systems, 1988.

Harris, Melvin. *Investigating the Unexplained.* Buffalo, N.Y.: Prometheus Books, 1986.

Harris, M., and R. Rosenthal. *Human Performance Research: An Overview.* Washington, D.C.: National Academy Press, 1988.

———. *Postscript to "Human Performance Research: An Overview."* Washington, D.C.: National Academy Press, 1988.

Hebb, D. O. "The Role of Neurological Ideas in Psychology." *Journal of Personality* 20 (1951): 39–55.

Herbert, Nick. *Elemental Mind: Human Consciousness and the New Physics.* New York: Penguin Books, 1993.

———. *Quantum Reality: Beyond the New Physics.* New York: Anchor Press, 1985.

Hines, Terrance. *Pseudoscience and the Paranormal.* Buffalo, N.Y.: Prometheus Books, 1988.

Hippocrates, *On the Sacred Disease.* See http://classics.mit.edu/Hippocrates/sacred.html. Accessed March 3, 2010.

Holden, Janice. "More Things in Heaven and Earth: A Response to 'Near-Death Experiences with Hallucinatory Features.'" *Journal of Near-Death Studies* 26, no. 1 (Fall 2007): 33–42.

Honorton, C. "Rhetoric over Substance: The Impoverished State of Skepticism." *Journal of Parapsychology* 57 (1993): 191–214.

Horgan, John. *The Undiscovered Mind.* New York: Simon and Schuster, 1999.

Houtkooper, Joop. "Arguing for an Observational Theory of Paranormal Phenomena." *Journal of Scientific Exploration* 16, no. 2 (2002): 171–85.

Hovelmann, Gerd. "Evidence for Survival from Near-Death Experiences? A Critical Appraisal." In *A Skeptic's Handbook of Parapsychology,* edited by P. Kurtz, 645–84. Buffalo, N.Y.: Prometheus Books, 1985.

Hutcheon, Pat Duffy. *Leaving the Cave: Evolutionary Naturalism in Social-Scientific Thought.* Waterloo, ON: Wilfred Laurier University Press, 1996.

———. "Popper and Kuhn on the Evolution of Science." *Book Review* 4, no. 1–2 (1995): 28–37.

Huxley, Aldous. *The Doors of Perception.* London: Chatto and Windus, 1954. Reprint, London: Granada Publishing, 1984.

Hyman, R., and C. Honorton. "A Joint Communiqué: The Psi Ganzfeld Controversy." *Journal of Parapsychology* 50 (1986): 351–64.

Hyman, Ray. "Comment." *Statistical Science* 6 (1991): 389–92.

———. "Evaluation of Program on Anomalous Mental Phenomena." *Journal of Scientific Exploration* 10 (1996): 31–58.

———. "Proper Criticism." *The New York Skeptic* 1 (Spring 1988): 1.

Inglis, Brian. *Natural and Supernatural.* London: Hodder and Stoughton, 1977.

———. *The Paranormal: An Encyclopedia of Psychic Phenomena.* London: Paladin, 1986.

Ingram, Jay. "Why I'm Skeptical—Even of the Skeptic." *Toronto Star,* March 16, 2003, A14.

Irwin, H. J. *An Introduction to Parapsychology.* 3rd ed. Jefferson, N.C.: McFarland and Company, 1999.

———. "The Near-Death Experience as a Dissociative Phenomenon: An Empirical Assessment." *Journal of Near-Death Studies* 12, no. 2 (Winter 1993): 95–103.

Jacobson, Nils. *Life Without Death?* New York: Dell Publishing, 1974.

James, William. *The Varieties of Religious Experience.* London: Longmans, 1903.

———. *The Will to Believe, Human Immortality, and Other Essays on Popular Philosophy.* New York: Dover, 1956. Original works published 1897, 1898.

———. *The Works of William James: Essays in Psychical Research.* Cambridge, Mass.: Harvard University Press, 1986.

Jansen, Karl, "The Ketamine Model of the Near-Death Experience: A Central Role for the N-Methyl-D-Aspartate Receptor." *Journal of Near-Death Studies* 16, no. 1 (Fall 1997): 5–26.

———. "Response to Commentaries on 'The Ketamine Model of the Near-Death Experience: A Central Role for the N-Methyl-D-Aspartate Receptor.'" *Journal of Near-Death Studies* 16, no. 1 (Fall 1997): 79–95.

Jeans, James. *The Mysterious Universe.* New York: Macmillan, 1948.

Johnstone, R. E. "A Ketamine Trip." *Anesthesiology* 39 (1973): 460–61.

Josephson, B., and F. Pallikari-Viras. "Biological Utilisation of Quantum NonLocality." *Foundations of Physics* 21 (1991): 197–207.

Kaiser, Jocelyn, ed. "Major EMF Report Warns of Health Risks." *Science* 269 (August 18, 1995): 911.

Kaku, Michio. *Hyperspace.* Oxford: Oxford University Press, 1994. Reprint, New York: Doubleday, 1995.

Keeton, M. T. "Some Ambiguities in the Theory of the Conservation of Energy." *Philosophy of Science* 8, no. 3 (July 1941): 304–19.

Kellehear, Allan. "Culture, Biology, and the Near-Death Experience." *The Journal of Nervous and Mental Disease* 181, no. 3 (1993): 148–56.

Kellehear, Allan, Ian Stevenson, Satwant Pasricha, and Emily Cook. "The Absence of Tunnel Sensations in Near-Death Experiences from India." *Journal of Near-Death Studies* 13, no. 2 (Winter 1994): 109–13.

Kelly, E., E. Kelly, A. Crabtree, et al. *Irreducible Mind*. Lanham, Md.: Rowman and Littlefield, 2007.

King, M. *Being Pakeha: An Encounter with New Zealand and the Maori Renaissance*. Auckland, New Zealand: Hodder and Stoughton, 1985.

Kircher, Pamela. *Love Is the Link*. Burdette, N.Y.: Larson Publications, 1995.

Koestler, Arthur. *The Roots of Coincidence*. London: Hutchinson and Company, 1972.

———. *The Sleepwalkers: A History of Man's Changing Vision of the Universe*. New York: The MacMillan Company, 1959.

Kuhn, Thomas. *The Structure of Scientific Revolutions*. 3rd ed. Chicago: University of Chicago Press, 1996.

Kurtz, Paul. "Committee to Scientifically Investigate Claims of Paranormal and Other Phenomena." *The Humanist,* May/June 1976, 28.

———. "The Growth of Antiscience." *Skeptical Inquirer* (Spring 1994): 255–63.

Lamont, Corliss. *The Illusion of Immortality*. New York: The Continuum Publishing Company, 1990.

Laudan, Rachel. "The Recent Revolution in Geology and Kuhn's Theory of Scientific Change." In *Paradigms and Revolutions,* edited by Gary Gutting. Notre Dame, Ind.: University of Notre Dame Press, 1980.

Lavy, S., and S. Stern, "Electroencephalographic Changes Following Sudden Cessation of Articial Pacing in Patients with Heart Block" *Confinia Neurologica* (Basel) 29 (1967): 47.

Leary, T. *Flashbacks*. Los Angeles: J. P. Tarcher, 1983.

Libet, Benjamin. "Do We Have Free Will?" *Journal of Consciousness Studies* 6, no. 8–9 (1999): 47–57.

Libet, B., A. Freeman, and K. Sutherland, eds. *The Volitional Brain: Towards a Neuroscience of Free Will*. Thoverton, U.K.: Imprint Academic, 1999.

Lindley, James H., Sethyn Bryan, and Bob Conley. "Near-Death Experiences in a Pacific Northwest American Population: The Evergreen Study." *Anabiosis: Journal for Near-Death Experiences* 1 (December 1981): 104–24.

Lorimer, David. *Survival? Body, Mind and Death in the Light of Psychic Experience*. London: Routledge and Kegan Paul, 1984.

Lycan, William. "Giving Dualism Its Due." www.unc.edu/~ujanel/Du.htm. Accessed March 31, 2010.

Masterman, Margaret. "The Nature of a Paradigm." In *Criticism and Growth of Knowledge,* edited by Imre Lakatos and Alan Musgrave. Cambridge: Cambridge University Press, 1970.

Mattuck, R., and Evan Harris Walker. "The Action of Consciousness on Matter: A Quantum Mechanical Theory of Psychokinesis." In *The Iceland Papers,* edited by A. Puharich, 111–60. Amherst, Wis.: Essentia Research Associates, 1979.

Mayer, J., and T. Marx, "The Pathogenesis of EEG Changes During Cerebral Anoxia." In McCullagh, Peter. *Brain Dead, Brain Absent, Brain Donors.* Chichester, England: John Wiley and Sons, 1993.

Milner, Richard. "Charles Darwin and Associates, Ghostbusters." *Scientific American* 275, no. 4 (1996): 96–101.

Moody, Raymond. *Life after Life.* New York: Mockingbird Books, 1975.

Morowitz, H. J. "Rediscovering the Mind." *Psychology Today* 14, no. 3 (1980): 12, 15–17.

Morse, Melvin, and Paul Perry. *Closer to the Light: Learning from Children's Near-Death Experiences.* New York: Random House, 1990.

———. *Transformed by the Light.* New York: Villard Books, 1992.

Morse, Melvin, David Venecia, and Jerrold Milstein. "Near-death Experiences: A Neurophysiologic Explanatory Model." *Journal of Near-Death Studies* 8, no. 1 (Fall 1989): 45–53.

Murchison, Carl, ed. *The Case For and Against Psychical Belief.* Worchester, Mass.: Clark University, 1927.

Myers, Frederic. *Human Personality and Its Survival of Bodily Death.* Vols. I and II. New York: Longmans, Green, and Co., 1903.

Neidhardt, John. *Black Elk Speaks.* Lincoln: University of Nebraska Press, 1932.

Nelson, R. D., and Y. H. Dobyns. "Analysis of Variance of REG Experiments: Operator Intention, Secondary Parameters, Database Structure." Technical Note PEAR 91004, Princeton Engineering Anomalies Research, Princeton University, School of Engineering/Applied Science, December 1991.

News and Comment. "Academy Helps Army Be All That It Can Be." *Science* 238 (December 11, 1987): 1501–2.

Nigro, Georgia, and Ulric Neisser. "Point of View in Personal Memories." *Cognitive Psychology* 15 (1983): 467–82.

Noble, H. B. *Next: The Coming Era in Science.* Boston: Little Brown, 1988.

Noyes, Russell. "Depersonalization in the Face of Life-Threatening Danger: A Description." *Psychiatry* 39 (1976): 19–27.

———. "The Experience of Dying." *Psychiatry* 35 (1972): 174–84.

———. "Near-Death Experiences: Their Interpretation and Significance." In *Between Life and Death,* edited by Robert Kastenbaum, 73–88. New York: Springer Publishing, 1979.

Office of Technology Assessment. "Report of a Workshop on Experimental Parapsychology." *Journal of the American Society for Psychical Research* 83 (1989): 317–39.

Osis, Karlis, and Erlendur Haraldsson. *At the Hour of Death.* New York: Avon Books, 1977.

Oteri, Laura, ed. *Quantum Physics and Parapsychology.* New York: Parapsychology Foundation, 1975.

Owens, J. E., E. W. Cook, and I. Stevenson. "Features of 'Near-Death Experience' in Relation to Whether or Not Patients Were Near Death." *Lancet* 336 (1990): 1175–77.

Parnia, Sam, and Peter Fenwick. "Near Death Experiences in Cardiac Arrest: Visions of a Dying Brain or Visions of a New Science of Consciousness." *Resuscitation* 52 (2002): 5–11.

Parnia, Sam; D. G. Walker, R. Yeates, and P. Fenwick. "A Qualitative and Quantitative Study of the Incidence, Features and Aetiology of Near Death Experiences in Cardiac Arrest Survivors." *Resuscitation* 48 (2001): 149–56.

Pasricha, Satwant. "A Systematic Survey of Near-Death Experiences in South India." *Journal of Scientific Exploration* 7, no. 2 (1993): 161–71.

Pasricha, Satwant, and Ian Stevenson. "Near-Death Experiences in India. A Preliminary Report." *The Journal of Nervous and Mental Disease* 174, no. 3 (1986): 165–70.

Pauli, Wolfgang. *The Influence of Archetypal Ideas on the Scientific Theories of Kepler: The Interpretation of Nature and the Psyche.* London: Routledge and Kegan Paul, 1955.

Penfield, Wilder. *The Cerebral Cortex of Man.* New York: The MacMillan Company, 1952.

———. *The Excitable Cortex in Conscious Man.* Liverpool: Liverpool University Press, 1958.

———. *The Mystery of the Mind.* Princeton, N.J.: Princeton University Press, 1975.

———. "The Role of the Temporal Cortex in Certain Psychical Phenomena." *Journal of Mental Science* 101, no. 424 (1955): 451–65.

Persinger, M. A. "Modern Neuroscience and Near-Death Experiences: Expectancies and Implications. Comment on 'A Neurobiological Model for Near-Death Experiences.'" *Journal of Near-Death Studies* 7, no. 4 (Summer 1989): 233–39.

———. "Near Death Experience: Determining the Neuroanatomical Pathways." In *Healing: Beyond Suffering or Death,* edited by Luc Bessette. Montreal: Publications MNH, 1994.

Pinch, T. J., and H. M. Collins, "Private Science and Public Knowledge: The Committee for the Scientific Investigation of the Claims of the Paranormal and Its Use of the Literature." *Social Studies of Science* 14 (1984): 521–46.

Planck, M. *Scientific Autobiography.* New York: Philosophical Library, 1968.

Plato, *Phaedo.* Edited by C. J. Rowe. New York: Cambridge University Press, 1993.

Polkinghorne, J. C. *The Quantum World.* London: Longman Group, 1984.

Popper, Karl. *Conjectures and Refutations.* New York: Harper and Row, 1965.

———. *The Philosophy of Karl Popper.* Edited by Paul Arthur Schilpp. Chicago: Open Court, 1974.

———. *The Logic of Scientific Discovery.* 2nd ed. New York: First Harper Torchbook, 1959.

———. "Natural Selection and the Emergence of Mind." *Dialectica* 22, no. 3 (1978): 339–55.

———. "Philosophy and Physics." In *Proceedings of the XIIth International Congress of Philosophy* 2 (1960): 367–74.

Popper, K., and J. Eccles. *The Self and Its Brain.* New York: Springer International, 1977.

Price, George R. "Science and the Supernatural." *Science* 122, no. 3165 (August 26, 1955): 359–67.

Puharich, A., ed. *The Iceland Papers*. Amherst, Wis.: Essentia Research Associates, 1979.

Putnam, Hillary. "The 'Corroboration' of Theories." In *The Philosophy of Karl Popper*, Part I, edited by Paul Arthur Schilpp. Chicago: Open Court, 1974.

Radin, Dean. *The Conscious Universe: The Scientific Truth of Psychic Phenomena*. San Francisco: HarperCollins, 1997.

Radin, Dean, and Roger Nelson. "Evidence for Consciousness-Related Anomalies in Random Physical Systems." *Foundations of Physics* 19, no. 12 (1989): 1499–1514.

Ramabadran, K., and M. Bansinath. "Endogenous Opioid Peptides and Epilepsy." *International Journal of Clinical Pharmacology, Therapy and Toxicology* 28, no. 2 (1990): 47–62.

Rao, K. Ramakrishna. "Consciousness." In Corsini, Raymond J., ed., *Encyclopedia of Psychology*, 2nd ed. Vol. 1. New York: John Wiley & Sons, 1994.

Ring, Kenneth. "Frightening Near-Death Experiences Revisited: A Commentary on Reponses to My Paper by Christopher Bache and Nancy Evans Bush." *Journal of Near-Death Studies* 13, no. 1 (Fall 1994): 55–64.

———. *Heading Toward Omega*. New York: William Morrow and Company, 1984.

———. *Life at Death*. New York: Coward, McCann, and Geoghegan, 1980.

———. "A Note on Anesthetically-Induced Frightening Near-Death Experiences." *Journal of Near-Death Studies* 15, no. 1 (Fall 1996): 17–23.

———. "Solving the Riddle of Frightening Near-Death Experiences: Some Testable Hypotheses and a Perspective Based on *A Course in Miracles*." *Journal of Near-Death Studies*, 13, no. 1 (Fall 1994): 5–23.

Ring, Kenneth, and Sharon Cooper. *Mindsight*. Palo Alto, Calif.: William James Center for Consciousness Studies, 1999.

Ring, Kenneth, and Stephen Franklin. "Do Suicide Survivors Report Near-Death Experiences?" *Omega* 12, no. 3 (1981): 191–208.

Ring, Kenneth, and Evelyn Elsaesser Valarino. *Lessons from the Light*. Portsmouth, N.H.: Moment Point Press, 1998.

Rodin, Ernst. "Comments on 'A Neurobiological Model for Near-Death Experiences.'" *Journal of Near-Death Studies* 7, no. 4 (Summer 1989): 255–59.

Rogo, D. S. *The Return from Silence*. Wellingborough, England: The Aquarian Press, 1989.

Rommer, B. *Blessings in Disguise: Another Side of the Near-Death Experience*. St. Paul, Minn.: Llewellyn, 2000.

Rosenblum, B., and F. Kuttner. "Consciousness and Quantum Mechanics: The Connection and Analogies." *The Journal of Mind and Behavior* 20, no. 3 (Summer 1999): 229–56.

———. *Quantum Enigma: Physics Encounters Consciousness*. Oxford: Oxford University Press, 2006.

Rosenthal, Robert. "Meta-analytic Procedures and the Nature of Replication: The Ganzfeld Debate." *Journal of Parapsychology* 50 (1986): 315–36.

Rush, Joseph. "Physical and Quasi-physical Theories of Psi." In *Foundations of Parapsychology,* edited by H. Edge, R. Morris, J. Rush, and John Palmer. Boston: Routledge and Kegan Paul, 1986.

Russell, Bertrand. *A History of Western Philosophy.* London: George Allen and Unwin, 1946.

———. *Portraits from Memory.* London: George Allen and Unwin, 1956.

———. *Why I Am Not a Christian, and Other Essays.* Edited by Paul Edwards. New York: Simon and Schuster, 1957.

Ryle, Gilbert. *The Concept of Mind.* London, England: Peregrine Books, 1963.

Sabom Michael. "Commentary on 'Does Paranormal Perception Occur in Near-Death Experiences?'" *Journal of Near-Death Studies* 25, no. 4 (Summer 2007): 257–60.

———. *Light and Death.* Grand Rapids, Mich.: Zondervan Publishing, 1998.

———. *Recollections of Death.* New York: Harper and Row, 1982.

Sagan, Carl. *Broca's Brain: Reflections on the Romance of Science.* New York: Random House, 1979.

Schiller, F. *Riddles of the Sphinx.* London: Swan Sonnenschein, 1891.

Schmidt, Helmut. "Addition Effect for PK on Pre-recorded Targets." *Journal of Parapsychology* 49 (1985): 229–44.

———. "Comparison of PK Action on Two Different Random Number Generators." *Journal of Parapsychology* 38 (1974): 47–55.

———. "PK Effects on Pre-recorded Targets." *Journal of the American Society for Psychical Research* 70 (1976): 267–91.

———. "The Strange Properties of Psychokinesis." *Journal of Scientific Exploration* 1, no. 2 (1987): 103–18.

Schmidt, Helmut, R. Morris, and L. Rudolph. "Channeling Evidence for a PK Effect to Independent Observers." *Journal of Parapsychology* 50 (March 1986): 1–15.

Schoolcraft, H. R. *Travels in the Central Portion of the Mississippi Valley.* New York: Collins and Hannay, 1825. Reprint, New York: Kraus Reprint Company, 1975.

Schorer, C. E. "Two Native North American Near-Death Experiences." *Omega* 16 (1985–1986): 111–13.

Schwartz, J. M., H. Stapp, and M. Beauregard. "Quantum Physics in Neuroscience and Psychology: A Neurophysical Model of Mind/Brain Interaction." *Philosophical Transactions of the Royal Society B: Biological Sciences* 360 (2005): 1309–27.

Searle, John R. *The Mystery of Consciousness.* New York: New York Review Books, 1997.

———. *The Rediscovery of the Mind.* Cambridge, Mass.: MIT Press, 1994.

Serdahely, William. "Pediatric Near-Death Experiences." *Journal of Near-Death Studies* 9, no. 1 (Fall 1990): 33–39.

———. "A Pediatric Near-Death Experience: Tunnel Variants." *Omega* 20, no. 1 (1989–1990): 55–63.

———. "Questions for the 'Dying Brain Hypothesis.'" *Journal of Near-Death Studies* 16 (Fall 1996): 41–53.

Sheldrake, Rupert. "Can Our Memories Survive the Death of Our Brains?" In *What Survives?* edited by Gary Doore, 111–21. Los Angeles: Jeremy P. Tarcher, 1990.

———. *Dogs That Know When Their Owners Are Coming Home.* New York: Crown Publishers, 1999.

———. *A New Science of Life.* Los Angeles: J. P. Tarcher, 1981.

———. *The Presence of the Past.* New York: Times Books, 1988.

———. *The Rebirth of Nature.* New York: Bantam Books, 1991.

Shermer, Michael. *The Borderlands of Science,* New York: Oxford University Press, 2001.

———. "Demon Haunted Brain." *Scientific American* 288, no. 3 (March 2003): 47.

Sherwood, Jane. *The Country Beyond.* London: Neville Spearman, 1969. First edition, 1944.

Siegel, Ronald. "Hallucinations." *Scientific American* 237 (1977): 132–40.

———. "The Psychology of Life after Death." *American Psychologist* 35, no. 10 (1980): 911–31.

Slade, Peter, and Richard Bentall. *Sensory Deception.* Baltimore: John Hopkins University Press, 1988.

Snow, C. P. *The Search.* 5th ed. London: Macmillan and Co., 1963. First edition, 1934.

Sperry, Roger. "Holding Course Amid Shifting Paradigms." In *New Metaphysical Foundations of Modern Science,* edited by Harman and Clark. Sausalito, Calif.: Institute of Noetic Sciences, 1994.

Squires, Euan. *The Mystery of the Quantum World.* 2nd ed. London: Institute of Physics Publishing, 1994.

Stanford, R. G., R. Zenhausern, A. Taylor, and Mary Ann Dwyer. "Psychokinesis as Psi-Mediated Instrumental Response." *Journal of the American Society for Psychical Research* 69 (1975): 127–33.

Stapp, Henry. "Attention, Intention, and Will in Quantum Physics." *Journal of Consciousness Studies* 6, no. 8–9 (1999): 143–64.

———. *Mind, Matter, and Quantum Mechanics.* Berlin: Springer, 2009.

———. *Mindful Universe.* Berlin: Springer, 2007.

———. "Quantum Interactive Dualism: An Alternative to Materialism." *Journal of Consciousness Studies* 12, no. 11 (2005): 43–58.

———. "Theoretical Model of Purported Theoretical Violations of the Predictions of Quantum Theory." *Physical Review A* 50 (1994): 18–22.

———. "Compatibility of Contemporary Physical Theory with Personality Survival." www-physics.lbl.gov/~stapp/Compatibility.pdf. Accessed April 1, 2010.

Stenger, Victor. *Physics and Psychics.* Buffalo, N.Y.: Prometheus Books, 1990.

———. *The Unconscious Quantum.* Buffalo, N.Y.: Prometheus Books, 1995.

Stevenson, Ian. *Children Who Remember Previous Lives.* Charlottesville: University Press of Virginia, 1987.

———. "Comments by Ian Stevenson." *Journal of the Society for Psychical Research* 55 (1988): 230–34.

———. *Reincarnation and Biology.* Vol. 2. Westport, Conn.: Praeger Publishers, 1997.

———. "Research into the Evidence of Man's Survival After Death." *Journal of Nervous and Mental Disease* 165, no. 3 (1977): 153–83.

———. *Twenty Cases Suggestive of Reincarnation.* Charlottesville: University Press of Virginia, 1966/1974.

Stokes, Douglas. "Promethean Fire: The View from the Other Side." *Journal of Parapsychology* 51 (September 1987): 249–70.

———. "Theoretical Parapsychology." In *Advances in Parapsychological Research,* edited by Stanley Krippner. London: McFarland and Company, 1987.

Strassman, Rick. "Endogenous Ketamine-Like Compounds and the NDE: If So, So What?" *Journal of Near-Death Studies* 16, no. 1 (Fall 1997): 27–41.

Teuber, Hans-Lukas. "Recovery of Function after Brain Injury in Man." In *Outcome of Severe Damage to the Central Nervous System,* edited by Ruth Porter and David Fitzsimons, 159–90. Amsterdam: Elsevier, 1975.

Thouless, R. H., and B. P. Wiesner. "The Psi Processes in Normal and Paranormal Psychology." *Proceedings of the SPR* 48 (1949): 177–96.

Toynbee, A., R. Heywood, K. Mant, N. Smart, J. Hinton, S. Yudkin, E. Rhode, and H. Price. *Man's Concern with Death.* London: Hodder and Stoughton, 1968.

Truzzi, Marcello. "On Some Unfair Practices towards Claims of the Paranormal." In *Oxymoron: Annual Thematic Anthology of the Arts and Sciences.* vol. 2, edited by Edward Binkowski. New York: Oxymoron Media, 1998.

———. "Reflections on the Sociology and Social Psychology of Conjurors and Their Relations with Psychical Research." In *Advances in Parapsychological Research 8,* edited by Stanley Krippner, 221–71. London: McFarland and Company, 1997.

Utts, Jessica. "An Assessment of the Evidence for Psychic Functioning." *Journal of Scientific Exploration* 10, no. 1 (1996): 3–30. Also in *Journal of Parapsychology* 59, no. 4: 289–320.

———. "The Ganzfeld Debate: A Statistician's Perspective." *Journal of Parapsychology* 50 (1986): 363–402.

———. "Rejoinder." *Statistical Science* 6, no. 4 (1991): 396–403.

———. "Replication and Meta-analysis in Parapsychology." *Statistical Science* 6, no. 4 (1991): 363–78.

———. "Response to Ray Hyman's Report." 1995. www.ics.uci.edu/~jutts/response.html. Accessed March 3, 2010.

———. "Response to Ray Hyman's Report of September 11, 1995, 'Evaluation of Program on Anomalous Mental Phenomena.'" *Journal of Scientific Exploration* 10, no. 1 (1996): 59–61. Also in *Journal of Parapsychology* 59, no. 4 (December 1995): 353–56.

Valarino, Evelyn Elsaesser. *On the Other Side of Life.* Cambridge, Mass.: Perseus Publishing, 1997.

Van der Drift, J. H., *Cardiac and Vascular Diseases/Handbook of Electroencephalography and Clinical Neurophysiology,* vol. 14A. Amsterdam: Elsevier, 1972.

van Lommel, Pim, Ruud van Wees, Vincent Meyers, and Ingrid Elfferich. "Near-Death Experience in Survivors of Cardiac Arrest: A Prospective Study in the Netherlands." *Lancet* 358 (2001): 2039–45.

van Lommel, Pim. *Endless Consciousness: A Scientific Approach to the Near-Death Exeperience.* New York: HarperCollins, 2010.

Vasiliev, L. L., *Experiments in Distant Influence*. New York: Dutton, 1976.

Wagner, Mahlon, and Mary Monet. "Attitudes of College Professors Toward Extra-Sensory Perception." *Zetetic Scholar* 5 (1979): 7–16.

Walker, E. H. "Consciousness and Quantum Theory." In *Psychic Exploration,* edited by J. White, 544–68. New York: Putnam's, 1974.

———. "Foundations of Paraphysical and Parapsychological Phenomena." In *Quantum Physics and Parapsychology,* edited by Laura Oteri, 1–44. New York: Parapsychology Foundation, 1974.

———. "Measurement in Quantum Mechanics Revisited." *Journal of the American Society for Psychical Research* 81 (October 1987): 333–69.

———. "The Quantum Theory of Psi Phenomena." In *Psychoenergetic Systems* 3 (1979): 259–99.

———. "A Review of Criticisms of the Quantum Mechanical Theory of Psi Phenomena." *Journal of Parapsychology* 48 (December 1984): 277–332.

Wallace, B. A. *The Taboo of Subjectivity: Toward a New Science of Consciousness*. New York: Oxford University Press, 2000.

Wheeler, John, and Wojciech Zurek, eds. *Quantum Theory and Measurement*. Princeton, N.J.: Princeton University Press, 1983.

Whinnery, James E. "Psychophysiologic Correlates of Unconsciousness and Near-Death Experiences." *Journal of Near-Death Studies* 15, no. 4 (Summer 1997): 231–58.

Wigner, Eugene. "Remarks on the Mind-Body Problem." In *Quantum Theory and Measurement,* edited by John Wheeler and Wojciech Zurek. Princeton, N.J.: Princeton University Press, 1983.

Wilson, Sheryl C., and Theodore X. Barber. "The Fantasy-prone Personality: Implications for Understanding Imagery, Hypnosis, and Parapsychological Phenomena." In *Imagery, Current Theory, Research and Application*, edited by Anees A. Sheikh, 340–90. New York: Wiley, 1983.

Zhi-ying, Feng, and Liu Jian-xun. "Near-death Experiences Among Survivors of the 1976 Tangshan Earthquake." *Journal of Near-Death Studies* 11 (1992): 39–48.

Zingrone, Nancy. "Failing to Go the Distance: On Critics and Parapsychology." Published by the Parapsychology Foundation. Presented at a meeting of the Society for Psychical Research, London, 1997. See www.skepticalinvestigations.org/exam/Zingrone_critics.htm. Accessed March 3, 2010.

Zollner, Friedrich. *Transcendental Physics*. Boston: Colby and Rich, 1888.

Zollschan, G. F., J. F., Schumaker, and G. F. Walsh, eds. *Exploring the Paranormal: Different Perspective on Belief and Experience*. Dorset, England: Prism Press, 1989.

INDEX

Page numbers in *italics* refer to illustrations.

BOOKS OF RELATED INTEREST

Transcending the Speed of Light
Consciousness, Quantum Physics, and the Fifth Dimension
by Marc Seifer, Ph.D.

The Biology of Transcendence
A Blueprint of the Human Spirit
by Joseph Chilton Pearce

The Spiritual Anatomy of Emotion
How Feelings Link the Brain, the Body, and the Sixth Sense
by Michael A. Jawer with Marc S. Micozzi, M.D., Ph.D.

DMT: The Spirit Molecule
A Doctor's Revolutionary Research into the Biology of
Near-Death and Mystical Experiences
by Rick Strassman, M.D.

Beyond the Indigo Children
The New Children and the Coming of the Fifth World
by P. M. H. Atwater, L.H.D.

The Akashic Experience
Science and the Cosmic Memory Field
by Ervin Laszlo

Chaos, Creativity, and Cosmic Consciousness
by Rupert Sheldrake, Terence McKenna, and Ralph Abraham

Radical Nature
The Soul of Matter
by Christian de Quincey

INNER TRADITIONS • BEAR & COMPANY
P.O. Box 388
Rochester, VT 05767
1-800-246-8648
www.InnerTraditions.com

Or contact your local bookseller